T0298969

E. H. Carr is widely remembered as an influential theorist of international relations. The scourge of inter-war idealists, he became the best-known Briton in a generation of predominantly American political realists. But Carr's realism differed greatly from that of his contemporaries: a vigorous advocate of social and economic planning and friend of the Soviet Union, he stood closer to Lenin than to Morgenthau. In this book Charles Jones makes sense of Carr's distinctive form of realism by examining his rhetoric and the reciprocal relationship between theory and policy-making in his writings. Close attention is paid to the period from 1936, when Carr left the Foreign Office, through his subsequent career as a one-man foreign ministry at Aberystwyth, the Ministry of Information, and above all *The Times*, culminating in the final frustration of his schemes for continued British world power in 1947.

CAMBRIDGE STUDIES IN INTERNATIONAL RELATIONS: 61

E. H. Carr and international relations

CAMBRIDGE STUDIES IN INTERNATIONAL RELATIONS

E. H. Carr and international relations
A duty to lie

Charles Jones

CAMBRIDGE
UNIVERSITY PRESS

CAMBRIDGE
UNIVERSITY PRESS

University Printing House, Cambridge CB2 8BS, United Kingdom

Cambridge University Press is part of the University of Cambridge.

It furthers the University's mission by disseminating knowledge in the pursuit of education, learning and research at the highest international levels of excellence.

www.cambridge.org
Information on this title: www.cambridge.org/9780521472722

© Cambridge University Press 1998

First published 1998

A catalogue record for this publication is available from the British Library

ISBN 978-0-521-47272-2 Hardback
ISBN 978-0-521-47864-9 Paperback

To Katharine Thomson

Few statesmen fail in an emergency to recognize a duty to lie for their country.

E. H. Carr, *German–Soviet Relations Between the Two World Wars, 1919–1939*

Contents

Preface

This book offers a critical introduction to the writings of E. H. Carr on international relations and assesses his sustained attempt to influence British policy between 1936 and 1946. The principal task of chapter 1 is to set out some problems of interpretation and reputation. Carr has long enjoyed the reputation of a political realist. This loosely implies excessive respect for power, structural constraints, and the state, together with a pessimistic attitude towards projects for radical political reform. His enemies repeatedly accused Carr of vacillation and lack of principle because of his advocacy of concessions on Central and East European issues to Germany in the 1930s and to the Soviet Union in the 1940s. The 'Carr problem' arises because those who read him with care generally find that he fails in certain respects to conform to the expectations aroused by the sobriquets 'realist' and 'appeaser'.

On the contrary, Carr favoured radical change in social and economic as well as foreign policy. Indeed, he stood very close to Leninism at times and later in life would describe his most widely read work on international relations, *The Twenty Years' Crisis*, as 'not exactly a Marxist work, but strongly impregnated with Marxist ways of thinking'.[1] Yet Carr regarded his ideological position as wholly consistent with a thoroughly patriotic pursuit of British interests. His case for radical economic change grew out of a conviction that Britain could maintain its position as a Great Power only on the basis of a greatly expanded economy, while the foreign policies he advocated

---

[1] R. W. Davies, 'Edward Hallett Carr, 1892–1982', in *Proceedings of the British Academy, 1983*, vol. LXIX (London: Oxford University Press for the British Academy, 1984), p. 485.

were generally in tune with significant factions in Whitehall and Westminster and were consistently directed towards the maximisation of British power in the long run. There was, as my colleague David Carlton patiently explained to me when I was inclined to overemphasise Carr's Leftward leanings, little of substance to have prevented the crypto-Marxist from voting Conservative in the 1930s (though it is most unlikely that he ever did). Throughout the Second World War he was to work in close and amicable partnership with a Christian Tory, Robin Barrington-Ward.

Those readers who know little of Carr or his work, having read perhaps no more than a few chapters of *The Twenty Years' Crisis*, may therefore prefer to leave chapter 1 aside. Since they have not yet been schooled into any systematic misunderstanding of Carr they hardly need to be cajoled out of it. They may find it best to read chapters 2 to 5 before returning to chapter 1. In this way they will become familiar with the arguments of Carr's books, essays, pamphlets, and journalistic writings on a wide range of foreign and social policy questions, the backdrop of crisis and world war against which they were formed, and the more abstract reflexions on the nature of international relations to which Carr was led by experience. They may then look once again at chapter 3, especially its central section, before concluding their reading of the book from the beginning of chapter 6. In the later chapters they will find a less expository and more critical assessment of Carr's ideas that pays close attention to some of the intellectual influences to which he was subject, the ways in which he manipulated ideas and language to attain his objectives, and the ethical implications of his approach to the study of international relations.

There can be no better moment to thank some of those who taught me history. Christopher Platt first attracted me to the history of Latin America and British international business, and so, by a circuitous route, to international relations. John Lonsdale and Ivor Wilkes ran such an inspiring course on African history that 9.00 a.m. lectures seemed no effort at all. The Crosby historian Frank Tyrer had earlier helped me to understand continuity and community. Last (or first) come E. A. Potts, and Ian (I. J. B.) Walker, the teacher who did more than any other to attract me to history as a profession. At a time when all that was required to pass A-level history with the highest grade was minimal knowledge culled from standard texts so long as this was combined with mastery of essay technique, Ian encouraged wide reading, introducing the class to recent controversies between historians in the pages of *Past and Present, Historical Journal,* and other academic publications, and also found time to foster a love of twentieth-century orchestral music. He cultivated discussion and thought in place of authority and rote learning. It was he who advised me to read E. H. Carr's *What Is History?* and much else when I was preparing for university entrance as a schoolboy in the 1960s.

I did not encounter Carr again until I began to teach international relations theory at the University of Warwick with Barry Buzan. Use of *The Twenty Years' Crisis* as a set text for two or three years in the mid-1980s, to be examined chapter by chapter – at times line by line – in small undergraduate classes, reawakened my interest, first made me aware of some of the more manipulative characteristics of Carr's rhetoric, and led, indirectly, to this book. This is an appropriate point to acknowledge the help of those students.

It was Barry Buzan who drew me around this time into a fruitful collaboration with himself and Richard Little which led me to think afresh about political realism. This work took Kenneth Waltz's *Theory of International Politics* as its point of departure, and close study of United States neorealism in the closing phase of the Cold War led to consideration of the moral and political gulf separating that arid world from what seemed to me a much more sympathetic British international society tradition. This led me to reconsider Carr's methodology and realise its distinctive quality. Early traces of the present project may therefore be found in the later chapters of *The Logic of Anarchy,* but it was only after completion of that book that I began to concentrate more completely on Carr. A succession of papers followed, only one of which appears in anything close to its original form in this book (as chapter 7), but all of which are here in some more or less ghostly shape. Each of these has been presented informally at seminars or conferences before moving forward to publication, and if I forget – as I certainly shall – to acknowledge every one of the many colleagues who helped me by their comments and questions I can only ask their pardon.

The first of these papers, 'E. H. Carr Through Cold War Lenses: Nationalism, Large States, and the Shaping of Opinion', was presented at the Sixth Lothian Conference at Mansfield College, Oxford, in March 1992 in belated commemoration of the seventieth anniversary of the foundation of the Royal Institute of International Affairs. I owe a particular debt to Andrea Bosco and Cornelia Navari because they took responsibility for editing the proceedings, later published as *Chatham House and British Foreign Policy, 1919–1945*. In this early paper I was concerned to account for the peculiarity of Carr's reputation by examining his own rhetorical practice and his distinctive place in the British intellectual Cold War. The main emphasis, however, was on one of the many aspects of Carr's work that had surprised me: the advocacy, by a political realist, of a functionalist approach to European regional integration. The special value of the Oxford conference lay in the view it gave me, as a newcomer in a field where I still feel myself a trespasser, of work by scholars, such as Christopher Brewin and Inderjeet Parmar, who had researched the social and political context within which Carr worked extensively.

Next came an invitation from Francis A. Beer and Robert Hariman, respectively of Drake University and the University of Colorado, Boulder, to consider Carr's rhetoric at greater length in a book finally entitled *Post-Realism*. Theirs was an exceptionally careful and thorough editing process which posed constructive questions. It also brought to my desk in draft some very thought-provoking contributions by others, including my then colleague Paul Chilton and the editors themselves.

A third contributory essay, and the only one to appear with relatively light revision as a chapter of the present volume, started life as a paper for the 1994 conference of the British International Studies Association, at York. Circumstances prevented me from attending, but the paper was presented to David Miller's philosophy of science seminar at Warwick and received unusually generous and extensive criticism from the anonymous readers to whom it was submitted by the editor of *Political Studies*.

My original intention was to expand this chapter to deal with Carr's debts to two other thinkers, Lenin and Reinhold Niebuhr. In the end it seemed wrong to do so. They may all swim in the same water, but Niebuhr survives only with the long-held breath of faith and Lenin by resort to the rusty aqualung of Marxism; only Mannheim, like Carr himself, moves easily through the waters considered here, breathing with the discreet and flexible gills of liberalism. Both the Lenin and the Niebuhr sections threatened to distract from the main thrust of the book and I concluded that they belonged elsewhere. At some point the place of Lenin as a pioneer of a genuinely systemic, though flawed, approach to international relations needs to be asserted against the customary accusations of reductionism, but this is neither the place nor the time. Equally, the reception of Niebuhr, not only by Carr but also by many others including Ken Waltz, deserves more extended treatment, but would have unbalanced the present book. Parts of chapter 7 were read to a lively group at the Centre for Studies in Democracy of the University of Westminster where John Keane, Chantal Mouffe, and their colleagues offered valuable advice, not all of which has been ignored. Finally, the shape of the book was altered, I hope for the better, by anticipation of the opportunity to speak about Carr's years at *The Times* at a conference to be hosted by the Aberystwyth Department of International Politics at Gregynog in July 1997.

Three other groups deserve acknowledgement: archivists, colleagues, and friends, among whom I include my family. I am grateful to Ursula Gavin, of Macmillan, for information about recent sales figures for Carr's books and to the staff of the British Library for help in consulting the Macmillan Papers. I also wish to acknowledge the generous access provided to papers relating to Carr by the University of Birmingham, the Royal Institute of International Affairs at Chatham House, and *The Times*. Along the way, drafts of papers or chapters relating to Carr were read and commented upon by David Carlton, Paul Chilton, Fred Halliday, and Robert Skidelsky. Barry Jones contributed a memorandum written by Carr while still at the Foreign Office which prefigured some of the ideas he was to develop at Aberystwyth. I gained from hearing Jonathan Haslam speak about Carr at an early stage in my own work and at the Gregynog conference on Carr in July 1997, and look forward to his biography to answer many puzzles about Carr that lie beyond the scope of my own book.

Finally there are those colleagues, friends, and members of my family who made the book possible by providing an environment in which study was possible. Of colleagues, Wyn Grant stands out, steering his department through difficult times with inexhaustible energy and patience. He made sure that I had a term's study leave in the autumn of 1994 to break the back of this task and has since encouraged me to snatch the tantalisingly few weeks without which the task could not be completed. Barry Buzan, without whom Warwick is the poorer, remains a good friend and collaborator and deserves my particular thanks for waiting so patiently for this book to be completed so that we (and Helge Hveem) can get on to the next. My wife Linda, attacking her own duties and projects with an energy I cannot match, has provided an example of dedication which I have followed only fitfully. We continue to exchange ideas about research, as we have always done since we were students together. My two teenage daughters, Kate and Ellen, have contributed in many small ways: through their cheerfulness and conversation, and by giving me the best possible reason to come down and cook at that point in the day where instinct says continue but reason recognises fatigue.

Last come two groups of Birmingham friends and musicians. The first of these is the Birmingham Bach Choir, but more specifically a past member of the choir, Nick Fisher, whose bold promotion of a Rochester Festival and commissioning of the setting by Paul Spicer of an excerpt from Rochester's 'Satire Against Mankind' drew my attention to what is surely the most elegant statement in English of the security dilemma and, taking the poem as a whole, of the threefold division between bleak structural realism, excessive idealist faith in reason, and the pragmatic or practical form of reason to which Carr aspired.

It happened that the final days of this book jostled with rehearsals for the revival of a multimedia anti-racist show which I scripted three years ago for another Birmingham choir, Clarion. On the one hand, the script draws loose analogies between the fascism and racism of the 1930s and 1940s and their resurgence in Europe since the end of the Cold War. On the other, it contains an extended meditation on the possibility of cultural resistance occasioned by the rediscovery, after his death, of a set of slides brought back from Brno by George Thomson, professor of Greek at Birmingham University, in the 1950s.

Of all the buildings they might have chosen for their Brno head-quarters, the Gestapo settled for the Law Faculty of the Tómas Masaryk University, named for the founder of the Czechoslovak state. Next they recruited political prisoners from a nearby concentration camp to paint murals to adorn a night club in the basement. The ironic deployment of a richly multicultural symbolic language by the Czech 'decadents' as they painted the Gestapo chiefs and their superiors into mock heroic scenes made the Nazi leaders look even more foolish than they realised. Alongside the music of Hanns Eisler and Kurt Weill, the murals stand as reminders that the cultural war against fascism was waged not only with words, as by Carr in his *Times* leaders, but also with graphic art and music.

Clarion, founded by a Birmingham doctor returning from service with the Republican cause in Spain, may have clung too long to the

Soviet alliance, as did Carr; but they have been valiant fighters over the years in pursuit of peace and democracy throughout the world. And if I choose to dedicate this book not to Clarion, but to one of its earliest members, Katharine Thomson, a member since 1940, it is because she is among the last of a generation close to Carr in its progressive radicalism: a child in Edwardian Cambridge, a critical eyewitness to Hitler's rise to power as she studied piano in Germany, confirmed in her lifelong commitment to the Left through marriage to the Marxist and classicist George Thomson, and a distinguished accompanist long ago to the prince of post-modernists, Ludwig Wittgenstein, who preferred to whistle than to sing his way through *Winterreise*.

And 'tis this very Reason I despise,
This supernatural gift that makes a mite
Think he's an image of the infinite;
Comparing his short life, void of all rest,
To the eternal, and the ever-blessed.
This busy, pushing stirrer-up of doubt,
That frames deep mysteries, then finds them out;
Filling with frantic crowds of thinking fools
The reverend bedlams, colleges and schools;
Borne on whose wings each heavy sot can pierce
The limits of the boundless universe:
So charming ointments make an old witch fly,
And bear a crippled carcass through the sky.
'Tis the exalted power whose business lies
In nonsense, and impossibilities.
This made a whimsical philosopher
Before the spacious world his tub prefer,
And we have modern cloistered coxcombs, who
Retire to think 'cause they have naught to do.
But thoughts are given for action's government;
Where action ceases, thought's impertinent:
Our sphere of action is life's happiness,
And he that thinks beyond thinks like an ass.
Thus, whilst against false reasoning I inveigh,
I own right reason, which I would obey:
That bounds desires, with a reforming will
To keep 'em more in vigour, not to kill.
Your reason hinders, mine helps to enjoy,
Renewing appetites yours would destroy.

From *A Satire Against Mankind*,
Lord Rochester

1   The trouble with Carr

Reputations and readings

Edward Hallett Carr enjoyed a long and productive life, leaving behind him not one but several reputations. In an affectionate memoir R. W. Davies recalled that Carr had pursued no less than six vocations with distinction.[1] One consequence of this has been that many readers who believe they know Carr turn out to be far more familiar with a single aspect of his work than with the whole.

What Is History? has been a prescribed text on historiography for a generation of students in British schools and colleges, many of whom will have remained unaware of anything else Carr wrote.[2] But the commentator on history and social theorist was also an academic historian. The last thirty-five years of his life were devoted principally to a fourteen-volume *History of Soviet Russia*. As Carr reached eighty, Abramsky declared that he would always be remembered for this monumental work, which ranked with Mommsen on Rome. Others have disputed such judgements vigorously, and the relative attention given to Carr-on-international-relations and Carr-as-historian in Abramsky's *Festschrift* hardly reflected his continued ascendancy in the first field and his dwindling reputation in the second.[3]

---

[1] R. W. Davies, 'Edward Hallett Carr, 1892–1982', *Proceedings of the British Academy, 1983*, vol. LXIX (London: Oxford University Press for the British Academy, 1984), p. 473.

[2] E. H. Carr, *What Is History?* (London: Macmillan, 1962). Provocative and valuable recent correctives have come from Keith Jenkins: *Re-thinking History* (London: Routledge, 1991) and *On What Is History* (London: Routledge, 1995).

[3] Leopold Labedz, 'E. H. Carr: An Historian Overtaken by History', *Survey*, 30:1–2, 1988, pp. 94–111, provides a damning assessment of the *History of Soviet Russia*.

1

Academic work does not exhaust Carr's repertoire. Before turning to his Soviet history, Carr had for six years been assistant editor of a great newspaper, *The Times*, with substantial responsibility for its attempts to channel British foreign and social policy in new directions. Before this he had served briefly in the wartime Ministry of Information and for twenty years, the best part of his youth, in the British Foreign Service. There he had managed, in a more leisured age, to combine diplomacy with an active literary career as essayist, reviewer, and biographer. However, the anonymity of the editorialist and the bureaucrat has in large measure protected Carr's continuing reputation as a theorist of international relations from being confronted with his spontaneous wartime outpourings on foreign policy, while much of the early work on Russian literature and politics, including the biography of the anarchist Bakunin which Carr regarded as his best book, is now referred to only by specialists.[4]

These diverse activities, the distinctive reputation to which each gave rise, and the complex pattern of relations between the several careers and reputations merit integrated, extended, and balanced attention in a general intellectual biography.[5] However, the focus of this book is considerably narrower and its scope of inquiry accordingly more limited. It is concerned above all with the contribution made by Carr to the practice and theory of international relations.

This emphasis does not mean that other facets of the man and his work are to be wholly ignored, but it does mean that they are considered here only to the extent that they shed light on the relatively brief period during which international relations was the dominant concern. Of this dominance there can be little doubt, for it was not to embark on a career as an academic historian but in order to be free to contribute to public debate about British foreign policy that Carr took the substantial personal and financial risk of resigning his post of first secretary at the Foreign Office in 1936 after twenty years' service, and it was in the main because of the defeat of his Centrist approach that Carr remained, for the first decade of the Cold War, without a secure

---

[4] Davies, 'Carr', p. 480.
[5] Jonathan Haslam, one of Carr's last research students, has generously undertaken this task, and has at his disposal personal papers including an extensive autobiographical sketch by Carr himself to which Davies also had access when writing his account of Carr's life and work for the proceedings of the British Academy.

academic post, victim of a genteel but remorseless British form of McCarthyism.[6]

It is because of this bold decision that Carr, more than a decade after his death, continues to be widely known among students of international relations as one of the most prominent classical realists of the middle of the twentieth century. His major contribution to this field of studies, *The Twenty Years' Crisis*, remains in print and is frequently recommended to students. However, familiarity with Carr has gone hand in hand with deep confusion about the interpretation of his work.

A first reason for this might seem mere carelessness. Even among those who have read it, the first nine chapters appear to be much better known than the remainder of the book, and the image of Carr's own views is too often based on the straw-man realism of chapter 5. Responsibility for such misreadings must be shared quite evenly between three parties. Readers, as well as anthologists and summarisers, may have concentrated unduly on the early chapters of *The Twenty Years' Crisis* to the exclusion of the remainder of this book and of Carr's other works on international relations, but Carr himself used a highly manipulative rhetoric in this book much more than in the rest of his extensive output, and this created rich possibilities of misunderstanding which his political opponents then proceeded more or less wilfully to exploit. This most complex of Carr's works is examined at some length in chapter 3 of this volume and again in chapter 6, where Carr's substantial intellectual debt to Karl Mannheim is explored.

Explaining the initial carelessness of readers and commentators is not difficult. It has not been laziness, but the distinctively academic vice of taxonomy that has been in large measure to blame. Many seem to have assumed that it is enough to know that Carr is a political realist. It may then be objected that reading Carr thoroughly and extensively is as little help in understanding political realism today as reading Marx or Keynes would be in seeking to understanding contemporary Marxism or neo-Keynesian economics. Some might think reference to the original ideas and their social context essential, but just as many would regard this as irrelevant, claiming that the

---

[6] Davies, 'Carr', p. 491; Timothy Dunne, 'International Relations Theory in Britain: The Invention of an International Society Tradition', University of Oxford, DPhil., 1993, p. 32, quoting Haslam, 'We Need a Faith', *History Today*, 33, August 1983, p. 39.

Realpolitik tradition and instead reserving it for a pragmatic and Centrist contemporary fusion of *Realpolitik* and the natural law tradition. Berki, himself a student of Carr, though exaggerating the identification of his erstwhile teacher with the *Realpolitik* tradition, anticipated McKinlay and Little by elaborating his own form of political realism, which was much less distant from Carr's views than he claimed.[19]

Sympathetic and perceptive accounts of Carr's contribution to international relations have been supplied by Ieuan John and his Aberystwyth colleagues as well as by William Fox, Hedley Bull, Kenneth W. Thompson, and, above all, by Graham Evans, whose essay remains the best short introduction to Carr on international relations.[20] The current revival of interest in Carr from the Left may best be dated from Ken Booth's 'Utopian Realism' of 1991.[21] More recently, the failure of Carr to conform to textbook realism has also been recognised with varying degrees of surprise, generosity, and enthusiasm by J. Ann Tickner, Andrew Linklater, and Timothy Dunne.[22] Yet in spite of this recent rediscovery of the idealistic aspects of his work, the level of confusion between Carr and the composite realism of the literature is such that the record needs to be put straight, and what follows may serve as a first approximation.

Classical realists including Carr and Morgenthau were, in their very

---

[19] Robert D. McKinlay and Richard Little, *Global Problems and World Order* (London: Pinter, 1986); Berki, *Realism*, passim.

[20] Ieuan John, Moorhead Wright, and John Garnett, 'International Politics at Aberystwyth, 1919–1969', in Porter, *Aberystwyth Papers*, pp. 86–102; Fox, 'Carr and Political Realism'; Bull, 'Theory'; Kenneth W. Thompson, *Masters of International Thought: Major Twentieth-Century Theorists and the World Crisis* (Baton Rouge: Louisiana State University Press, 1980); Graham Evans, 'E. H. Carr and International Relations', *British Journal of International Studies*, 1:2, July 1975, pp. 77–97.

[21] Ken Booth, 'Security in Anarchy: Utopian Realism in Theory and Practice', *International Affairs*, 67:3, July 1991, pp. 527–45.

[22] J. Ann Tickner, 'Re-visioning Security', in Ken Booth and Steve Smith, eds., *International Relations Theory Today* (Cambridge: Polity Press, 1995), pp. 175–97; Andrew Linklater, 'The Transformation of Political Community: E. H. Carr, Critical Theory, and International Relations', *Review of International Studies*, 23:3, July 1997, pp. 321–57; Dunne, 'International Relations Theory in Britain'. Linklater recalled an earlier paper in which he described Carr as 'an unadulterated realist' and went on to characterise his later paper as 'a confession; an exercise in delayed repentance'. One task for the sociology of knowledge is to pose the question of why the same individual will read an author quite differently in changed social circumstances. Integrity of response trumps consistency, but only at the cost of exposure to the charge of opportunism.

different ways, explicitly concerned to create a scientific discipline of international relations. If none anticipated the kind of approach pioneered by Kaplan and others in the 1950s, this not a consequence of methodological naivety. They were already well aware of positivism in the 1930s, but knew that it was by no means the only method available to the social scientist, and found it more or less repugnant. For his part, Carr introduced an alternative strand of the emerging social scientific methodology of the day into international relations at the end of the 1930s. This was Karl Mannheim's sociology of knowledge, a critical approach which bore a strong family resemblance to the views of Marx on ideology and false consciousness.[23]

Sociology of knowledge allowed for the possibility of fundamental change in history. Realism is generally held to privilege continuity over change. On this question, classical realists divided broadly into those, like Morgenthau, who derived continuity from a supposed facet of human nature and those who followed a more explicitly structuralist path, stressing the necessarily though unintendedly conflictual outcome of rational action in an anarchic state system. Though fitting neatly into neither of these categories, Carr was much closer to the second than the first. Far from being a historian in any traditional sense, Carr was a historicist. Here, little more is meant by this than that he believed history to be a progressive working out of the unchanging and fundamental structural dilemma of international anarchy over time through the rise and fall of states, through wars of adjustment, and through international negotiation.[24]

A history of this sort, in which the fundamental rules of the game do not change, is sometimes described by its critics as synchronic. The

---

[23] Fox, 'Carr and Political Realism', p. 1, is among the few to draw attention to this move, though Carr is very open about it in the preface to the first edition of *The Twenty Years' Crisis*. Carr's debt to Mannheim is traced in detail in ch. 6 of this volume.

[24] An excellent contemporary example of this style of history is to be found in Paul Kennedy, *The Rise and Fall of the Great Powers: Economic Change and Military Conflict from 1500 to 2000* (New York: Random House, 1988). For challenges to Kennedy's synchronic and structuralist approach to war which stress discontinuity, see David Kaiser, *Politics and War: European Conflict from Philip II to Hitler* (London: I. B. Tauris, 1990), or John J. Weltman, *World Politics and the Evolution of War* (Baltimore and London: Johns Hopkins University Press, 1995). The most frequently cited twentieth-century debate concerning historicism, between Karl Popper and Karl Mannheim, is referred to in ch. 6 in this volume. For Carr's vitriolic, if justified, contribution see Carr, *What Is History?*, p. 86, n. 1. References to this book are to the first edition unless the second is specified.

clock has been stopped and all the events take place in what is in essence a single moment. In a more familiar phrase, drawn from classroom science, the investigation is conducted 'with other things being equal' (*ceteris paribus*). Many historians strongly object to this methodological principle. Carr was aware of the danger and attempted fitfully to avoid it; but he consistently voiced a belief, albeit a carefully qualified belief, in progress. In short, at the time he wrote his major works on international relations, Carr was neither a historian nor a positivist, but a social scientist of some sophistication, espousing a form of pragmatism tempered by structuralism.

It is certainly true that *The Twenty Years' Crisis* was a polemic, and that much of its energy was directed against the naive view that international law and the League of Nations might somehow replace the play of power politics. Yet the book is more than a polemic. It was offered by Carr as 'An Introduction to the Study of International Relations'. This will have been partly, no doubt, to impress the reader, but partly because Carr took seriously the broader implications of the methodological position that he had adopted, and because its later and less frequently read chapters were given over to positive policy suggestions grounded in the analysis of parts I and II. Conciliation of the Soviet Union, maintenance of Britain as a third major power alongside the USA and the USSR, and the creation of a welfare state in Britain: these main strands of Carr's programme were pursued with vigour in subsequent publications and through the leader column of *The Times* over the next few years, and not without some measure of success.

Rhetoric, relativism, and realism

The frequent but misleading association of Carr with post-war North American realists, taken together with inconsistencies among the current profusion of textbook definitions of realism, may provide a clue that what realists have in common is less a matter of academic agreement on the nature of international politics or the issues of the day than an approach to political practice. In such an approach the study of politics is co-opted by and subordinated to the process of official deliberation and the practical conduct of politics, becoming thereby thoroughly implicated not only in the formulation of policy but also in its implementation. Other recent scholars, examining major realists, have remarked on inconsistencies which are conformable with a shared willingness to sacrifice intellectual integrity in pursuit of political objectives or, to put it another way, to allow the end to justify the means.[25]

One obvious weakness of such an approach is that it sacrifices a useful commonsense distinction by placing realists in the same camp as idealists: all of them equally *engagé* and morally committed, differing simply in their affiliations. However, it is possible for the distinction between realist and idealist to be re-established as a disagreement over permissible means to influence policy: the relative merits of truth and persuasion, transparent and manipulative texts, and universally accessible as opposed to restricted media. A more interesting corollary is that the positivist stance adopted by some self-proclaimed realists may be no more than that: a rhetorical ploy calculated to disarm the reader by the profession of objectivity and disengagement.

This hypothesis about the primacy of rhetorical technique and moral commitment over content in political realism is one reason why Carr is studied, throughout the early chapters of this book, in the context of his times and with close attention to his choice of genres, media, and forms of expression. It may be possible, by working back from the advocacy of specific policies, to delineate recurrent concerns and principles. Carr certainly seems to imply this. His Mannheimean social constructivist method constantly pointed to the circumstances and interests that had moulded the policy choices of others, though Carr was careful to indicate that, precisely because they were socially determined, interests and preferences were apt to change.[26] But this

---

[25] A salient example is the treatment of Machiavelli in R. B. J. Walker, *Inside/Outside: International Relations as Political Theory* (Cambridge: Cambridge University Press, 1993).

[26] I do not intend, in this volume, to enter into discussion of the variety of claims to social constructivism that have developed within academic international relations over the past decade. Post-Marxists and Marxists of the Frankfurt or critical tradition, post-structuralists, post-modernists, and late liberals all use the term and agree on the importance of recognising the malleable and historical character of belief systems, knowledge, and sources of personal and social identity. Yet they disagree profoundly on other matters. My own position is that of a late or 'ironic' liberal, much less inclined now, after closer study of Carr and Mannheim, to persist in nostalgic attempts to keep structuralism in play than I was six years ago as *The Logic of Anarchy* went to press, but still impressed by the possibility of building a pragmatic liberalism growing out of the tradition to which Mannheim and Carr both belong. An excellent introduction to these debates is provided by Alexander Wendt, 'Anarchy Is What States Make of It: The Social Construction of Power Politics', *International Organization*, 46:2, Spring 1992, pp. 391–425.

methodology is plainly reflexive, and Carr deserves the same treatment he metes out to the luckless idealists of the 1920s. It makes sense to examine everything Carr wrote during the 1930s and 1940s in the context of the roles he undertook, the predicaments he encountered, the interests he espoused, and the practical political intention of each work. It is through this method that a reading of Carr is developed that attempts to represent his oeuvre fairly, locating and accounting for the essential features of his distinctive brand of realism.

Whatever the purpose of Carr's rhetorical tricks, their effect was sometimes less to manipulate than to confuse the reader. More generally, some of the blame for the crudity of standard characterisations of political realism must be laid at the door of the realists themselves. A favourite tactic, especially beloved of theorists working in a British political culture that idealises fudge, has been to outline two opposing ideals – realism and idealism or justice and order – before disavowing both in order to push through what may then be presented as a compromise between extremes. Hedley Bull pursued just such a plan in *The Anarchical Society*.[27] J. H. Herz also played this trick, dismissing the extremes in favour of his own 'realistic liberalism'.[28]

More than a decade before, Carr had adopted the same stratagem, and it is hardly surprising that this should have led to confusion between Carr's own position and the straw-man realism of the early chapters of *The Twenty Years' Crisis*: the set of beliefs that Carr himself consistently refers to as 'realism'.[29] To this day, there are textbooks on international relations in circulation contaminated by confusion between the positions argued for by acknowledged realists and the grotesquely caricatured views that they sent forward on their Right flank to draw fire away from the main advance. The former were seldom if ever called 'realism' by their authors; the latter generally were. This has made life difficult for generations of students. One of the objectives of this book has therefore been to make a bonfire of Carr's straw-man realism and identify more clearly the more prag-

---

[27] Hedley Bull, *The Anarchical Society: A Study of Order in World Politics* (Basingstoke: Macmillan, 1977).
[28] J. H. Herz, *Political Realism and Political Idealism: A Study in Theories and Realities* (Chicago: University of Chicago Press, 1951).
[29] E. H. Carr, *The Twenty Years' Crisis, 1919–1939: An Introduction to the Study of International Relations* (London: Macmillan, 1939).

matic and Centrist realism which he consistently advocated and inconsistently pursued.

A controversial figure

The contribution of straw-man realism to the misinterpretation of Carr would, however, have been much less severe had it not been seized upon and exploited by critics whose deep opposition to his views led them to disregard all scruples. The distorted readings of Carr that prevailed throughout the Cold War were in some measure a symptom of his association with the losing side. British and American academics performed similar duty in another theatre by their sustained suppression of Lenin's flawed but intriguing structuralist theory of war.[30] Within weeks of Carr's death, Norman Stone took the opportunity of a review of his *The Twilight of the Comintern* to consider his life and work as a whole.[31] In the columns that followed, Carr was accused of cruelty, unfairness, cowardice, intellectual autism, and padding around College in 'sand-shoes'. Old charges of appeasement and duplicity were repeated. The account was, to say the very least, intemperate. Letters followed – from family, colleagues, and former students – convincingly challenging the accuracy of Stone's account on several points and charging him with selective quotation.[32] It was a late public echo of disagreements dating back to the late 1930s and 1940s.

Since Carr's notoriety as much as his celebrity provides the motive for this book, it is worth asking how it came about that he was still capable of arousing such fierce opposition after the lapse of forty years. There were at least five reasons. First of all, Carr had, in the opinion of his opponents, consistently been far too kind in his judgement of the Soviet achievement. 'Clearly, to him [Carr], the Bolsheviks had taken a howling desert of illiteracy . . . and turned it into a sort of

---

[30] The tradition continued. Norman Etherington's masterly study, which reveals the slight of mind practised on Lenin by Fieldhouse and others, appeared five years too soon and failed to receive the attention it deserved among international relations scholars: Norman Etherington, *Theories of Imperialism: War, Conquest, and Capital* (Beckenham: Croom Helm, 1984).

[31] Norman Stone, 'Grim Eminence', *London Review of Books*, 5:1, 20 January–2 February 1983, pp. 3–8.

[32] Letters from Rachel Kelly, *London Review of Books*, 5:2, 3–16 February 1983, and from R. W. Davies, Eric Hobsbawm, John Barber, and Jonathan Haslam, *London Review of Books*, 5:3, 17 February–2 March 1983.

Welwyn Garden City.'[33] He had underestimated the substantial economic progress achieved by Russia under tsarist rule and he had closed his eyes to Stalinist suppression of non-Russian nationalities within the Soviet Union. Secondly, Carr was felt to have erred in his views on British policy, both foreign and domestic. He had urged appeasement of Hitler right up to the outbreak of war, before changing his tune to argue for British acquiescence in Soviet expansionism in Eastern Europe. At the same time he had urged Churchill's government to turn, prematurely so his critics claimed, from the conduct of war to planning for peace – and for a peace that left little room for private enterprise. In the third place, Carr was held to be guilty of methodological sins. He had opened the door to relativism and economic determinism by arguing that the social conditioning of scholarly opinion, just as much as other kinds of opinion, robbed it of any claim to universal truth or superior moral judgement.

In short, Carr-the-realist was thought too tolerant of the centralised and bureaucratic superstate as the major actor in international relations, too dismissive of the significance of the ideologies and values that distinguished one superpower from another, and too ready to acquiesce in the supposedly inevitable outcome of Great Power rivalries. As if this were not enough, two further charges against Carr were present in Stone's review, though each was obliquely expressed. Carr, according to Stone, 'never quite said what he meant'. Finally Stone observed, in an unsuccessful attempt at irony, 'the curious thing about Carr, the historian of power, was that he never had much himself'.

The first of these two charges might be thought no more than a peevish complaint from a critic unable to find clear evidence in Carr's work of the views he supposed his opponent to have held. But it is rather more profound and accurate than this. Carr very frequently wrote not simply to express his views, but with a highly developed awareness of the persuasive impact his text might have. He was, as has already been indicated, a self-conscious rhetorician or propagandist. There was no point in speaking the truth if it did not achieve one's objective; far better to write what would be effective, even if it did not quite tally with one's inner beliefs. Later chapters will argue not only that Carr took such a position, but also that it is of a piece

---

[33] Stone, 'Grim Eminence, p. 6. For a most illuminating early example of the deep antipathy of the British Right to the garden city, see John Buchan, *Mr. Standfast* (London: Hodder & Stoughton, 1919).

with his realism on foreign policy questions and was a predictable consequence of his adoption of a social constructivist methodology. The final accusation, of lack of power, is an odd one. Why should one expect a professional student of power to exercise it any more than one would expect a theatre critic to tread the boards? The British political system, then as now, was less conducive than that of the United States to the movement of talented academics into posts within the administration and the diplomatic service. Indeed, it can be argued not only that Carr attempted to influence public policy but also that, given the constraints of the British system, he was remarkably successful. Detailed examination of Carr's years at *The Times* in chapter 5 will show that, notwithstanding Churchill's intemperate attack over Greece, Carr's position – and that of the newspaper he served – was not decisively defeated until Bevin's mind hardened against the Soviet Union in the early spring of 1946. Had Carr not been of some consequence it is hard to imagine why Stone and his predecessors should have felt the need to attack with such vigour and to sustain the attack into the 1980s.

Contemporary relevance

Carr died in 1983. He was already an adult when the First World War broke out and would later candidly admit that the progressive drift of his work was a consequence of his Edwardian upbringing.[34] How can the ideas and antagonisms of Carr and his generation be of more than antiquarian interest to citizens and politicians at the close of the twentieth century? The answer lies in an understanding of what constitutes contemporary history of ideas.

To clarify this concept it is still helpful to call on the mildly counter-intuitive definition of contemporary history derived by Carr himself from Benedetto Croce and R. V. Collingwood and popularised a generation ago by Geoffrey Barraclough.[35] Barraclough contrasted modern history and contemporary history. Modern history studied the effects of great events of the past such as the Reformation, the rise of manufacturing industry, or the French Revolution. It was firmly rooted in the study of documentary sources and, partly for that

---

[34] Carr, *What Is History?* (2nd edn; London: Penguin, 1987), p. 6.
[35] Carr, *What Is History?*, p. 15; Geoffrey Barraclough, *An Introduction to Contemporary History* (London: Watts, 1964).

reason, profoundly Eurocentric. It proceeded chronologically, looking forward to the present from what were held to have been crucial moments in the past.

Contemporary history, by contrast, set out to understand current predicaments by delving back into the past. This led it to be more concerned than modern history with the non-European world. In Barraclough's day, modern history was generally held to have begun in the later 1400s, perhaps with the fall of Constantinople in 1453, perhaps with the first successful European settlements in the Americas, or the revival of European interest in its classical past. But contemporary history had no clear frontier. In explaining the contemporary politics of the Balkans it is hard to avoid delving back before 1400 to the battle of Kosovo (1389) and the Great Schism (1054).[36] In short, contemporary history was not concerned exclusively with very recent events; it was not current affairs by another name; it was a method rather than a body of facts.

In spite of this, Barraclough found that, by and large, his contemporary world could be explained in terms of a cluster of features that all originated at the end of the nineteenth century. He shared with Lenin the belief that the contemporary world had been formed by the economic, social, and administrative consequences of electricity, steel, the internal combustion engine, new metallurgical techniques, telegraphy, and the like, which had completely transformed the world between 1870 and 1900.

Since Carr and Barraclough addressed this topic in the early 1960s and since Carr made his contribution to international relations more than a decade earlier, there have been further, equally profound, changes. It is easy to exaggerate the extent of contemporary economic interdependence. Ratios of international trade and investment to domestic activity may or may not exceed the historically high levels of the late nineteenth century. Changes in institutional forms, especially the rise of more bureaucratic transnational corporations and intrafirm trade, make comparisons hazardous.[37] What seems rather clearer is

[36] As does Rebecca West in one of the greatest works of contemporary history, *Black Lamb and Grey Falcon: The Record of a Journey Through Yugoslavia in 1937*, 2 vols. (London: Macmillan, 1942).

[37] Charles Jones, 'Institutional Forms of British Direct Investment in South America', *Business History*, 39:2, April 1997, pp. 21–41, deals with one aspect of the problem, namely concurrent but independent changes in the form and the definition of foreign direct investment.

that a revolution in information technology has facilitated unprecedentedly high levels of cultural integration and social control and almost equally marked reactions against these tendencies in the shape of fundamentalist religious movements, fissiparous nationalisms, and the proliferation of ephemeral popular movements and subcultures. Coupled with the breakdown of bipolarity, this profound cultural revolution has thrown into relief the ways in which changes in weaponry and tactics have destroyed the military invulnerability of even the largest, wealthiest, or most remote states to nuclear or terrorist attack. The general political consequence of these changes has been that, even where the extensive multinational state has survived, declining ability to provide welfare through autarky and security through military might has sapped its legitimacy, forcing a substitution of co-optation, pluralism, and accommodation for the unselfconsciously assimilative nationalism and bureaucratic authoritarianism of the previous era.

The extent to which the territorial state has been able to retain control during this transformation has varied greatly. Its greatest achievements to date appear to have been the creation of a European Union and the broad extension of neoliberal disciplines of market economic and political democratisation from growth points in the United States, Britain, and Chile in the 1970s. Its failures have included the breakdown of the federal states of Yugoslavia, Czechoslovakia, and the Soviet Union. In Turkey, Brazil, China, and India, it is still touch and go.

One outcome of the transformation has been to make a great deal of history redundant. Barraclough's contemporary history is no longer contemporary. What practical value is there in a history, however meticulous and scholarly, of a trade union, a corporation, or even a state that has not simply gone out of business but encapsulates a style of mass organisation no longer considered relevant? The lessons of such a history are largely irrelevant when no one any longer intends to try to improve on past performance. Carr's massive history of the Soviet Union falls into precisely this category. Thought by many of his contemporaries to have been the most substantial of his works, it is currently the least interesting, quite regardless of its merits.

Indeed, it can plausibly be claimed that the changes of the last twenty years have been so fundamental that the world has now entered a new contemporary era of which Fordist industry, mass organisation, and Great Power warfare are no longer the defining features. A new contemporary history is therefore required in order to overcome the bewilderment and alienation of life in an unfurnished apartment. Where is one to look?

As in every past era, the warp of the new contemporary history will be spun from contemporary experience; its softer weft will consist in a reinterpretation of more or less distant pasts. For there is certainly no guarantee that the new contemporary historians will settle, or would be right to settle, as Barraclough did, for a privileging of the very recent past. Competitive reinterpretation may delve deep into the past as parties to current disputes seek to legitimate their positions. In the crisis of the First World War the extent to which ancient, rather than modern, historians responded to the challenge of offering policy advice and formulating war aims is remarkable. In the present crisis the process of competitive historiographic revision has already been under way for some time, and the battlefield stretches over at least the past two hundred and fifty years, bringing into question long-cherished assumptions about the industrial revolution, the French Revolution, the American Revolution, and the rise of the welfare state.

Carr might seem the worst possible author to turn to at this point because he turned out to be such a poor prophet in his own day. The most obvious point of vulnerability in Carr's vision of society was his attachment, however carefully qualified and hedged, to historical progress. This was both a methodological and a practical weakness. In the preface to the second edition of *What Is History?*, drafted towards the end of his life and published posthumously, Carr remarked on the tone of optimism with which he had first concluded his book in 1961 and drew attention to the many events of the subsequent twenty years that might have frustrated his earlier hopes, including the economic crises of the 1970s and the more recent intensification of the Cold War.

Against these grounds for pessimism Carr characteristically deployed a weapon he had carried at his side for almost half a century: the sociology of knowledge. Who were the prophets of doom? Why were they so despondent? His answer was that 'belief in annihilation is confined to a group of disgruntled intellectuals'. The masses in the leading economies were cheerfully improving their lot. Elsewhere whole nations were gaining ground relative to the West. Carr concluded that the prevailing gloom could be dismissed as 'a form of elitism – the product of elite social groups whose security and whose privileges have been most conspicuously eroded by the crisis, and of elite countries whose once undisputed domination over the rest of the world has been shattered'.[38]

Charmingly, disarmingly, Carr went on to characterise himself, by resort to the same logic of social conditioning, as a dissident among intellectuals, one of the 'very few . . . still writing who grew up, not in the high noon, but in the afterglow of the great Victorian age of faith and optimism'. Given this background, he found it impossible to share in the gloom and felt bound to adopt 'if not . . . an optimistic, at any rate . . . a saner and more balanced outlook on the future' than his juniors.[39]

The argument is thin to vanishing. If social conditioning dismissed the disgruntled pessimists by providing a causal explanation of their views, it could be applied with equally damaging effect to his own optimism. Carr was well aware of this, and had argued elsewhere that the self-conscious intellectual was in great measure liberated from the constraints of upbringing, free to be as optimistic or pessimistic as he chose within the relatively flexible constraints of the available evidence.[40] He was simply up to his old tricks, selecting from the available facts such material as would allow him to interpret world affairs in a way that satisfied him before presenting the interpretation as an objective tendency; and his interpretation at the start of the 1980s was, in essence, much the same as his interpretation in the very different circumstances of the later 1930s.

Inequalities of power, within his own country and between the world's Great Powers and their challengers, could hardly be maintained in the long run, even by force, in the face of changes in underlying material and technological conditions. So long as currently powerful classes and states accepted this and developed policies of graceful acquiescence, the transition could be handled in an orderly and peaceful fashion. They might even, provided they limited their foreign military commitments and adopted economic and social

---

[38] Carr, *What Is History?* (2nd edn), p. 5.

[39] Carr, *What Is History?*, p. 6.

[40] A good example is to be found in the very work for which this preface was written. 'I shall venture to believe that the historian who is most conscious of his own situation is also more capable of transcending it, and more capable of appreciating the essential nature of the differences between his own society and outlook and those of other periods and other countries, than the historian who loudly protests that he is an individual and not a social phenomenon. Man's capacity to rise above his social and historical situation seems to be conditioned by the sensitivity with which he recognizes the extent of his involvement in it' (ibid., p. 38).

policies calculated to support sustained power projection, succeed in stemming decline. This bundle of policies is generally called appeasement. It was the argument which, in its general features, was to provide Paul Kennedy with a remarkable best-seller when applied to United States decline a few years after Carr's death.[41]

Yet even if Carr's claims about material progress in general are conceded, and the doubts of ecologists dismissed as elitist stratagems, it cannot be denied that many of his favourite specific trends petered out or turned tail within his own lifetime. The passages in his works that drew most fire at the time and are least defensible in retrospect are those founded in an assessment of the supposedly dominant tendencies of contemporary history. In addition to the progressive equalisation of power, Carr assumed the progressive elimination of nationality as a basis for statehood and the ability of a system of extensive multinational states to provide security through economic management and territorially based defensive systems, confidently entrusting this task as readily to the Soviet Union as to the United States of America or a West European union under British leadership. But the most interesting features of attempts to reconcile security and cultural identity through the formation of extensive states have turned out to be the moral and practical differences between them, not their similarities. The devil was in the detail.

Carr was not alone in marginalising the detail. His assumptions about the progressive erosion of privilege and the superiority of the extensive state were commonplace throughout the middle decades of the twentieth century. From the 1920s to the mid-1970s – during almost the whole of Carr's adult life – they sustained those elites whose members attempted to manage aggregate demand in the world's richest economies in ways that would avoid global crisis of the kind experienced in the early 1930s, those who attempted to manage collective security through the League of Nations and the United Nations in ways that would avoid a recurrence of war between the major powers, those who managed the economic development of less industrialised and poorer economies, those who fostered regional integration in Western Europe and elsewhere, and those in authority over the massive bureaucratic structures spawned by political conflict and market competition alike.

These assumptions are now shattered. Yet for precisely this reason

---

[41] Kennedy, *Rise and Fall of the Great Powers.*

the practical choices that Carr faced in the 1930s and 1940s during the transition from classical to managed liberalism – choices between *laissez-faire* and intervention, between Great Power management and collective security, or between federation and nationalism – are once again the focus of public attention today in radically changed circumstances. It is Carr's questions and his proposed method, rather than his answers or the implementation of his methodology, that give his work a particular contemporary resonance.

One response to this set of choices, intellectually perhaps the most prevalent one in much of the Western world, has been to revert to the supposedly self-regulating liberal forms of an earlier period: pull back the state, downsize the company, abandon conscription, open the frontiers. But the more doctrinaire manifestations of this reaction share precisely the methodological weakness of the old orthodoxy they replace. They do little more than reverse the direction of Carr's favoured tendencies. About turn! *This* way to the end of history! Big government? Fordist corporations? Planned economy? – Dinosaurs all!

A more radical and arduous course is to negate Carr's abiding weakness, not simply by tilting the see-saw of progress once again, but by reformulating his core concepts of democracy, pragmatism, and progress in ways that avoid the pitfalls of a crudely linear historicism.[42] That is what is sketched in a very preliminary way in the concluding chapter, where the contemporary value of Carr's earlier attempt is compared to that of a ranging shot for a team of gunners. The ranging shot generally misses but is the precondition for later success. It cannot therefore be said to have failed in its purpose by missing the target. In this sense, itself a foretaste of what may be understood by a pragmatic yet non-historicist formulation of realism, Carr's work may regarded as redeemable, not just salutary.

---

[42] Here, and throughout the early chapters, I follow Carr's example by conceding that the generally accepted meaning of the term 'historicism' was established, misleadingly but irrevocably, by Popper, in *The Poverty of Historicism* (London: Routledge & Kegan Paul, 1957). See Carr, *What Is History?*, p. 86, n. 1.

2   Before the war

Carr's life

Born on 28 June 1892, Edward Hallett Carr was educated at the Merchant Taylors' School, London, and Trinity College, Cambridge, before entering the Foreign Office in 1916 as a temporary clerk. During the war he worked under Robert Cecil in the Contraband Department, dealing with Russia and Scandinavia. Posted to Paris for the peace conference, he was appointed secretary to the Committee on New States, assisting Sir James Headlam-Morley.[1]

When the conference came to an end Carr remained in Paris, working with the Conference of Ambassadors, under Sir Orme Sargent, who became his mentor. The work concerned relations with the newly created states of Central and Eastern Europe. Carr subsequently regularised his position, formally entering the service in November 1921 as a third secretary in the Foreign Office. Promoted to second secretary in January 1925, he was transferred to Riga and remained there until May 1929, acting as chargé d'affaires in the absence of the regular head of mission on two occasions, in 1926 and 1928. A final overseas posting took him to Geneva as assistant adviser on League of Nations affairs from 1930 to 1933 and was followed by his promotion to first secretary in August 1933. Between these overseas postings he worked in the Central and Southern Departments of the Foreign Office, dealing with European affairs.

As capital city of the newly independent Latvian republic, Riga was a watching post for developments in neighbouring Soviet Russia

---

[1] Sir James Headlam-Morley, *A Memoir of the Paris Peace Conference, 1919*, edited by Agnes Headlam-Morley (London: Methuen, 1972), p. 92.

though, if George Kennan is to be believed, the watching consisted more in the perusal of mundane economic and political documentation than in exchanges with glamorous clandestine agents.[2] Although most communications went out over the signature of the head of mission, Carr emerges from the shadows now and then, in the absence of his chief, reporting in September 1925 on matters as various as the political situation in Latvia, relations between Poland and Lithuania, and the vexatiously intricate problem of League of Nations representation on the Memel Harbour Board.[3]

The British mission kept a sharp eye on the arms trade in the Baltic, balancing commercial and strategic considerations. On one occasion Carr appealed to the Foreign Office to grant a licence for the export of 1,200 BSA machine guns to Lithuania, since 'refusal to allow them to meet their reasonable requirements from United Kingdom would not prevent their obtaining arms but merely drive them into closer relations with our competitors', in this instance France.[4] Such was the daily round of diplomatic life.

For all the tedium, Riga was Carr's first exposure to grass-roots nationalism. Latvian nationalism relied heavily on a story of supposed medieval high culture suppressed by the Teutonic Knights. Carr's colleagues took the view that this history had no authenticity or historical continuity, having been manufactured in the last third of the nineteenth century by a handful of intellectuals, relying heavily on the folk song tradition.[5] This lordly contempt for cultural nationalism was to be a consistent feature of his approach to international relations. Twenty years later he would quote approvingly Rosa Luxemburg's dismissive description of Ukrainian nationalism as 'the ridiculous farce of a few university professors and students'.[6]

In July 1936, Carr resigned from the Foreign Office to take up the Wilson Chair of International Politics at the University of Wales, Aberystwyth. Here he found an independent academic base from which to take part in the quickening national debate on foreign policy through a succession of books and essays, culminating in *The Twenty Years' Crisis* and *Britain: A Study of Foreign Policy*, both of which were published late in 1939 following the outbreak of war. For two years,

[2] George F. Kennan, *Memoirs, 1925–1959* (London: Hutchinson, 1968), pp. 47–9.
[3] PRO FO371/10975 N5602/26/59, 29 September 1925; FO371/10980 N5334/N5335.
[4] PRO FO371/10975 N4104.   [5] PRO FO371/10875.
[6] Norman Stone, 'Grim Eminence', *London Review of Books*, 5:1, 20 January–2 February 1983, pp. 3–8.

from 1936 to 1938, he chaired a research group on nationalism for the Royal Institute of International Affairs at Chatham House, which published a substantial report in 1939.[7] Also through Chatham House, he played a part in peacetime preparations for the establishment of a Ministry of Information (MoI).

As the international situation deteriorated, Carr sought additional opportunities to contribute to the policy debate. He was commissioned by Guy Burgess of the BBC in 1937 as anchorman for a series of scripted interviews on the Mediterranean.[8] He was also being consulted by *The Times* on Soviet matters as early as July 1937 and contributed two series of articles on the USSR (1937) and the United States (1938). This led to an invitation from Geoffrey Dawson, editor of *The Times*, to join the editorial team on a trial basis during the last month of the 1939 long vacation. Carr accepted, warning only that 'in the event of war (which, from my present detached position looks rather improbable), I am earmarked for the Ministry of Information'.[9]

It was indeed to the MoI that Carr went on the outbreak of war three days later. Barely a month after this he wrote from the ministry, this time to Robert (Robin) Barrington-Ward, Dawson's deputy. The two had already discussed the possibility of Carr joining the staff of *The Times*, but Barrington-Ward had been concerned lest staff react against the appointment of a man from outside the profession, let alone the institution, to such a senior position, while Carr seemed happy enough at the ministry for the time being. 'After three weeks of indescribable chaos', he wrote, 'I have got my little section here efficiently organised and . . . am quite content with my present job.'[10]

At the MoI, Carr helped draft British war aims and develop propaganda for use abroad. As director of the Foreign Publicity Directorate, he waged a brief but unsuccessful battle with his minister, Sir John Reith, before resigning in March 1940.[11] At this point he rejected the possibility of a return to the Foreign Office and seems to have tried to revive discussions about a post at *The Times*. For his part,

---

[7] *Nationalism: Its Nature and Consequences* (London: Oxford University Press for the Royal Institute of International Affairs, 1939).

[8] W. J. West, *Truth Betrayed* (London: Duckworth, 1987), p. 57.

[9] News International, Archives of *The Times*, Carr to Dawson, 31 August 1939.

[10] Ibid., Carr to Barrington-Ward, 29 September 1939.

[11] Robert Cole, *Britain and the War of Words in Neutral Europe, 1939–1945: The Art of the Possible* (Basingstoke: Macmillan, 1990), p. 22. See also Ian McLaine, *Ministry of Morale: Home Front Morale and the Ministry of Information in World War II* (London: George Allen & Unwin, 1979).

Barrington-Ward was cautious. Unable to make any definite offer, he was concerned lest he had earlier been too positive about prospects for Carr; but by June 1940 Carr was on the *Times* editorial team, and after contributing twenty-six leaders over the summer he found that he had enjoyed the past three months, having been able 'to get across one or two things which seemed . . . important'.[12] He proceeded to set out his terms for joining the staff.[13] By November a deal had been struck by which he would join the staff of *The Times* for the duration of the war on an annual salary of £1,200 from the start of the new year.

In the event, Carr was to stay at *The Times* for more than six years, up to the end of July 1946, as assistant editor, and even after that date would retain an office and a personal secretary at *The Times* under a contract guaranteeing him a minimum of £500 a year. During these years Carr kept up a constant stream of leading articles – more than four hundred in all – while at the same time producing two substantial works, *Conditions of Peace* and *Nationalism and After*. The strongest of Carr's 1940 leaders, which constituted a personal statement of war aims with a marked emphasis on welfare, were also published in the form of an anonymous booklet, *Planning for War and Peace*, in December 1940.[14]

After the war, more narrowly academic than ever before, Carr devoted himself primarily to a massive history of the Soviet revolution and its consequences, in fourteen volumes, on which he continued to work right up to his death in 1983. He remained, as he had been before the war, a regular reviewer for the *Times Literary Supplement*, and also found time to deliver four sets of lectures, each subsequently published in book form. *The New Society* and *What Is History?* both grew out of radio broadcasting, and contain interesting reflections on methodology. A third set, *German–Soviet Relations Between the Two World Wars, 1919–1939*, was more narrowly concerned with foreign policy. A further general work, *The Soviet Impact on the*

[12] News International, Archives of *The Times*, Carr to Barrington-Ward, 15 September 1940.

[13] As late as 1943 he was still drawing his salary from Aberystwyth, though the bulk of it was paid into a charitable trust. This continued in spite of objections from Lord Davis, who had endowed the chair. Carr did not finally resign the chair until 1946: Timothy Dunne, 'International Relations Theory in Britain: The Invention of an International Society Tradition', University of Oxford, DPhil., 1993, p. 31.

[14] *Planning for War and Peace: Ten Leading Articles Reprinted from 'The Times'* (London: The Times Publishing Co., 1940). Anonymity was maintained in this pamphlet, but all ten leaders were by Carr.

Western World, originated as a set of lectures delivered in Oxford early in 1946.

Reviewer and essayist

Carr's literary output was considerable. His views changed over the years, though neither as much nor in quite the way that some of his critics have claimed. He also adopted a number of distinct genres: the book review, the newspaper editorial, and the pamphlet, as well as biography, lecture, monograph, journal article, and textbook. The remainder of this chapter provides a summary of his work up to 1939, giving particular attention to international relations and reserving treatment of *The Twenty Years' Crisis* to chapter 3. Carr's work at the MoI, his early leading articles for *The Times*, and *Conditions of Peace* are discussed in chapter 4, while chapter 5 deals largely with the later years at *The Times* together with *Nationalism and After* and *The Soviet Impact*.

During the first phase in his career, from 1916 to 1936, Carr's energies were less than fully absorbed by official duties. There was time to read widely in preparation for the succession of books on writers and intellectuals that would appear between 1931 and 1937.[15] From the end of the 1920s he became a regular reviewer, contributing one or two reviews each week to the *Spectator, Christian Science Monitor, New Statesman, Fortnightly Review, Times Literary Supplement, Sunday Times,* and *Slavonic Review.* Some of these reviews were signed, some carried no more than the initials 'E. C.', while some were anonymous. Many dealt with Russian literary and biographical works. Taken together, they display considerable erudition. Riga, for Carr as for Kennan, had evidently afforded a great deal of time for reading.[16]

At the same time, Carr was contributing short articles on recent and contemporary foreign policy to the press, mostly signed John Hallett or 'J. H.'. 'Hallett' was generally used as a *nom de plume* to avoid any

---

[15] Carr, *Dostoievsky* (Boston: Houghton Mifflin, 1931); Carr, *The Romantic Exiles* (Boston: Beacon Press, 1933); Carr, *Karl Marx: A Study in Fanaticism* (London: Dent, 1934); Carr, *Michael Bakunin* (London: Macmillan, 1937).

[16] Kennan, posted to the United States Mission in Riga from 1931 to 1933, found the place 'empty and dreary'. Most winter and spring evenings at home with his young wife 'were whiled away with readings aloud from Conrad'. 'In general, this period of service in Riga was simply a continuation of study': Kennan, *Memoirs*, pp. 37–49.

embarrassment to the Foreign Office whenever Carr touched on post-tsarist Russia, even when policy was not discussed. A note in the *Fortnightly Review* in January 1930 on the memoirs of a White Russian officer was signed 'John Hallett', as was a piece the next month on 'The Poets of Soviet Russia'.

By the mid-1930s, themes that would recur years later were already becoming evident – among them contempt for nationalism and for United States idealism, both eloquently expressed in a June 1933 article in the *Fortnightly Review* on 'Nationalism, the World's Bane'. Here, Carr noted the strange partnership of nationalism and democracy in the nineteenth century, attributing the separation of 'these Siamese twins of nineteenth-century political thought' to the extension of nationalist sentiment into Eastern and Central Europe and the anachronistic identification of democracy and nationalism that had guided Woodrow Wilson in post-war decisions about national self-determination and statehood.[17] The roots of Carr's consistent proposal for cultural nationalism within a world of large integrated economic and security communities are to be found here. 'There is a point up to which we are all Marxists now', he wrote. 'We all seek to explain political history in terms of the underlying economic realities. The main problem which confronts us at the present time is not the strife between the principles of Nationalism and Democracy. It is the apparent impossibility of reconciling Nationalism with the economic exigencies of modern civilization.'[18] Carr contended that the greatest post-war disaster had been economic nationalism, with its doctrine of self-sufficiency and its breaking up of large customs areas in the Danube basin and the Russian Empire.

By 1935 the compelling welfare argument in favour of large states, coupled with a belief in the injustice of the Versailles settlement, had led Carr to the brand of appeasement that he would uphold consistently up to the outbreak of war in 1939. For fifteen years British government had tried to curry favour with France by repeated protests against German behaviour. Germany had long since discovered that Britain lacked the resources and resolve to take action when these protests were ignored. The best policy was therefore to

[17] John Hallett [E. H. Carr], 'Nationalism, the World's Bane', *Fortnightly Review*, 133 (new series), January–June 1933, p. 695.
[18] Hallett, 'Nationalism', p. 699.

keep quiet for a time and disentangle the country from all but those core interests that could realistically be defended.[19]

Given the economic vulnerability of small states, the aggressive tendencies of some of the newer European powers towards them, and the limited preparedness of others to underwrite the new nations, the question arose of whether small states could survive in the modern world. If only the two forces – nationalism and aggression – could be separated, then a world with more and smaller states might yet permit the operation of a thriving capitalist world economy. But Carr was sceptical. He argued that, for want of a clear national identity, Austria had become the seat of a struggle between the extreme nationalism of Nazi Germany, and the anti-nationalism of Jewry and the Catholic Church.[20] Other small and peaceable states could expect little better.

Professor of international politics

During the second phase of his career, extending from 1936 to 1947, of which only the first three years are considered in this chapter, the main purpose of Carr's work was to influence policy, both by addressing policy-makers directly and by seeking to win over a broader swathe of elite opinion. For Carr, theory was always subordinate to policy. This is why it makes sense to approach his theoretical and methodological positions through the more immediate policy objectives of his work.

The first substantial work on international relations that Carr published was also the least obviously self-consciously intellectual or theoretical in content. *International Relations since the Peace Treaties* provides a largely chronological narrative of events from the end of the First World War to the beginning of 1937.[21] Clearly written and informative, accessible to a wide readership, the book lacks scholarly apparatus to the point where even the quotations are to be taken on trust. This, or something like it, may have been the fare of Carr's undergraduate students at Aberystwyth in the later 1930s. Already, however, a number of themes were discernible, some of them

---

[19] PRO FO371/19498 C2201/55/18, Minute by E. H. Carr, desk officer in the Southern Department of the Foreign Office.
[20] John Hallett [E. H. Carr], 'The Austrian Background', *Fortnightly Review*, 135 (new series), January–June 1934, pp. 569–76.
[21] E. H. Carr, *International Relations since the Peace Treaties* (London: Macmillan, 1937).

common to a large swathe of British opinion, others more distinctive of Carr.

At the heart of it all lay the post-war settlement. Carr blamed the peace-makers for the political and economic disruption that had followed. The territorial settlement in Europe had been so favourable to the victors and so tough on the vanquished that it could provide security for neither in the long run. The economic impact of the creation of so many new states in Central Europe had also been disruptive, as had the system of reparations.

The key distinction in international relations lay between the satisfied and the dissatisfied powers: those who already had what they wanted could only lose by war; those who still hoped for territorial rectification or expansion came to regard war as the only practical means to achieve their objectives. This did not coincide neatly with the divide between victor and vanquished, for the consequence of failure to reward them adequately had been to place two of the Britain's former allies, Japan and Italy, in the group of dissatisfied powers. Nor did it coincide with any ideological division between democracy and totalitarianism, for Japan – though no democracy – was not fascist. It did not even find a basis in mutual interest, for numerous points of potential conflict between Germany and Italy remained, as too, Carr implied, did real possibilities of further movement between alliances. Much more than anything else, the basis for common action in international affairs was revealed to be a shared predicament.

Chief among the satisfied powers, with their general preference for peace and the status quo, were to be found three of the victors: Britain, the United States, and France. Chief among the dissatisfied powers were Germany, Italy, and Japan. Already, one of the central arguments that was to run through Carr's work was evident in his response to this divide. As time went by, the relative power of states changed, rendering agreements obsolete. In the absence of a generally accepted and consensual system for treaty revision and dispute settlement, war was the sole means of removing mounting anomalies between past agreements and current realities. It was precisely the possibility of providing a substitute for war that the League of Nations had offered before 1930, and that might have been developed further if only the satisfied powers, and above all France, had been more conciliatory at that time.

To this prudential argument it was easy to add a moral case for concessions. The Treaty of Versailles had included provisions that were either impractical or unjust, and Germany had had no option but to accept it.[22] The British and the French had reneged on their commitments to Italy under the Treaty of London in the face of pressure from the United States. Carr presents the cases of both Germany and Italy persuasively and with a measure of sympathy.

A second strand of analysis concerned economic life. Here Carr was impressed by the scale of economic disruption caused by the creation of new states following the war and by the intensification of economic nationalism after 1929. In particular he condemned the refusal of the satisfied powers to allow a start to be made on repairing the damage through the formation of a customs union between pre-Hitler Germany and Austria. Large national economies with strong and interventionist states were his recipe not only for economic but also for political security. He was therefore encouraged to find the United States under Roosevelt moving towards intervention and planning, taking the re-election of the president in 1936 as evidence of how 'wholeheartedly the mass of the American people had accepted the new principle of state regulation'.[23]

In addition to this comprehensive primer, Carr also published four shorter essays on international relations during the first year of his tenure of the Aberystwyth chair. Two of these appeared in the *Fortnightly* and one in *International Affairs*, while the fourth – and most interesting – received minimal circulation as a publication of the University of Nottingham.

The League of Nations

In October 1936, Carr used the *Fortnightly* to set out his view of the League of Nations in advance of its seventeenth assembly. Notable for its general support of the League, this short essay is interesting as much for its form as for its content. Here, for the first time, was the dialectical structure of what would prove to be his most popular work on international relations, *The Twenty Years' Crisis*. There were, Carr insisted, three Leagues: the League of the Idealists, the League as seen

---

[22] The moral case had first been put by British radicals – both Liberal and Labour – in May 1919, when the draft terms of the Treaty of Versailles were first published: A. J. P. Taylor, *The Trouble Makers: Dissent over Foreign Policy, 1792–1939* (London: Hamish Hamilton, 1957), p. 160.

[23] Carr, *International Relations*, p. 245.

by the French, and 'the League as it will appear to the historian'.[24] The British interpretation of the League was, in essence, an idealist interpretation in which the Covenant was regarded as the constitution of a moral community of sovereign states. Against the vision proposed by British idealists, Carr set the more realistic vision of the French, for whom the League was little more than 'a defensive alliance against Germany designed to perpetuate the territorial settlement of 1919'.[25]

These two opposed visions were men of straw: extreme positions, considered only to be dismissed, on the dialectical path to Carr's own interpretation of the League as, at its best, 'the busy and effective centre of European political life'.[26] The League in the 1920s had been, he felt, more consensual and more inclusive than it was to be in the subsequent decade, and all the better for that. It had been more consensual because it had sought international co-operation mainly under Article XI of its charter, which required the consent of the parties to a dispute, rather than Article XVI, with its sanctions provisions and largely impractical threats of force. ('Moral suasion was the only way of settling anything.'[27]) It had been more universal or inclusive because Germany soon joined, while, of the non-members, the Soviet Union was not sufficiently strong to matter and United States administrations took a constructive interest.

Carr therefore urged that Article XI of the Covenant should be retained and French proposals to exempt it from the current unanimity rule resisted, that Article XVI should be abandoned, that regional pacts should be forgotten and the long-term objective of universal membership reasserted, and that Article XIX should be given a more central position in the deliberations of the League.

Article XIX allowed the League to advise members to reconsider treaties that were felt to threaten peace. The greatest contribution the British could make at this juncture, Carr felt, was to make clear to states consumed by resentment that injustices imposed by past settlements would be taken seriously, should they constitute a threat to world peace, by a League that did not exist to protect vested interests. Only in this way could revisionist Germany and Japan be dissuaded from further unilateral action in defiance of international law.[28]

---

[24] E. H. Carr, 'The Future of the League – Idealism or Reality?', *Fortnightly,* 140 (new series), July–December 1936, p. 386.
[25] Ibid., p. 389.   [26] Ibid., p. 391.   [27] Ibid., p. 392.   [28] Ibid., p. 396.

Inaugural

October 1936, the same month in which the essay on the League was published, saw Carr deliver his inaugural lecture at Aberystwyth, later published in *International Affairs*.[29] Under the title 'Public Opinion as a Safeguard of Peace', he undertook a survey of the variety of British opinion on resort to war. Accepting at the outset the conventional if ambitious view that the study of international politics was capable of enhancing the mutual understanding of nations and promoting peace, Carr moved quickly to dismiss explanations of war that rested primarily on class, natural aggression, or demography, and which consequently looked for solutions in revolution, psychology, or the restriction of population. In each of these, the deterministic character of the analysis missed the essentially contingent character of political life and the consequent requirement that any rational response to it be pragmatic.

The duty of a professor of international relations, Carr suggested, was 'to promote a truer understanding of the nature of international relations, and thereby contribute to the creation of a balanced and well-informed public opinion'.[30] From this declaration, he set out at once to survey, but also to mould, public opinion. Pure pacifists, he believed, were few in number. Their ranks were currently swollen by those who believed war to be inevitable and were determined to avoid responsibility for it and by a second group, no less sincere in their attachment, whose pacifism derived from the belief that Britain had nothing to gain from war, and who might therefore be expected to melt away should that circumstance change. In uneasy alliance with these supporters of peace were to be found some socialist internationalists and those who, while condemning all wars of aggression, accepted the legitimacy of defensive warfare.

Coming closer to his own position, Carr next examined those whom he termed 'isolationists' or 'imperialists', precursors of the much later theory of hegemonic stability, who presented no principled opposition to war but felt that, for purely practical reasons, the global good was best served by the continued existence of a British Empire with the ability to police the world's trade routes, and who based their

[29] E. H. Carr, 'Public Opinion as a Safeguard of Peace', *International Affairs*, 15:6, November–December 1936, pp. 846–62.
[30] Ibid., p. 847.

opposition to war on the assumption that British capability was far more likely to be reduced than enhanced by any major conflict.

From pacifists and isolationists, Carr turned his attention to 'collectivists': his term for those who freely accepted the need for war as an instrument of foreign policy, differing only about how order might best be tempered with justice. One possibility was the creation of a supra-national authority that would control its own forces, while the second, clearly preferred by Carr himself, was collective security: 'an arrangement by which sovereign States agree to combine together against any one of their number who may be guilty of an act of aggression'.[31]

It was within this last group, with their attachment to Article XVI of the League of Nations, that Carr identified what was to become one of his principal targets: those intellectuals or idealists – liberal hawks? – who believed that the mass of voters in democratic states could be relied upon to support the use of force to punish aggression even in the absence of any direct threat to their perceived interests. Carr was struck by the discrepancy between the six and three-quarter million British householders who had supported such action in response to question 5 (b) of the Peace Ballot of October 1934, and the blunt refusal of the British government and opposition, a few months later, to risk war with Italy over Abyssinia. Was it that the British governing elites had flagrantly ignored the sentiment of the country? Quite the contrary, Carr declared. It had been the liberal interventionist intellectuals who erred by taking the earlier vote at face value. Ordinary voters had been ready enough, when asked by the League of Nations Union, to express as a matter of principle their readiness to use war if necessary, but sensible enough, when presented with a practical case, to shrink from any mechanistic application of their moral preference.[32]

What was the empirical basis for Carr's enlistment of Middle England in support of policies of bluff and appeasement? It was a curiously old-fashioned and ingenuous piece of a priori reasoning. To

---

[31] Ibid., p. 853. Mention of a force under supra-national control was an acknowledgement of the views of David Davies, author of *An International Police Force* (London: Benn, 1932) and other works, who had endowed the Wilson Chair, vigorously opposed Carr's appointment, and found little support for his utopian schemes from any of the incumbents. See Brian Porter, 'David Davies and the Enforcement of Peace', in David Long and Peter Wilson, eds., *Thinkers of the Twenty Years' Crisis: Inter-War Idealism Reassessed* (Oxford: Clarendon, 1995), pp. 58–78.

[32] A. J. P. Taylor, *English History, 1914–1945* (Oxford: Oxford at the Clarendon Press, 1985), pp. 379–81.

find out what the voters really think, he suggested, one should examine the behaviour of their representatives. 'Speeches and votes in the House [of Commons], whenever military sanctions are the issue, are dictated by the opinions of the man in the street.'[33] Had the seven million who voted positively on question 5 (b) of the Peace Ballot meant what they said literally, a policy of appeasement could not possibly have been maintained. From the fact that it was so firmly embraced by their representatives, it may be inferred that the people were content, and that some interpretation of their earlier vote other than a strictly literal one must be found.

Stripped of its rhetorical and taxonomic pretensions, this lecture boiled down to an attempt by Carr, through declaration rather than on any basis of evidence, to enlist public opinion in favour of his own views and against those of his 'isolationist' opponents. Setting aside this dubious rhetorical tactic, these views repay brief attention, as the earliest general statement of Carr's general position on international relations.

Public opinion, he declared, was now firmly opposed to 'automatic' military commitments of the form: 'The country will certainly go to war if such-and-such happens.' The decision to go to war must always be subject to final deliberation in the light of the full circumstances prevailing on the eve of war. Secondly, it was possible to isolate or contain war, and from this it followed that Britain need not concern itself directly with each and every threat of war on the spurious grounds that world peace was indivisible. Next, war weariness was so great in Britain, Carr argued, that British opinion could not be relied upon to support war as 'an instrument of any kind of policy at all' for many years to come. In the fourth place, Carr enlisted public opinion in support of his view that, since the effective application of economic sanctions could so easily bring a country to the brink of war, it would be best to desist from using Article XVI of the Covenant against any Great Power. Finally, Carr discovered that, rather than being pro-German, British public opinion was 'simply anti-Versailles', because 'the sound instincts of British democracy', almost intuitively recognised that, 'if European democracy binds its living body to the putrefying corpse of the 1919 settlement, it will merely be committing a particularly unpleasant form of suicide'.[34]

While there might have been much sound sense in these views, the

---

[33] Carr, 'Public Opinion', p. 858.   [34] Ibid., p. 860.

fact remains that Carr had no evidence to justify presenting them as British public opinion beyond the fact that the government had espoused some of them without unleashing a storm of protest. The supposed opinion of Middle England served simply as a rhetorical stick with which to beat idealist intellectuals.

The Mediterranean

An invitation to lecture at Nottingham University gave Carr an opportunity to refine his personal doctrine of appeasement and apply it in a much less abstract manner to events of the day.[35] Tracing the rise of British power in the Mediterranean from the seizure of Gibraltar in 1704 to the occupation of Palestine in 1918, Carr located the most urgent contemporary threat to British pre-eminence in the rising power of Italy.[36] The Italian attack on Abyssinia in October 1935 is often remembered as one of the sharpest nails in the coffin of the League of Nations. Carr notes that it was also a direct threat to British interests and prestige, not least because it strengthened Italian ability to disrupt British imperial communications beyond Suez and relied for its achievement on large troop movements through the Suez Canal, carried out in the face of clear but ineffectual British disapproval with consequent grave damage to British prestige.

It was hard to interpret the British decision not to intervene, which might legally have been attempted under cover of the League, as other than a sign of weakness. Britain looked weak for having failed to exploit the League as a cloak for a pre-emptive attack on Italy in much the same way that the United States would have looked weak had it failed to lead a United Nations coalition force against Iraq following the 1990 invasion of Kuwait. Large naval vessels were judged very vulnerable to air and submarine attack. The British naval

---

[35] E. H. Carr, 'Great Britain as Mediterranean Power', Cust Foundation Lecture, 1937, University College, Nottingham, delivered 19 November 1937 (published by the University).

[36] Dunne understates Carr's assessment of the Italian threat. Seeming at first to contest Eden's claim that freedom of movement in the Mediterranean was a vital interest, he goes on to develop a profile of British interests there as 'something less than life but something more than a convenient route' (Carr, 'Mediterranean', p. 8), claiming that the replacement of Britain by Italy as the dominant power in the Mediterranean would entail Italian political control of Egypt and Palestine and, more importantly, a marked relative decline in the prestige of Britain (pp. 9–10): Dunne, 'International Relations Theory in Britain', p. 45.

base at Malta was only twenty minutes' flying time from Italy. Far from facing down the threat, the British Mediterranean fleet had retreated to the relative security of Alexandria in anticipation of the Italian move on Abyssinia.

The consequences of growing Italian power, when coupled with these new technologies of offensive warfare, were threefold. First of all, British naval power in the Mediterranean was put on the defensive. To expose the Mediterranean fleet in a war against Italy in 1935 would have been to risk the loss of several capital warships, which might in turn, so Carr argued, have brought nearer a more serious challenge to British naval supremacy from Germany. Secondly, Britain was forced to make concessions in order to balance Italian power in the Mediterranean and nurture possible allies against it. Thus Britain had felt obliged to concede peacetime access to the Mediterranean to Soviet naval vessels by the Convention of Montreux in July 1936 and to grant fuller recognition of Egyptian independence, including membership of the League of Nations, through the Anglo-Egyptian treaty of August 1936. Thirdly, the deteriorating position and defensive posture of the British in the Eastern Mediterranean emboldened Italy to make a further challenge in the west once League sanctions were withdrawn in July 1936. The following month saw the offer of substantial Italian military assistance to General Franco, with decisive consequences for the intensity and outcome of the Spanish Civil War and for the integrity and prestige of British and French naval power.

Here, the arguments and even the imagery of *The Twenty Years' Crisis* are anticipated. Italy is presented as a revisionist power – a latecomer – doing nothing that other European states had not attempted before and consequently dismissive of their opposition. 'To put it bluntly', Carr wrote, 'most Italians regard us as hypocrites. We are depicted as old men preaching to the young and vigorous a morality which we did not ourselves practice so long as we were capable of enjoying vice.' 'It is useless to deny', he concluded, 'that we have begun, rather late in the day, to advocate a higher international morality which is convenient to ourselves and highly inconvenient to certain other countries.'[37] Concession to Italy in the Mediterranean would not lead to the exclusion of Britain or the interruption of British trade, as crude realists might fear. Conversely, liberal claims that there was no conflict between British and Italian interests were beside the

[37] Carr, 'Mediterranean', pp. 4–5.

point. The issue, Carr made clear, was 'not whether Great Britain and Italy shall both continue to use the Mediterranean for their trade (in any event they will both continue to do so), but whether Italy will use it by the good grace of Great Britain or whether Great Britain will use it by the good grace of Italy'.[38]

The distinction between the status quo and revisionist perspectives and the importance of viewpoint in understanding political disagreements – themes later to be developed in *The Twenty Years' Crisis* – are already evident. So too is the central preoccupation of the later work with the substitution of effective threat for outright coercion. Concession to Italian power in the Mediterranean would produce a greater change in the relative prestige of Italy and Great Britain than of their objectively measured military and naval might. But it was prestige that mattered, Carr concluded, because, 'if your strength is recognised, you can generally achieve your aims without having to use it'.[39]

Carr's policy recommendation was not made fully explicit. He favoured appeasement, but was undecided between appeasing Italy and appeasing Germany. Because Britain was strategically overextended and had not yet developed effective responses to new threats from aerial and submarine attack, its strategists could not afford to risk uniting the revisionist powers by resolute and consistent resistance to their demands. Bluffing in international affairs has always been a dangerous business. Every time the British bluff was called, credibility and prestige were diminished and the revisionist powers were alienated to no good purpose. 'We cannot afford to pursue a policy which leads straight to the consolidation of a German–Italian–Japanese bloc confronting the rest of the world', Carr insisted.[40] The best policy for Britain was therefore to make concessions to one or other of the revisionist powers in order to avert the prospect of a hostile Axis while freeing resources from one theatre for firmer ultimate resistance in the others. Japan could not be conciliated without damage to British relations with the United States, which Carr regarded as 'the firmest foundation-stone of our whole foreign policy'.[41] This left Italy and Germany; and while Carr declined to choose between them in the peroration of his lecture, his estimate of direct and serious nature of the Italian threat to British interests and of the relative indifference of Britain towards Central Europe as compared with the Mediterranean seems to have been calculated to lead

[38] Ibid., p. 9.   [39] Ibid., p. 10.   [40] Ibid., p. 4.   [41] Ibid., p. 24.

his audience towards concession to Germany as the lesser of two evils.[42]

It is hardly surprising, in the light of his assessment of the Italian threat, that Carr should have interpreted the Spanish Civil War as in large measure a facet of Italian imperialism. In strictly domestic terms, the conflict appeared to him to be much more a struggle between anarchist and ultra-conservative than between Communist and fascist. Besides, the civil conflict mattered less than its wider implications. With Italy in occupation of the Balearic Islands, both British and French naval power and communications in the Western Mediterranean were threatened. Viewed in terms of Mediterranean security, the war was 'a drive to make Italy paramount in the Western Mediterranean', complementing earlier expansion in the Eastern Mediterranean and east of Suez.[43]

But in the greater part of his discussion, Carr ranged far beyond Spain and the Mediterranean to consider the global implications of the Civil War. Here he was concerned to demonstrate that the foreign policies of states were seldom driven by ideological considerations. 'There is . . . plenty of sound and fury, but far less substance, in this fashionable conflict of ideologies', he insisted, 'and the fundamental division is not between Fascism and "the Left", but between those who are in the main satisfied with the present distribution of the world's goods as between States and those who, for various reasons, are not.'[44]

From a British point of view, the attraction of this interpretation lay in the doubt it cast on the prospects of solidarity between fascist powers. For the national interests of Germany and Italy as two dissatisfied powers were no better as a basis for enduring co-operation than their ideological kinship. Therefore, the worst error that Britain could commit in the prevailing circumstances, Carr maintained, was

[42] The strategic argument for appeasing Germany in order to face up to Italy has not always been fully appreciated. This is mainly because the Italians turned out to be a less effective force than had been feared. It was by no means unique to Carr. Churchill persisted in concentrating British forces in the Mediterranean well into 1943, threatening further delay to the invasion of France. The Americans 'were convinced that the British approach was above all political and aimed at maintaining . . . long-term influence in the Mediterranean': Clive Ponting, *Churchill* (London: Sinclair-Stevenson, 1994), p. 599; see also p. 613.

[43] E. H. Carr, 'Europe and the Spanish War', *Fortnightly*, 141 (new series), January–June 1937, p. 26.

[44] Ibid., p. 32.

to be panicked by a false estimate of the cohesion of the Right in Europe into a close and irrevocable association with the Franco-Soviet group. British intervention on the Republican side in Spain was therefore out of the question. It might be the one policy best calculated to create a firm alliance between Germany and Italy. Instead, observing the reluctance of the British to resist fascist expansion, Carr urged that the time had come to attempt a reconciliation with Germany based on treaty revision under Article XIX of the League that would offer this dissatisfied power a just settlement by a legal process and without resort to unilateral aggression.[45]

Ideology, morality, and interest

Two further essays in the *Fortnightly*, in 1938 and 1939, dealt respectively with the fallacy of ideological foreign policy and the distinction between national interest and universal morality. 'The Twilight of the Comintern' simply represented a more detailed exploration of the anti-ideological theme of 'The Spanish War'. The Comintern, or Third International, established by Soviet Russia in 1919 to foment worldwide revolution, had been a real force in Germany and Asia for a few years. But, as the military position of the Bolshevik regime became more secure, it became apparent that Lenin had been mistaken in believing that the success of world revolution was indivisible. The Soviet state began to engage in more or less normal relations, settling, after the death of Lenin, for 'socialism in one country'. Carr took the view that the Comintern was a spent force by 1924, and that it was only under the stimulus of the diametrically opposed ideological foreign policy of Adolf Hitler, in 1934, that it was revived, though now as a means to bolster popular fronts and bourgeois allies rather than to advance social revolution. In Britain, where the prospects for revolution were barely perceptible, Communism had acquired a measure of respectability, especially among intellectuals. But Carr found the British Communist Party to the Right of some sections of the Labour Party and unquestionably patriotic in its defence of British interests against fascist and Nazi aggression.

Most decisively, the USSR, through the Comintern, had displayed the pragmatic character of its foreign policy by its suppression of Anarchist and Trotskyist forces in Spain. The objective of Soviet

[45] Ibid., p. 34.

intervention was a stable Spanish republic functioning as an effective ally against Germany and Italy, not the encouragement of a social revolution that might threaten to spill over into neighbouring France, weakening the Soviet Union's strongest ally. The policy had failed, of course, but not without providing more material with which policy-makers in Italy, Germany, and Japan could sharpen the apprehensions and stiffen the resolve of the more gullible of their adherents, both at home and abroad. Opposition to a supposed Communist menace, Carr insisted, was a delusory basis for foreign policy and the merest mask for the pursuit of specific German, Japanese, and Italian national interests.[46]

It was the tendency to mask national interest, not with ideology but with supposedly universal morality, that provided the theme for a last pre-war contribution to the *Fortnightly*.[47] To pursue national interest while consciously cloaking it in universal morality was no more than the customary business of diplomats. In 'Honour among Nations', Carr attacked the modern tendency of statesmen to go further, convincing themselves of the rightness of their policies. 'We want to be bamboozled into thinking ourselves moral', he writes, 'and since few can successfully bamboozle others without first bamboozling themselves, clear thinking has become a disqualification for a states-man.'[48] Hypocrisy was worse than *Realpolitik*, because the hypocrite could not, when the occasion demanded it, take off a mask that had come to feel natural.

The particular targets of the attack on hypocrisy, here as elsewhere in Carr's work, turn out to be the insistence on peace as a universal good and on the sanctity of treaties. Both favoured the status quo. Quoting Rousseau and Adam Smith, Carr concluded that '"law and order", both in domestic and in international politics, is the natural slogan of the well-to-do and of the conservatives'.[49] The contrary view, beloved of the dissatisfied powers, that change was to be welcomed almost for its own sake, was dismissed as a kind of madness. The only way out of the impasse, Carr suggested, was self-knowledge. To be aware of, and so to discard, the more obvious layers of national hypocrisy was the essential precondition that had to be

---

[46] E. H. Carr, 'The Twilight of the Comintern', *Fortnightly*, 143 (new series), January–June 1938, pp. 137–47.

[47] E. H. Carr, 'Honour among Nations', *Fortnightly*, 145 (new series), January–June 1939, pp. 489–500.

[48] Ibid., p. 494.   [49] Ibid., p. 497.

met before nations could attempt 'a synthesis . . . or conglomeration . . . of national moralities'. The path lay, in part, through international law and international organisation, both of which had suffered considerable reverses since the Great War by being used to mould rather than consolidate public opinion, or as tools of vested interests. It lay also in recognition of the extent to which a truly international morality already existed. 'So much has been written in the last few years of the "international anarchy"', Carr pointed out, 'that people tend to overlook the wide field of everyday life in which international law is recognized and, on the whole, observed.'[50]

Each of these shorter works had its occasion, but each was also in part a sketch for one or other of the two books that appeared in 1939 and summed up Carr's pre-war position. The first, a short account of British foreign policy since 1918, was ready for publication before war broke out in 1939.[51] Lord Halifax, as foreign secretary, contributed a friendly preface, dated 3 August, in which he commended Carr's past service in the Foreign Office. The outbreak of war the following month delayed publication, allowing Carr to make appropriate revisions.

Carr's diagnosis

From its title, Carr's *Britain: A Study of Foreign Policy* might sound like a thinly disguised second edition of *International Relations since the Peace Treaties*. It was nothing of the sort. The later book was more directly concerned with British policy than with international relations in general. But the major difference was that Carr now adopted a thematic approach in place of the narrative structure of two years before. Successive chapters dealt with Britain and democracy, Britain as a world power, British economic policy, Britain and the League of Nations, Britain and Europe, and the advent of war.

Undoubtedly, the most innovative aspects of the book are the treatments of methodology and of the nature of British foreign policy. These are considered in chapter 7, where the character of Carr's realism is more extensively discussed. Here, only some highlights of the policy analysis are noted.

---

[50] Ibid., p. 499.
[51] E. H. Carr, *Britain: A Study of Foreign Policy from the Versailles Treaty to the Outbreak of War*, in *Ambassadors at Large: Studies in the Foreign Policies of the Leading Powers*, general ed., E. H. Carr (London: Longman Green, 1939).

In the first place, Carr showed an acute awareness of the material base of state power. The British economy was nowhere near as large, relative to the United States and Germany, as it had been before 1914. Other states, too, were catching up. But just as important as relative national economic strength, measured in steel output or the consumption of electricity, were the deployment or mobilisation of that economic capability and the implications for national military power of technological change. Carr acknowledges, for the first time, that one good reason for the British policy of appeasement had been a lack of military preparedness. Rearmament had not begun until 1935. Britain had therefore been in no position to face the losses anticipated from successful Mediterranean and African campaigns against Italy in 1936. As to the strategic implications of technology, Carr refers once again to the vulnerability of a first-class naval and industrial power to submarine and aerial attack, but to this theme of his lecture on Mediterranean policy he adds the move from coal to oil and the implications of air travel and radio for communications and logistics. Unlike the USSR and the USA, Britain was obliged to import petroleum. The strategic and economic importance of routes to the Middle East and the Dutch East Indies was accordingly increased by the change from coal to oil. This new vulnerability was to some extent offset by improved communications and logistics, facilitating military and economic co-operation between the British Dominions. Only war would finally answer the question of where the balance of advantage lay, but Carr was convinced that one consequence of war in Europe was bound to be a relative decline in British power in the Far East. He judged the much delayed naval base at Singapore inadequate 'even if conditions in Europe were sufficiently tranquil to permit the concentration of a major part of the British navy at Singapore; and this', he concluded, 'has not been the case for many years.'[52]

A second theme that began to emerge in this pre-war survey, and that was to become much more insistent in Carr's writing of the 1940s, was international integration. Here, relations between Britain and the self-governing Dominions were offered as a model of consensual international relations, economic co-operation, and military collaboration based in a shared democratic political culture and requiring minimal institutional apparatus.[53] Carr was still near the

---

[52] Ibid., p. 60.   [53] Ibid., p. 39.

beginning of a search for a model of international integration and co-operation that avoided the formalism of the League of Nations.

The now familiar contrast between satisfied and dissatisfied powers was drawn once again. This time, Carr's main objective seems to have been to explain the reluctance of the satisfied powers to honour their military commitments to the League, and account for their preference for policies of appeasement. Clutching at straws, some might say, Carr still claimed appeasement to have been a success, in spite of the recent British declaration of war against Germany, on the grounds that it had secured Italian neutrality and thereby avoided simultaneous European and Mediterranean campaigns at a time when British industrial and armaments production was still not yet at full stretch.[54]

In the space of three years, against a background of deteriorating relations between the major European powers, Carr had developed and enunciated a robust and coherent view of Britain and its place in the world. The British economy was too weak, its people too weary, and its forces too thinly stretched across the world for it to be able to gain from war. To stand cheek by jowl with France in defence of the Versailles Treaty was simply to hasten a final breakdown of international relations. Recognising the injustice, the instability, the obsolescence, and the sheer economic dysfunctionality of the post-war settlement, Carr argued that interest and justice alike favoured adoption of the policy that was to become notorious as appeasement. His preferred course of action consisted in renunciation of the kinds of unsupported provocation and bluster – intended to substitute for capability – that fooled no one and needlessly soured relations. In their place he favoured measured and morally defensible concessions – the most obvious example being agreement to an economic union of Germany and Austria – of a kind calculated to placate a potential enemy while lengthening the odds on the formation of any grand coalition of dissatisfied powers.

Carr believed that neither a capitalist world economy nor the principles of secular democracy could easily coexist with a plethora of nationalistic micro-states, while modern techniques of warfare had largely put paid to neutrality. He was therefore especially sympathetic to any revisions of the post-war settlement that tended towards an international system based on consensual and law-governed relations

---

[54] Ibid., ch. 5.

between large multi-ethnic groupings of states of approximately similar economic and military capability.

Nationalism did not provide a natural basis for political self-determination or territorial statehood any more than 'national interest' offered a satisfactory basis for policy. 'Did the Czech working-man, for instance, have a more natural affinity with the Czech noble than with the German working-man?'[55] He certainly saw no proof that the outcome of rational pursuit of national interest in a world of nation-states would be generally optimal. But, what is much more remarkable, he did not shrink from the consequence, that 'from the international point of view, it would surely be necessary for certain nations to disappear'.[56]

This was a view which was to lead Carr into a great deal of controversy during the 1940s, as he persistently advanced the proposal that the Soviet Union be allowed a free hand in the shaping of Eastern Europe after the war. Already, G. M. Gathorne-Hardy had written to Michael Balfour, secretary of the Chatham House study group on nationalism, drawing attention to words given to Brand by his creator, Ibsen. '"Let the great powers hear the call; / Let the others man the wall; / We are small, and lack the might / To do battle for the right."' 'I suppose', Gathorne-Hardy mused, 'Carr would regard this attitude, which roused the scorn of Ibsen, as mere obvious common sense.'[57]

The central problems in this view of the world were its failure to appreciate the acute desire for authentic sources of personal identity in the modern world and a lack of clarity and discrimination in Carr's conceptualisation of the typical actor in his ideal international system. Less similar political entities could hardly be found than the USSR, the British Commonwealth, and the inter-American system. Carr was to turn to each, almost indiscriminately, as he developed his idea of post-war political organisation in Western Europe. A constant feature of his position was that Britain should remain at the head of at least one such multinational grouping.

If the nature of the political actor that was to replace the nation-state remained poorly defined, Carr was rather clearer about the principles that should underlie relations between actors in any system of states.

---

[55] Archives of the Royal Institute of International Affairs (RIIA), Nationalism Study Group (NSG), Minutes, 8 March 1937.

[56] Ibid., Minutes, 15 November 1937.

[57] Ibid., Gathorne-Hardy to Balfour, 16 May 1938.

The basic division between states was defined neither by ideology nor by interest. States that had done well in the past, whether militarily or economically, favoured the status quo. Peace, free trade, international treaties, and law all served to protect their position and might easily preserve it past the point where, if put to it, they would be able to defend themselves by force of arms. For their part, rising powers were apt to find the status quo obstructive. It was often to their advantage to break the rules, even to the point of waging war. States of each kind were adept in justifying their action by appeal to universal moral principles. The only way to resolve the conflict of interest between them, short of war, was to build on the existing element of law-governed behaviour in international relations, extending this gradually, in conformity with the distribution of military capabilities and at a pace no faster than public opinion would allow, on the basis of inter-state consensus. If states could not impose good relations on themselves, they could not impose them on each other. Here, surely, was a vision of international relations that was Fabian and functionalist in tone, and clearly idealistic in the Kantean manner of being made sense of by reference to a standard (or ideal) that was intelligible, though in principle unattainable. For Carr, that ideal was democracy, but democracy defined – as will become clearer in chapter 7 – in a most eccentric manner.

3   The Twenty Years' Crisis

The early chapters

Conceived in peacetime as a polemic in favour of appeasement, the book that was to prove the most enduring of all that Carr wrote in the 1930s, joining the small company of classic works on international relations, had reached proof stage by the time Britain went to war on 3 September 1939.[1] Yet to admit *The Twenty Years' Crisis* to the international relations canon is not to accept – though many have – its status as an authoritative realist text. The book is treacherous: its rhetoric is complex and its true intentions are never clearly or fully disclosed. Between Carr and his reader one searches in vain for open covenants openly arrived at. This is why the summary that occupies the first part of this chapter is followed by a treatment of the manner in which Carr addresses his readers, while assessment of his specific policy concerns is reserved to the final section.

For, by contrast with Carr's other works, *The Twenty Years' Crisis* is drenched in erudition. Reference piles upon reference. Bismarck is there. Indeed, there are statesmen in profusion. Sun Yat-sen, Hitler, Mussolini, Woodrow Wilson, and Taft all stalk its pages. From closer to home come Winston Churchill, Anthony Eden, and three past prime ministers. Then there are the philosophers and social theorists. German thought is well represented by Kant, Hegel, Marx, and a host of lesser figures. But this Teutonic display does not occlude other traditions. Machiavelli is referred to. So are Lenin, Lukacs, and Bakunin, Sorel, Croce, and Halévy, Montesquieu, Rousseau, and

---

[1] E. H. Carr, *The Twenty Years' Crisis, 1919–1939: An Introduction to the Study of International Relations* (London: Macmillan, 1939). References to this book are to the first edition unless the second is specified.

Comte, Alexander Hamilton, Reinhold Niebuhr, Salvador de Madariaga, Peter Drucker, and the international lawyers, Lauterpacht and
Schwartzenberger. A veritable catalogue of British thought is paraded,
from Bacon, through Smith, Hume, Burke, John Stuart Mill, Bagehot,
Bright, T. H. Green, Bosanquet, and Dicey, to moderns such as
Hobson, W. T. Stead, Bertrand Russell, Laski, Hobhouse, Ginsberg,
Keynes, and the supposed idealists, Norman Angell, Arnold Toynbee,
and Alfred Zimmern. The list is not exhaustive: exhausting, rather, for
the reader who picks up a book that seductively pronounces itself to
be 'An Introduction to the Study of International Relations' and finds,
instead, a *tour de force*.

What was Carr up to? Was his purpose to instruct or rather to
dazzle? It will be best to sketch the book in outline before attempting a
more critical survey. In a brief introductory chapter, heightened public
interest in international affairs is presented as a reaction to the horrors
of the Great War of 1914–18 and the part played by secret diplomacy
in bringing that war about. International relations as a field of
academic inquiry owed its existence to public concern. It was therefore to be expected that it would, at least in the early days, be a highly
instrumental activity, concerned above all to prevent war. Carr argued
that there was much more opportunity in the social sciences than in
the physical sciences for the observer to participate in the process
under examination. Analysis and purpose could hardly be separated
and the social scientist was unlikely to feel bound by circumstances
which it was his chief intention to transform. But the experience of the
1930s had brought this early utopian phase in the study of international relations to an end. The alliance of will and description had
proved insufficient to overcome the countervailing power of dissatisfied states. Utopianism gave way to realism, with its emphasis on the
objective, predictable, and unmalleable character of the social as of the
physical world, and its inclination to forswear morality in favour of
acquiescence.

The opposition of utopia and reality is elaborated in a second
chapter, which establishes a set of related dichotomies. The utopian,
or idealist, is inclined to overemphasise free will; the realist is more
likely to be a determinist, perhaps to the point of abandoning any
attempt at political action. The idealist theorises, and the typical
representative of his school is the intellectual. The realist is less
interested in political theory than the day-by-day practice of politics
and administration; his ideal type is the bureaucrat. The idealist

stands on the Left in politics; the typical realist on the Right. The idealist is a legal naturalist, convinced that there is a moral standard to which political behaviour and law ought to conform; the realist by contrast regards law and morality as little more than rationalisations of the will of each sovereign power.

With this set of dichotomies in place, Carr goes on to outline the utopian tradition of thought about international relations in chapters 3 and 4 before criticising it from a realist perspective in chapter 5. Realism itself is then disposed of in a brief but devastating sixth chapter, leaving the road clear for Carr to present his own synthesis of utopianism and realism, which occupies the remaining eight chapters, constituting fully three-fifths of the text.

Carr derives the liberal tradition of politics, which he dubs utopianism, from the secularisation of natural law in early modern Europe. As sovereignty in Christendom passed from Pope and Emperor to the sovereigns of territorial realms, the naturalist supposition that law represented an imperfect approximation to a universal ethic gave way to an admission of legal positivism in which law was starkly characterised as the command of a sovereign backed by force. Utopianism, in Carr's characterisation, had its origin in the attempt to find, in or through human reason, a substitute for God that might somehow revive the corpse of moral universalism. 'The optimism of the nineteenth century was based on the triple conviction', he averred, 'that the pursuit of the good was a matter of right reasoning, that the spread of knowledge would soon make it possible for everyone to reason rightly on this important subject, and that anyone who reasoned rightly on it would necessarily act rightly.'[2] Applied to international affairs, this led to the conclusion that, if, once the making of foreign policy were removed from the exclusive control of monarchs and aristocrats, whose sectional interest disposed them towards warfare, and subjected instead to the democratic control of an educated populace acting under a republican constitution, then war would be a thing of the past. Europeans, for the most part, had seen enough of the corruptibility of the middle and lower classes by the end of the nineteenth century to have abandoned their initial unconditional faith in reason and democracy. But it survived in its naive form in the United States, and so came to be applied through the influence

[2] Ibid., p. 34.

of Woodrow Wilson to the creation of new states and the formation of the League of Nations following the First World War.

Carr conceded, as he had done in his *Fortnightly* essay of 1936, that the League, as originally established, sacrificed theoretical tidiness to a realistic recognition of the distribution of power in many respects, and was the better for it.[3] But he was now more dismissive and less patient than in the earlier essay, claiming that the League had begun, as early as 1922, to fall prey to the sins of excessive rationalism, expressed through abstraction, automaticity, and formalism.[4]

The second great failure of the League, deriving just as surely as its rationalism from the nineteenth-century liberal tradition, was its uncritical faith in international public opinion. Wilson and other advocates of the League were convinced of the responsibility of secret diplomacy and lack of democratic control for the outbreak of war in 1914. It followed that transparency alone would bear the main weight of the system of collective security. Exposed to public scrutiny, the victors would be shamed into disarmament. No government could survive resolute public reaction to its refusal to comply with a decision of the Council or the Assembly of the League. Sanctions, let alone coercion, hardly needed to be considered. For, as Lord Cecil had declared when defending the League in the British Parliament, 'What we rely upon is public opinion . . . and if we are wrong about it, then the whole thing is wrong.'[5]

Carr, of course, concluded that the whole thing *was* wrong, and that the failure of the League to prevent the breakdown of international relations in the 1930s and the decline into war were to be attributed neither to the stupidity and wickedness of policy-makers and electorates, nor to the exceptional or transitional character of the times, but to fundamental flaws in the liberal assumptions that had guided its design.

While these flaws included excessive faith in reason, education, and public opinion, they rested in turn upon a deeper fallacy, deriving from the eighteenth-century Enlightenment belief in a harmony of interests. The extraordinarily audacious and counter-intuitive liberal claim that had crystallised most perfectly in the work

---

[3] E. H. Carr, 'The Future of the League – Idealism or Reality?', *Fortnightly*, 140 (new series), July–December 1936, pp. 385–402.

[4] Carr, *Crisis*, p. 40.

[5] House of Commons, 21 July 1919: *Official Report*, cols. 990, 992; quoted in Carr, *Crisis*, p. 47.

of Adam Smith was that pursuit of self-interest by each individual provided the surest guarantee of the best possible collective outcome. Generalised, the theory of harmony of interests suggested that there was no conflict between selfishness, cupidity, aggression, and right conduct, because natural human drives were mediated by intervening structures (of which the market was simply the most obvious) in ways that produced outcomes no individual had either designed or desired, yet which could hardly be improved upon. And conditions for much of the nineteenth century seemed to confirm the theory, as apparently related advances in industrial production, trade, and standards of living spread steadily outward from their West European epicentres.

In international relations, as in economic affairs, the precondition for the satisfactory realisation of a harmony of interests was the removal of artificial constraints on natural action. In the market, this required a policy of *laissez-faire*. Rolling back the range and intensity of state intervention in social and economic life would permit the emergence of a free and perfect market: free in the sense that no actor was excluded, perfect in the sense that none was so powerful as to be able to change the rules of the game.

In relations between states it was much the same. Identification of the natural actors in world politics by the formation of the German and Italian nation-states in the nineteenth century was extended, in the 1919 settlement, through more general application of the principle of self-determination. Nationality based on language, shared history, or religion was assumed to be the best title to statehood. Fragmentation of the pre-war Habsburg, German, and tsarist empires and the inclusion in the League of non-European powers went some way – so the utopians might claim – to meet the second condition, of widely distributed power.

In short, utopians could see, in the post-1918 world, political conditions analogous to those which they believed had secured the economic prosperity of the nineteenth century. The trouble was, as Carr observed, that the flaws in economic liberalism were already apparent, and that they applied equally, by the remorseless logic of analogy, to the supposed political harmony of interests on which the League was premised.

At root, the problem lay in market imperfection. British manufacturing firms tended, by the early twentieth century, to be smaller, and for that reason less competitive in world markets, than their United

States and German rivals. Going back to the middle of the nineteenth century, the picture was rather more complicated. Although the typical British merchant house was small, legal and financial independence sometimes masked close co-operative relations with other firms under a more or less centralised management, constituting what have come to be described investment groups, some of them very large and powerful.[6] Certainly, British corporations providing international financial, transport, and communications services were large relative to those of other nations.

The industrialists and traders of other nations therefore faced an international service economy of merchants, bankers, insurers, railways, telegraphs, and shipping lines that was dominated by the British and favoured British commerce in a thousand small ways. And behind this world-wide service economy stood the British state and the Royal Navy. Far too haughty ever to be at the beck and call of mere businessmen and sufficiently liberal to allow others besides British traders through most of the doors it opened, British naval power nevertheless conferred advantage. Recall Carr's aphorism about Britain and Italy in the Mediterranean, where the question was 'not whether Great Britain and Italy shall both continue to use the Mediterranean for their trade . . . but whether Italy will use it by the good grace of Great Britain or whether Great Britain will use it by the good grace of Italy'.[7]

In a world where others traded by the good grace of Britain, free trade, though never universally adopted, had yielded widespread benefits, just as the classical political economists had promised. But the gains had been unevenly distributed, with the strongest economies gaining disproportionately. Britain had initially attained economic and naval dominance by mercantilist policy and force of arms. Soon policy-makers and entrepreneurs in Germany and the United States drew the moral that they could make inroads into British industrial pre-eminence only through protectionism. Equally, increasing concentration of economic power in the leading sectors of all the major

---

[6] Stanley Chapman, *Merchant Enterprise in Britain from the Industrial Revolution to World War I* (Cambridge: Cambridge University Press, 1992); Charles Jones, 'Institutional Forms of British Direct Investment in South America', *Business History*, 39:2, April 1997, pp. 21–41.

[7] Carr, 'Great Britain as a Mediterranean Power', Cust Foundation Lecture, 1937, University College, Nottingham, delivered 19 November 1937 (published by the University), p. 9.

economies towards the end of the nineteenth century contradicted the utopian premise of free and perfect competition.

The near universal response to these imperfections, some of which arose from the seemingly self-destructive nature of the competitive process itself while others were attributable to state intervention, was to call for countervailing intervention. This move away from individualist liberalism and towards compensatory or collectivist liberalism, already well established before 1914, was confirmed after 1918, as new and old states alike raised barriers to trade and embarked on programmes of import-substituting industrialisation. While economists continued to believe that, provided the international economy was allowed to function, it would take care of individual national economies, politicians preferred the reverse argument, hoping in vain that their pursuit of short-term national interest would prove consistent with the general interest. Only in the United States, Carr maintained, where trade protection was the sole though significant breach in the liberal system, did *laissez-faire* remain largely intact as domestic policy up to 1929, contributing largely to the continued faith of North American officialdom in individualist liberalism and a consequent readiness to apply utopian political remedies in the post-war settlement.

Content in chapter 4 to observe and explain the collapse of a harmony of economic interests, first as belief and then as policy, Carr reserves his most damaging criticism of utopianism for the next chapter. Given the extent and persistence of market imperfections, why had anyone ever believed in the practical possibility of a harmony of interests? The answer was that thought was in large measure the product of circumstances and interests. Far more than they knew or, knowing, were willing to admit, people tended to believe what it was to their advantage to believe.

It was easy for those manufacturers and traders who received relatively large shares of the benefits of industrial capitalism to believe that they shared with their workers a common interest in *laissez-faire* policies. It was correspondingly easy for those already powerful states that stood to lose most by war to believe that all states had a common interest in world peace. Workers who disrupted production in an attempt to increase their own share of the cake, or new states prepared to risk war in pursuit of territorial expansion, colonies, market access, or the revision of past treaties, were irrational and misguided. They risked losing their own share of the spoils by attacking the system. Theirs was a politics of envy.

Conversely, it was easy for those whose relative gains from these systems were less to become suspicious of the motives of the powerful and fearful of the use that they might make of their cumulative relative advantages of wealth and power. From this suspicion it was a short step to belief in the merits of revolution or war as a means to the elevation of equality of distribution over maximisation of utility. Internationalism, then, was the natural philosophy of those powerful states – Britain, France, and the United States – dubbed by Carr the satisfied or status quo powers; nationalism, of dissatisfied or revisionist states such as Germany, Italy, and Japan. Rather than providing a universalist calculus that would lead all right-thinking people to identical conclusions, reason turned out to be – quite literally – the means of rationalising beliefs which were rooted in social conditions, material interest, culture, and history.

It is at this point that Carr suddenly changes tack. Having deployed realist criticism to expose the interested character of supposedly universalist liberal doctrines, he next proceeds to expose the poverty of realism as a basis for political action by subjecting it to its own critical method. If the thought of one's opponents is a function of their class or national interest, why not one's own? Not only error, but truth turns out to be the result of social conditioning. Since it is, by definition, the most powerful who rule, truth turns out to be no more than the story told by the victors, a changeable function of historical processes driven by impersonal and unmotivated causes. Truth, so defined, is neither permanent nor universal, and is devoid of moral content.

No one who fully accepted such a bleak vision could embark upon a course of political action calculated to make a difference for the better; consistent determinism would put paid to the 'difference' and nihilism to the 'better'. Instead Carr discovers that his great realists of the past, from Machiavelli to Marx, had uniformly found themselves to be exceptions to the rule, sufficiently liberated from causal determination to apprehend universal truths and identify moral objectives which, at one and the same time, were guaranteed by the progressive drift of history and yet required resolute and organised human action for their attainment. From such inconsistency had arisen revolutionary Marxism as a political movement.

The boxing match of parts I and II of *The Crisis* reaches a curious conclusion. Both the idealist champion and the realist challenger are flat out on the canvas. The commentator takes the microphone. But before we hear what Carr has to say for himself, we had better review his account of the contest a little more carefully. For the story takes on a new dimension now that the author, too, is by implication exposed as one of those realists with an ideal.

Regard *The Twenty Years' Crisis* as a polemic, written to persuade, rather than the scientific work of instruction that it purports to be, and it is not difficult to see that the main rhetorical strategy of these first six chapters has been to place the author in the political centre and consign other voices to the extremes of Left and Right. The assumption is that those readers who matter most will feel more comfortable and receptive if asked to join Carr for a stroll down the middle of the road than they would if called to the barricades. In short, the early chapters are little more than scene-setting and manipulation. Anyone concerned simply to know what Carr thought about international relations and believed should be done to improve them had better start reading at the beginning of chapter 7. Yet the earlier chapters of *The Twenty Years' Crisis* are, perhaps, the most instructive of all his writings for their insights into the underlying methodology and morality of Carr's realism, and it is with this in mind that they are re-examined here before the burden of Carr's mature pre-war positive policy recommendations is set out in the closing section of the chapter.

Carr's rhetoric

How does *The Twenty Years' Crisis* work? The most frequently employed argumentative figures in *Crisis* are dichotomy and dialectic. The first two parts of the book work through a series of pairings which echo the basic division between utopia and reality. Utopia is associated with free will, theory, law, naivety, and radicalism; reality, conversely, with determinism, practice, power, sterility, and conservatism.

Alongside dichotomy, especially in the early chapters of the book, Carr deploys a set of anthropocentric metaphors which are tri- rather than di-chotomous, resting on the terms 'infancy', 'maturity', and 'senility'. The pairing of 'infancy/old age' may seem just one more dichotomy; but poised between the two lies maturity, which, by implication, is the leading intellectual characteristic of the third part of the book, where Carr is to put forward his own views following his presentation and subsequent dismissal of both utopianism and realism. The problem is that the order in which the book unfolds is

Table 3.1 *The sequence of* The Twenty Years' Crisis

Not:	Infancy	Maturity	Senility
But:	Infancy (thesis)	Senility (antithesis)	Maturity (synthesis)

not the natural, but the dialectical, order, as shown in table 3.1. Both utopianism and realism, as Carr portrays them in the early chapters, are stalking horses. They display discreditable extremes in order to win support, from those readers who think of themselves as moderate, for the compromise that Carr will pull out of the hat in the later chapters. One must assume the prime target readership to be the British policy-making elites of the day: almost entirely male, largely middle-aged or elderly, and for the most part conservative in politics. To flatter these readers into concurrence Carr very early on introduces the notion of utopianism as youth or immaturity. 'The science of international politics is in its infancy', he announces in the opening sentence of the book.[8] Realism, however, is the philosophy of sterile old age.[9] In place of the two extremes, Carr offers a seductive compromise of romantic pragmatism – 'mature thought', as he calls it – standing perfectly poised between youth and age, just as Titian had once pictured the cardinal virtue of prudence. 'Ex praeterito praesens prudentur agit ni futura actione deturpet': 'From past experience the present acts prudently lest future action be vitiated.'[10]

Table 3.2 *Youth and age in* The Twenty Years' Crisis

Youth	Senility	Maturity
Female	Male	Offspring

A second problem with Carr's deployment of this set of terms arises from his implicit gendering of 'youth' and 'maturity'. The contradictory coding of patriarchy into sexuality is shown in table 3.2, where application of the dialectic produces 'maturity' in the first case, and a youthful 'offspring' in the second. Realism is associated with analysis which is 'hard' and 'ruthless', and therefore with an inability to alter, act, or create in isolation. When the political scientist reaches the limits of what may be achieved by utopianism – the stage of

[8] Carr, *Crisis*, p. 3.   [9] Ibid., p. 15.
[10] James Hall, *Dictionary of Subjects and Symbols in Art* (London: Murray, 1974), p. 255.

Table 3.3 *Ambiguities in Carr's use of anthropocentric imagery*

Time:	Past	Present	Future
Age:	Infancy	Maturity	Senility
Dialectic:	Thesis	Antithesis	Synthesis
Gender:	Female/juvenile	Male	Offspring
Reference:	Utopianism (idealism)	Carr's own view *or* realism	Realism *or* Carr's own view

adolescence – the moment will come 'when purpose by itself is seen to be barren [rather than sterile or impotent], and when analysis of reality has forced itself upon him'.[11] Whether this rational rape is homosexual or heterosexual is scarcely the point; its patriarchal character is clear enough.

Carr's use of such images is summed up in table 3.3. What do they amount to? Because of the mismatch of organic and dialectical images, there is space in them for the elderly to read an offer of resumed maturity and potency, and for the realist (as male) to assume authority over and anticipate acquiescence from the utopian (female/ juvenile). There is certainly room for readers to develop quite divergent readings of Carr's realism.

The possibly unthinking identification of the author as mature male, through the use of anthropocentric terms, is reinforced by the authoritative stance that Carr develops towards his readers. Instead of adopting the Machiavellian ploy of an apparently simple and literal language in which author and reader are fully complicit, one with another, Carr chooses to present himself as the professor addressing his pupils (maturity speaking to adolescence). *The Twenty Years' Crisis* is announced as 'An Introduction' to international relations.[12] On the same title page Carr describes himself, truthfully of course, as 'Professor'. The immediate implications are of authority as well as authorship, but, secondarily, of a more utopian address and accessibility to a wide and untutored audience.

Carr moves quickly to provide a further boost for his own authority as initiate, or revealer of mysteries. In the preface the reader is promised analysis of 'the underlying and significant, rather than the

---

[11] Carr, *Crisis*, pp. 13–14. [12] Ibid., p. iii.

immediate and personal, causes of the disaster [the outbreak of war]'.[13] The theme of induction, even initiation, into a public science of social relations formerly conducted in secret, is persisted in through the titles of part I and chapter 1: 'The Science of International Politics' and 'The Beginnings of a Science'.[14] Authority is further reinforced by a barrage of references to the classics of European political philosophy far in excess of anything required for the achievement of the book's polemical aim.

There is no deceptively innocent Machiavellian style here. Instead, one group of readers is held in thrall while nods and winks are offered to the initiate, as Carr playfully risks subverting the authority he has assumed in this most Marxist of all his works. He is scathing towards the 'metaphysicians of Geneva [who] found it difficult to believe that an accumulation of ingenious texts prohibiting war was not a barrier against war itself'; yet he *writes* to offer a method of averting war through the appeasement of rising powers.[15] He quotes with approval Churchill's claim in 1932 that at no previous time had 'the gap between the kinds of words which statesmen used and what was actually happening in many countries [been] so great as it is now'.[16] Is this to be taken as a general invitation to mistrust propaganda and, more generally, to reject the claim of political texts to represent or act upon the world? But Carr's intention is not destructive; rather it is to succeed in the attempt to persuade readers of the possibility of translating his own policy proposals into reality.

Discussing propaganda, or 'power over opinion', in a text intended precisely to exert power over opinion, Carr argues at length for the inseparability of military and economic power from each other and from control of the media. He concludes that state control over the media is inevitable, and that ideas of independent world opinion as a political force are illusory, since 'propaganda is ineffective as a political force until it acquires a national home and becomes linked with military and economic power'.[17] Yet he puts this view as a private person and a forceful independent critic of the government of his own country on the brink of war.

In such ways as this, Carr attempts an extraordinary balancing act. As realist, he strives to maintain control and superiority over his readers. As idealist or liberal, he seeks in Kantean fashion to extend

---

[13] Ibid., p. ix.   [14] Ibid., p. xiii.   [15] Ibid., p. 41.   [16] Ibid.
[17] Carr, *The Twenty Years' Crisis* (2nd edn; London: Macmillan, 1946), pp. 135, 139.

the public use of reason to the conduct of foreign policy.[18] The invitation to a wider public is there, but it is as much an invitation to submission as an offer of empowerment.

Carr employs dichotomy and dialectic for substantive reasons, to set limits, as it were, to the position he intends to take in the later, longer parts of his book. He employs them, also, for their rhetorical value in affirming his authorial power and hooking a Conservative readership. But in seeming contradiction to this second objective, Carr uses dichotomy to keep the Left on board. For the dialectical method is also the German, and so the Marxist, method. *The Twenty Years' Crisis* moves in stately progress from thesis (utopianism/liberalism) to antithesis (realism/nationalism) and on to synthesis (Carr's own position). This first, theoretical, synthesis is then played out through a further, practical, dialectical progression. Small linguistic clues of Carr's familiarity with the German philosophical tradition and with Marxism abound, as, for example, his use of the term 'reproduction' in the context of dialectical reasoning.[19]

Very early in the book, a more specific mason's handshake is offered to the observant Marxist. Carr distinguishes between the physical and the social sciences. In the latter, the purpose of the investigator must always be numbered among the facts to be examined; there can be no complete objectivity. 'Purpose and analysis become part and parcel of a single process.'[20] Immediately, Carr goes on to cite Marx in support. Straight away, then, he has disclosed an understanding of a central Marxist attitude towards scientific methodology and a familiarity with the canonical works. But at the same time he has playfully negated his own standing as scientist and authority by the clear implication that he too, like any political scientist, must be regarded as purposive – a negation, however, that might easily float past the untutored reader.

Elsewhere, Carr's account of the origins of the First World War is the purest Leninism both in its stress on 1900 as the turning point in international relations and the linking of territorial and economic aspects of imperialist competition.[21] Indeed, the specific debt to Lenin, among authors in the Marxist canon, becomes more and more obvious as the book proceeds; direct references to Lenin's works (eleven)

[18] Onora O'Neill, 'The Public Use of Reason', *Political Theory*, 14:4, November 1986, pp. 523–51.
[19] Carr, *Crisis*, p. 26.   [20] Ibid., p. 6.   [21] Ibid., p. 78.

exceed those to Marx and Engels singly (two and three, respectively) and jointly (four).

Nor are these the only whiffs of Marxism in the book. Germany and Italy, regimes of the totalitarian Right, are highlighted as the have-not or revisionist states to which Britain and the other status quo powers are urged to make concessions proportionate to the current, rather than to some bygone, distribution of power, so that general war may be avoided. Yet the argument applies with equal force to the Soviet Union. Carr may have reckoned he had much more chance of persuading British Conservatives to allow the Soviet Union to resume its place among the Great Powers by first putting forward the parallel and equally necessary – if less palatable – case for Germany. He was certainly quick to put the Soviet case openly as soon as circumstances allowed. Days after Hitler's attack on the Soviet Union, taking his cue from a speech by Churchill, Carr noted that 'the experience of twenty years has shown the flimsy foundations of any settlement in Eastern Europe in which Russia does not whole-heartedly participate'.[22]

Also intriguing is the sheer space offered to the Marxist reader within Carr's dichotomous schemes. Utopianism is aligned with the Left. Realism, however, is a little confusingly derived by Carr through German idealism and Marxism.[23] Earlier, the strategy of opposition to individualist liberalism pursued through the early chapters and, most of all, the assault upon liberal political economy pander just as much to the critical appetites of Marxists as of British Conservatives and Unionists. Again, the seemingly Rightist characterisation of the Left as more theoretical and the Right, by contrast, as wise and pragmatic is implicitly nuanced in favour of the 'realist' Soviet regime by the observation that 'when Left parties . . . are brought into contact with reality through the assumption of political office, they tend to abandon their "doctrinaire" utopianism and move towards the Right'.[24]

Yet for all this barely concealed appeal to the socialist Left, Carr was to be able to hold a large section of the Tory readership of *The Times* in thrall, at least during the middle passage of the war. Soon after Carr's arrival, Robin Barrington-Ward expressed admiration for his willingness to work in partnership, moulding his 'advanced views in such a way that they will seem to our constituency the most normal and

---

[22] 'Aid to Russia', *The Times*, 25 June 1941.   [23] Carr, *Crisis*, pp. 83–6.
[24] Ibid., p. 28.

inevitable truths'. This enthusiasm began to dwindle only in mid-1943, as Barrington-Ward, having more and more to 'tone down' the leaders of his deputy, ruefully noted that 'the political effects of what he writes are not always plain to him'.[25]

Policy recommendations

Carr does not restrict himself to addressing two ideologically opposed readerships simultaneously in *The Twenty Years' Crisis*; he also attempts to deploy two versions of realism in order to exploit the space between them.

To this end, dichotomy, so powerful a technique in the first and second parts of the book, is re-deployed in part III. Where utopianism–radicalism–theory and realism–conservatism–practice had formed neat columns in the first half of the book to provide the two extremes, now *theoretical* positions of whichever political orientation – whether radical or conservative – are pitted against their *practical* or pragmatic counterparts. In privileging practical over theoretical reason at this point, Carr perhaps reveals Kantean, rather than Anglo-Saxon, liberal antecedents.[26] Doctrinaire conservatism, just as much as doctrinaire liberalism, is to be subordinated in concrete political situations to the needs of the moment. 'Every political situation contains mutually incompatible elements of utopia and reality, of morality and power.'[27]

The reason for this switch in the use made of dichotomy was to retain the powerful rhetorical tool of a supposed spirit of pragmatism, compromise, and moderation in order to seduce the Right into adoption of what might otherwise seem doctrinally unacceptable policy proposals. So while the merits of Carr's second realism, the pragmatic blend of power and morality which he finally preferred to the reflexive critique of chapters 5 and 6, will be subjected to closer scrutiny in chapter 7, it is enough for the present to note its policy implications, spelt out in the fourth section and the conclusion of *The Twenty Years' Crisis*.

Here there is a difficulty. For most of the specific proposals made by Carr are very much of their time, as policy proposals must necessarily

---

[25] Barrington-Ward's diary, quoted in Stephen Koss, *The Rise and Fall of the Political Press in Britain*, vol. II, *The Twentieth Century* (Chapel Hill and London: University of North Carolina Press, 1984), pp. 608 and 616.
[26] O'Neill, 'Use of Reason', p. 531.   [27] Carr, *Crisis*, p. 119.

be, and may also appear technical and narrow in character, the fruits rather more of Carr's career in the Foreign Office than of his subsequent years of reflection. Moreover, the outbreak of war meant that, by the time the book was published, they were redundant, at least in the short run.

In brief, Carr proposed that observance of international law had been subverted rather than secured by post-war emphasis on the doctrine of the sanctity of treaties and judicial settlement of international disputes. In seeking to substitute law for war, the peacemakers had neglected the more practical possibility of substituting alternative institutions for war that were political or social, rather than legal, in character. Taking the essential problem to be how changes in the relative economic and military power and consequent status and privileges of states could be accommodated without resort to war, Carr quickly rejected the formation of a world state or global legislature. While this would certainly bring an end to the problem of international anarchy, it would do so by abolishing rather than solving the intellectual problem of security under anarchy.

Instead, Carr turned to the model of bargaining, developing the analogy between international relations and relations between capital and labour in the absence of statutory regulation. Violence in labour relations in the form of strike or lock-out had steadily given way to conciliation and arbitration, but outcomes continued to reflect the relative strengths of the parties because the threat of force remained. The implication was that negotiation backed by force might be extensively substituted for war in international relations, and the consent even of the loser secured, provided all parties viewed the negotiated outcome as being very close to what might most probably have been obtained by force of arms, given the prevailing balance of power.

To explain how this new style of international politics would differ from traditional *Realpolitik*, Carr does little more than refer the reader to two examples: the 1921 Irish settlement and the Munich agreement of September 1938. The second, which is treated at greater length than the first, is unambiguously identified as 'the nearest approach in recent years to the settlement of a major international issue by a procedure of peaceful change'.[28] Germany originally had been forced, under threat of a resumption of hostilities, to accept a peace that was

---

[28] Ibid., p. 282.

both unrealistic and unjust. Versailles had ignored the irrepressible social and economic strength of Germany and displayed moral inconsistency, riding roughshod over its own general principle of self-determination by leaving more than three million Germans within the newly created Czechoslovak state.

Germany having finally begun to recover from the war of 1914–18 by the mid-1930s, Carr attributed the subsequent acquiescence of the status quo powers in the renunciation of the military clauses, the reoccupation of the Rhineland, and the *Anschluss* as much to their appreciation of the justice of the German case as to their relative weakness. The only fly in this ointment, he suggests, was that the status quo powers squandered the goodwill that should have come from their policy of appeasement, and the moderating influence this might have had on subsequent German policy, by accompanying every concession with blustering condemnations of German action. Refusal to accept their moral complicity in German foreign policy of the 1930s instead conveyed the impression that British and French appeasement was pure *Realpolitik*, springing simply from simple weakness. This, in turn, intensified and quickened the audacity of German policy, when a less hypocritical stance might easily have moderated it.

Thus far, Carr remained well within the confines of Conservative foreign policy debate. Only in a final speculative chapter, 'The Prospects for a New International Order', did he turn from the relatively narrow attack on legal formalism to the broader concerns which were soon to occupy him, first as a propagandist in the employ of the state and, soon afterwards, as little short of a one-man alternative government, installed at the offices of *The Times* in Printing House Square. Here, it becomes difficult to separate description from advocacy. Carr was willing to identify the decisive issues in the new order that he believed must replace the old liberal system if chaos was to be averted. He was even willing to anticipate some probable outcomes. But he was, as yet, evasive and diffident in the role of advocate. Yet advocacy there was, as Carr set out his normative account of a new world order, identifying the characteristic political actor, the locus of hegemonic power, and the source of legitimacy.

The most notable political change of the nineteenth century had been the substitution of inter-state conflict, still based largely on material inequalities, for intra-state class conflict. Class solidarity had proved less fundamental than the solidarity of politically consolidated national communities. For Carr, Disraeli and Bismarck had been 'the great figures' of the nineteenth century.[29] The territorial nation-state had become 'the supreme unit'.[30]

This current supremacy of the state, and of inter-state conflict, might prove no more enduring than the class conflict of Marx's day. Excessive attachment to it held, for the modern student of international relations as for Marx, the threat of irrelevance. Yet rather than speculate about fundamental political transformations, Carr confines himself to shorter-term speculation about the likely configuration of power in a still territorial system.

Here he remarks on two concurrent but opposing tendencies. The first, as exemplified in European maritime imperialism and the national unifications of Germany and Italy (and, one might add, the contiguous continental imperialisms of the United States and the Soviet Union), was towards extensive, more or less economically integrated multinational units. To the historian of this oligopolistic imperialism, the settlement of 1918, with its creation of new, small states, seemed 'a dangerous fiasco'.[31] But another story could as easily be told, in which fissiparous cultural and political tendencies within the British Commonwealth, the United States, and other potential or emerging blocs proved stronger than the logic of economic integration.

'While technical, industrial and economic development within the last hundred years has dictated a progressive increase in the size of the effective political unit', Carr mused, 'there may be a size which cannot be exceeded without provoking a recrudescence of disintegrating tendencies.' 'The issue', he concluded with remarkable prescience, was 'likely to become more decisive than any other for the course of world history over the next few generations'.[32]

The solution offered by Carr, nicely anticipating the post-1945 settlement, was of a world in which the effective unit of power would 'consist in groups of several formally sovereign states [in which] the effective (but not necessarily the nominal) authority is exercised from a single centre'.[33] Anticipating the subsequent development of Carr's thought, one may here detect the germ of a vision in which, within such groupings, continued formal sovereignty or autonomy would

---

[29] Ibid., p. 290. [30] Ibid., p. 291. [31] Ibid., p. 294. [32] Ibid., p. 295.
[33] Ibid., p. 296.

placate the forces of cultural nationalism while alliance systems and customs unions provided security.

Pursuing his formula of accommodation between power and morality to its conclusion, Carr next attempts to identify, and in some measure to justify, the probable hegemon of the new international order. Britain, clearly, had had its day. Hegemonic status had been offered to but declined by the United States in 1918. Carr acknowledged the aspirations of Germany and Japan, accepting that no compelling universalist grounds existed for justifying a *pax Americana* over a *pax Germanica* or a *pax Japonica*. He dwells briefly upon the 'romantic idea' of a union of English-speaking peoples, a favourite of a vociferous minority in Britain ever since the days of Cecil Rhodes, noting its appeal to the beleaguered British, but warning of its irrelevance to United States policy-makers. He concludes, with never a mention of Russia, that the most likely outcome for the foreseeable future would be a *pax Americana* 'imposed on a divided and weakened Europe'.[34]

What was to provide the moral basis for this new hegemony? Fully aware of his own vulnerability to realist charges of hypocrisy, Carr nevertheless settled upon the greater development of consent and conciliation within Anglo-American than German or Japanese political culture, recalling his earlier analogy between industrial and international relations. A world order organised on this basis, rather than on the equally bankrupt alternatives of ready resort to force and legal formalism, would from time to time require material sacrifice as well as restraint from its ruling elites. This, Carr felt, was more to be hoped for from the elites of the United States and Britain than from those of any other Great Powers. No very convincing account is offered of why this should be so. Implicitly, the argument seems to be that they would make concessions to equality when effectively threatened with insecurity. In Roosevelt's United States, as in Chamberlain's Britain, the experience of the 1930s had established that the state could provide social security through public expenditure, and that those who ruled would be willing to continue and extend this provision, even at some sacrifice of their relative wealth, since they had glimpsed the abyss of social collapse and political revolution. Correspondingly, revisionist powers of the future, knowing that their political and economic collapse held almost as many dangers for the

---

[34] Ibid., pp. 298 and 300.

status quo powers as for themselves, would be able to exploit a general perception, extending even to the policy-makers of the most powerful states, that security, in international as in domestic affairs, demanded sacrifices in the form of international economic assistance.

Only in these closing and very possibly least read pages of his best-known book did Carr take the first steps that would take him beyond the parameters of conventional foreign policy debate towards the more radical posture that was soon to earn him the sobriquet 'the Red professor of Printing House Square'. But the essence is there. The practical, achievable utopia offered by Carr was one in which a small number of loose agglomerations of sovereign states, with the United States and its satellites foremost among them, maintained world peace through a system of compensatory liberalism characterised by state intervention, at home and abroad, designed to maintain both social and international security by conceding progressive equality under the implicit threat of disruption.

4 War aims

The Ministry of Information

The economic and social foundations of a peaceful international order, hardly more than sketched towards the close of *The Twenty Years' Crisis*, were rapidly to be forged into an integrated and radical programme of social welfare, economic management, and foreign policy over the next six years as Carr worked to make his voice heard, firstly through the Ministry of Information (MoI) and later as drafter of a succession of editorials or 'leaders' in *The Times*.

It is possible to draw a very rough distinction between the chief preoccupations of the early months of the war, on which Carr would finally publish under his own name early in 1942, and those that came into sharper relief during the later phase.[1] The first and essential propaganda task was to secure the widest possible support for the British government, both at home and abroad, by setting out a practical and desirable set of war aims. This would at one and the same time reassure neutral states, undermine popular support for enemy governments, win allies, and motivate the British people. Besides, it would ensure that Britain did not come to the conference table unprepared in the event of a negotiated peace in 1940 or 1941.

When the balance of probabilities shifted during 1941, as first the Soviet Union and then the United States entered the war, definition of British war aims in general gradually gave way to much more specific

---

[1] E. H. Carr, *Conditions of Peace* (London: Macmillan, 1942). Part of the book, on nationalism, was published earlier in pamphlet form. See below, n. 72. Carr's preface to *Conditions of Peace* is dated January 1942, from which it may be inferred that the book was substantially written in 1940–1.

questions of applying them to the delineation of post-war frontiers and spheres of influence, the design of international organisations, more detailed implementation of domestic social policy, and how best to reward allies and deal with enemies. During the long counter-attack of 1942–5 a debate ensued about the coming peace that looked back to the supposed failures of the post-1918 settlement and forward to the hoped-for outcomes of military campaigning and inter-Allied diplomacy. Accordingly, consideration of Carr's work during the Second World War is roughly divided along these lines, those issues that were to dominate the later years being deferred to the next chapter.

Among the topics to be dealt with when methodological and theoretical aspects of realism are considered at greater length in chapter 7 will be the related concepts of authorship and authority. If the paramount concern of the realist political leader is to win, then the highest priority of the realist intellectual is to persuade. Should this require some sacrifice of vanity, as authorship and public recognition are traded for the superior authority of a government department or a prestigious newspaper, consistent realism demands that pride be swallowed and the most effective path preferred.

No wonder then that Carr embarked on a career of hugely produc-tive anonymity following the outbreak of war, in what was almost certainly the most influential phase of his life. Memoranda he drafted at the MoI were secret. His authorship of *Times* leading articles was anonymous, subject to amendment by his editor, and occasionally subcontracted.[2] The tradition of anonymity was stoutly maintained when the strongest of the 1940 leaders, for all ten of which Carr had been responsible, were published in pamphlet form.[3] The other side of this exchange was that MoI memoranda reached ministerial desks, and might stand some chance of determining British policy, while *The Times* was widely viewed as a quasi-official publication, allowing Carr to disseminate what was increasingly a personal alternative foreign

---

[2] Jonathan Haslam, unpublished conference paper, Gregynog, July 1997, suggests that some of Carr's leaders may have been drafted by, or drafted from notes supplied by, members of Political and Economic Planning. Donald McLachlan, *In the Chair: Barrington-Ward of 'The Times', 1927–1948* (London: Weidenfeld & Nicolson, 1971), p. 212, goes less far, but does identify some candidates.

[3] *Planning for War and Peace: Ten Leading Articles Reprinted from 'The Times'* (London: The Times Publishing Co., 1940).

policy to a readership – at home and abroad – that far exceeded the circulation of his earlier publications.

The role of any single individual in the drafting of papers prepared in a civil service department is often less than clear. This problem is compounded for anyone examining the British Ministry of Information by uneven survival of records. Moreover, Carr held the post of director of foreign publicity for a very short time, from the end of 1939 until his resignation in April 1940. So while some documents bearing his signature have survived, and many others generated within the ministry in the early months of the war bear Carr's stamp in their ideas, and even their style, it can seldom be determined whether this or that phrase came from his pen, reflected his influence, or simply expressed a more broadly derived collegiate view in which he concurred.

In spite of this, there is no doubt that Carr was among the more senior figures in the ministry during the months when the very first attempts were being made to draft a statement of British war aims. He contributed directly to the debate through a report on propaganda policy at the start of 1940.[4] Moreover, early drafts of British war aims from other hands included a number of ideas already familiar to readers of *The Twenty Years' Crisis* and many that Carr himself would go on to voice in *The Times* and in *Conditions of Peace*. These included the military obsolescence of the smaller European states and the consequent need for post-war international co-operation, the irretrievable nature of the breakdown of the pre-1914 liberal international order and the consequent impossibility of a return to the *status quo ante*, the need to back law with force in any future international security system, and the importance of creating a welfare state in Britain and offering constitutional concessions to British dependencies in order to appear fully democratic and post-imperial in the eyes of potential allies.[5]

The focus of the manifesto on the conduct of British propaganda that Carr submitted to his political masters on taking over the Foreign Publicity Directorate (FPD) was rather narrower than this, concerned

---

[4] 'Principles and Objectives of British Propaganda in Foreign Countries', 2 January 1940, PRO INF1/848 14478, Minutes of Information Policy Committee, PC Paper No. 5. Another copy, referred to by Robert Cole, *Britain and the War of Words in Neutral Europe, 1939–1945: The Art of the Possible* (Basingstoke: Macmillan, 1990), p. 199, n. 46, is to be found in the Foreign Office general series: FO371/25174.3839.

[5] PRO INF1/862.

chiefly with the question of motivation. Foreigners must be convinced, he argued, not only that Britain was capable of winning the war, but also that this outcome was desirable. While British propaganda was bound to be adapted to local needs, it must show a basic uniformity, stressing political freedom, freedom of expression, the degree of independence achieved by self-governing states within the Commonwealth, and the strength of British commitment to respect for other nations, international economic co-operation, and peaceful settlement of disputes. Tactically, it would be important to stress the future rather than dwelling on the past and, so far as was possible, to associate other countries with these values, developing the idea of an extensive free world from which few states besides Germany had defected. Consistency of moral judgement was also vital to the credibility of British claims and meant that Italy and the Soviet Union must be condemned for their past and current aggressions in spite of the value of their neutrality. Beyond this, the memorandum consists chiefly in discussion of how to adapt the British message in such a way as to optimise its effect in a wide range of neutral states.

Why did Carr not stay at the MoI to see through his programme? The reasons are quite clear, and have to do with his personal ambition and vanity, with the ambivalent position of the Foreign Publicity Directorate, originally set up within the Foreign Office (FO) following an announcement by Chamberlain in June 1939, but billeted on the Ministry of Information (MoI) at the outbreak of hostilities, and lastly with the more general weakness of the MoI itself.

Personal absorption within the state machine was something that Carr had anticipated and even advocated by implication in his treatment of propaganda – 'power over opinion' as he termed it – in *The Twenty Years' Crisis*. There he had recognised the prevalence and intensity of propaganda in the post-1918 period. He had also argued that it was inseparable from other expressions of power, such as military force and economic bargaining power.[6] This was because, like them, it was effective only as an attribute of the state. 'International slogans only become real and concrete when they are translated into terms of national policy', he declared. 'Power over opinion cannot be dissociated from military and economic power.'[7] But when it came to

---

[6] For an illuminating alternative view of propaganda at this time, see Sidney Rogerson, *Propaganda in the Next War* (London: Bles, 1938).

[7] E. H. Carr, *The Twenty Years' Crisis, 1919–1939: An Introduction to the Study of International Relations* (London: Macmillan, 1939), p. 179.

it, Carr was not willing to submit to the disciplines of civil service life if this were to inhibit the clarity and effectiveness of his views. After only three weeks at the MoI – and three weeks of war – Carr was starting to chafe at the bit. 'I should very much like, when the thing comes to an end, to be in a position to have a say about terms of settlement, and this job gives me little prospect of that', he complained to the then assistant editor of *The Times*, Robert – more often Robin – Barrington-Ward.[8]

Carr was guided by one supreme concern, which was to have an effective voice in British foreign policy and the post-war settlement. To achieve this, he needed an institutional base with just the right blend of authority and autonomy from which to advocate his personal foreign policy. Hence his move to the MoI. The problem was that relations between the Foreign Office and the MoI, and between the Foreign Publicity Directorate and the MoI, when taken together, made the prospect of his exerting any substantial influence very slight indeed. A combination of his powerlessness within the ministry and the powerlessness of the ministry itself led Carr to resign in April 1940.

Taking the personal position first, Carr had not figured in the pre-war planning for the MoI and was not on the list of more than twenty names earmarked for specific administrative positions in a progress report of February 1938. This may well have been because the pre-war formation of the FPD took place within the Foreign Office.[9] Yet even after succeeding Lieutenant-General Charles as director of the Foreign Publicity Directorate at the end of 1939, Carr only once attended the Information Policy Committee, the most senior committee in the ministry. This was on 2 February 1940, when his paper on foreign propaganda policy was one of three for discussion that day.

To this personal marginalisation should be added the doubts Carr must have felt about both the current and the potential political impact of his directorate – lodged in the way it was within a newly formed ministry – and about the effectiveness of the ministry as a whole. Though Lord Macmillan had resisted strong Foreign Office pressure to take over the FPD, his successor, Sir John Reith, was not

[8] News International, Archives of *The Times*, Carr to Barrington-Ward, 29 September 1939.
[9] PRO INF/1, Progress Report for the period ending 31 January 1938. For the FO role in the genesis of the FPD, see PRO INF/1/859, Halifax to Macmillan, 20 October 1939.

willing to allow it the autonomy that Carr believed necessary. The early months of 1940 witnessed wrangles between Carr and Reith over staffing difficulties and the structure of the ministry. The personnel supplied to him by the MoI Establishments Division were just not good enough. Carr asked instead for authority to make his own arrangements, but this was refused. Worse, Reith now set up a separate Commercial Relations Department, hiving off matters that Carr felt to be essential concerns of his own directorate.[10]

As well as internal rivalries, there were jealousies between ministries. Robert Cole, in his authoritative study of British wartime propaganda in neutral Europe, perceptively remarked that 'E. H. Carr regarded the FPD as a "miniature Foreign Office".'[11] It had been partly the danger that it might develop along these lines that had led the foreign secretary, Lord Halifax, to try to reclaim it from the upstart MoI. Halifax had argued in October 1939 that the FPD could not work effectively without direct contact with British overseas missions, but that it was unacceptable for the Foreign Office monopoly of such contacts to be breached. His conclusion was that the FPD should return to the Foreign Office. Macmillan discussed the matter with Chamberlain, explaining that in his opinion 'the removal of the Foreign Publicity Division . . . would really involve the total dissolution of this Ministry', and Halifax climbed down when it became clear that the prime minister had sided with Macmillan.[12] Behind this exchange lay a further concern, shared by Halifax and Carr, about the competence of many of the MoI propagandists.[13]

Carr enjoyed some success in improving relations between the two ministries, but may nevertheless have inferred from this early clash between Macmillan and Halifax that, even if he had proved able to win his bureaucratic battles within the MoI, the FO would have watched his subsequent attempts at empire-building jealously.[14] Nothing comparable to Toynbee's Foreign Research and Press Service (FRPS) at Balliol, regarded by Eden as so indispensable that its 177 professional staff were recalled to London in 1943, was ever likely to

---

[10] Cole, *Britain and the War of Words*, p. 22.
[11] Ibid.
[12] PRO INF/1/859, Macmillan to Halifax, 26 October 1939; Halifax to Macmillan, 26 October 1939.
[13] Cole, *Britain and the War of Words*, p. 16.
[14] On Carr's responsibility for improved FO–MoI relations, see ibid., p. 24.

be achieved from within the MoI.[15] Its place in the Whitehall pecking order and its influence on the Cabinet were both low. Not until Duff Cooper took over from Reith at the MoI as the third incumbent in less than a year would a determined effort made to establish a Cabinet committee on war aims, duly formed under the chairmanship of Neville Chamberlain in July 1940.[16] 'If we are going to get anything useful decided and approved by Government, we must get a small committee, on which Government departments, and perhaps the War Cabinet itself, are represented', Cooper reasoned.[17] But this was all too late for Carr, who had experienced the ministry at its worst and weakest under Lord Macmillan and Sir John Reith.

The Times

Add the potential hostility of the Foreign Office and the apparent weakness of his own ministry to the purely internal obstacles he faced, and it is not difficult to see why Carr moved to *The Times* in April 1940. Perhaps there he would find the independent power-base he was seeking. The fact that he remained for seven years, producing more than 350 editorial articles or leaders, suggests that he did. At the outset there were at least three reasons to expect that he would be successful: the intelligence network of *The Times*, its circulation, and its relationship with the British government.

In those days *The Times* was, above all else, a news paper. It had a comprehensive network of correspondents at home and abroad, and its editorial team consequently worked on the basis of copious and generally reliable information which both fuelled and disciplined the broad views of British policy which it was their business to formulate.

---

[15] Inderjeet Parmar, 'Chatham House, the Foreign Policy Process, and the Making of the Anglo-American Alliance', in Andrea Bosco and Cornelia Navari, eds., *Chatham House and British Foreign Policy, 1919–1945: The Royal Institute of International Affairs During the Inter-War Period* (London: Lothian Foundation, 1994), p. 312.

[16] PRO INF1/862, 863. The Foreign Office was very co-operative. See INF1/862, Halifax to Cooper, 30 July 1940; see also the exchange of letters dated 27 July 1940 between Cadogan and Cooper. Wickham Steed wrote to Duff Cooper on 24 July 1940 suggesting that senior policy committee to clarify war aims. It may have been this letter that prompted Cooper to press for the Cabinet committee, which was formed 'to make suggestions in regard to a post-war European and World system with particular regard to the economic needs of the various nations, and to the problems of adjusting the free life of small countries in a durable international order': PRO INF1/863.

[17] PRO INF1/862, Cooper to Cadogan, 27 July 1940.

In this respect a great newspaper came rather closer than did the Ministry of Information to the ideal propaganda instrument as envisaged by Duff Cooper. 'It is an awfully difficult matter, this formulating of war aims', the minister mused. 'There are two extremes between which we want to steer a middle course. We do not want to have a lot of professors, out of touch with realities, thinking brilliantly in an academic void, nor do we want purely opportunist propagandists, changing their views from day to day with the course of events. We want something between the two – people who do know what is going on and can keep closely in touch with the course of events, but who are also capable of taking long views and planning for the future.'[18] Here, three months too late, was the brief Carr had wanted at the MoI, and which he now set out to work to at *The Times*.

Propaganda by the middle of the twentieth century was fast becoming a matter of numbers through a kind of informational Fordism. With a circulation of 192,000 on the eve of war, *The Times* fell far short of the *Daily Express* or the *Daily Herald*, each with over 2 million.[19] It did not even come near to the 637,000 claimed by the *Daily Telegraph*. But it had an unchallenged position on the breakfast tables of the British policy-making elites.[20] Viewed from a different perspective, a daily readership of 192,000 dwarfed the 8,965 print run, distributed over two and a half years, of the first edition of *The Twenty Years' Crisis*, the 15,000 copies of *Conditions of Peace* printed during 1942 and 1943, or even the 20,000 copies of *Nationalism and After* printed in January 1945.[21]

The political alignment of *The Times* was just as important as the class or number of its readership. Under Geoffrey Dawson, the paper had been closely associated with Chamberlain and the policy of

---

[18] Ibid. From the context it is clear that the professors with whom Cooper was losing patience were Toynbee's team at Balliol, and Lionel Curtis and others at Chatham House.

[19] Iverach McDonald, *The History of 'The Times'*, vol. V, *Struggles in War and Peace, 1939–1966* (London: Times Books, 1984), p. 63. Wartime paper shortages produced an artificial restriction in circulation, which, however, never fell below 150,000 during the war.

[20] Political and Economic Planning, *Report on the British Press* (London: PEP, 1938), quoted in Richard Cockett, *Twilight of Truth: Chamberlain, Appeasement, and the Manipulation of the Press* (London: Weidenfeld & Nicolson, 1989), p. 25.

[21] These and other figures for the print runs of works published by Macmillan are derived from the Macmillan Edition Books in the British Library, Add. MSS 55909–55930.

appeasement, as Lord Halifax had been because of his 1937 talks with Hitler, and Carr himself now was since the publication of *The Twenty Years' Crisis*.[22] This reinforced a long-standing assumption that *The Times* favoured the government of the day. Richard Cockett has suggested that it was regarded as a semi-official organ overseas throughout the 1930s because of Dawson's very close Cabinet contacts, above all with Halifax.[23] It was to be the general presumption, especially overseas, that Carr's policy was identical with official policy which was so to exasperate officials and ministers as the divide between the two grew steadily wider, until the day in 1945 when Churchill, on the floor of the House of Commons, finally attacked *The Times* over Greece to loud Tory cheers.[24]

Consistent with this close relationship was the willingness of *The Times* to publish editorials to order, in support of government policy. When Sir Samuel Hoare cabled from Madrid in 1941 requesting energetic efforts to prevent Spain from joining the Axis, a Foreign Office official minuted that 'an inspired *Times* leader would be helpful and no doubt the News Dept. could arrange for one'. Carr and Iverach McDonald were spoken to and provided with notes for a leader, which they promised for the next day. 'Independent Spain', written by Carr, duly appeared on 24 April 1941.[25] Wartime leaders on Latin American affairs were generally offered for comment to R. A. Humphreys of the Foreign Office Research Department, and some were drafted by him.[26] In Buenos Aires, the local *Times* correspondent made a habit of submitting all his copy to the British Embassy.[27]

In a similar spirit, Carr himself submitted material to the Foreign Office prior to publication for approval and comment, as did some of the foreign correspondents working for the paper.[28] And sometimes,

---

[22] Cockett, *Twilight of Truth*, p. 27, quoting *History of 'The Times'*, vol. V, *150th Anniversary and Beyond, 1912–1948* (London: The Times Publishing Co., 1952), p. 915.
[23] Cockett, *Twilight of Truth*, p. 13.
[24] McLachlan, *In the Chair*, pp. 239 and 252–3.
[25] PRO FO371/26950 C3968/484/41.
[26] An example is 'Nutrition and Trade', *The Times*, 21 July 1943, which deals with Latin America and is identified in the *Times* editorial notebooks as being by Humphreys.
[27] PRO FO371/33517 A11406/11/2.
[28] PRO FO371/26819 C13599/214/36; FO371/33517 A11406/11/2, David Kelly, Buenos Aires, to Victor Perowne, 2 December 1943, makes clear that the Buenos Aires correspondent of *The Times*, anxious not to damage relations with the new Argentine regime, had been submitting material to the embassy for comment only to find that the staff of *The Times* in London consistently rendered his copy more hostile to the Argentine government before publication.

when he found himself out of line with government policy, he was willing to back-pedal in an attempt to reduce the damage. This was done after one notorious leader, 'Security in Europe', which appeared on 10 March 1943 and gave great offence to the Poles. As far as possible, the damage was made good through the correspondence columns and by a further, more moderate leader, also by Carr.[29]

Given this generally close relationship, it was hard for government to dissociate itself from the line taken by Carr in *The Times*. One of Carr's 1941 leaders, 'Peace and Power', had suggested that a stable post-war Europe could not be assured without recognition of both Soviet and German power. This simultaneously offended Turks, Yugoslavs, Romanians, Greeks, Poles, and Czechs. The Turkish minister in Madrid was not alone in regarding *The Times* as 'a spokesman of the British Government'. Knatchbull-Hugessen, in Angora, found it 'virtually impossible to convince any foreigners . . . that the "Times" is not officially inspired'. A weary official in London minuted: 'We are at the mercy of *The Times* and can only hope for a longish interval before the next lapse.'[30] On another occasion, State Department officials in Washington were in doubt about whether a *Times* leader opposing the post-war dismemberment of Germany was or was not inspired by Her Majesty's Government.[31] Part of the problem posed by Carr's editorials was, indeed, that they were seldom so extreme that they did not reflect opinion within some section of government or of the Foreign Office. Worse, they sometimes advanced the official view, but at a moment that seemed to the official mind to be tactically unsound and therefore damaging to British interests.

Times leaders are anonymous, their authors shielded by collective responsibility. Moreover, the paper always claimed to be resolutely independent. On the first of these issues, the official line was nicely expressed by the editor in response to criticism from the Foreign Office. 'It is never safe to attribute the views of *The Times* to this or that individual', he wrote. 'Whoever may write a given article the opinions expressed are the opinions of the paper. There is really no

[29] PRO FO371/34566 C2822/258/55, Cadogan to P. M., 23 March 1943.
[30] PRO FO371/30096 R7715/R7720/240/44 1941. The debate as fought out in the correspondence columns of *The Times* and in *The Economist* is summarised in P. M. H. Bell, *John Bull and the Bear: British Public Opinion, Foreign Policy, and the Soviet Union, 1941–1945* (London: Arnold, 1990), p. 60.
[31] PRO FO371/39079 C2867/C2868/146/18 1944.

distinction to be drawn between the Editor and any of his team of leader-writers.'[32]

But this official line was disingenuous. A set of notebooks survives in which are written lists allocating responsibility for each topic of the day to one or, very occasionally, two of the small team of leader writers. They also establish who was duty editor for each edition of the paper.[33] The notebooks help establish authorship but do not entirely settle the matter, for a draft might easily be passed from one member of the team to another, and the whole argument of an editorial changed by a few strokes of the editor's pen. So where a topic assigned to Carr is treated in an uncharacteristic manner, this cannot be treated as clear evidence of a development in his thought. However, it is evident from Foreign Office correspondence and the archives of *The Times* that Carr was personally responsible for the great majority of the leaders that stand against his name in the notebooks, and, taken as a whole, the Carr leaders are consistent with (and on occasion even identical to!) the remainder of his published work.[34] Four other features make them especially useful to the historian of ideas.

To begin with, they were written under pressure of time and have therefore the freshness of water-colour preparatory sketches for the more studied oils of this period, *Conditions of Peace* and *Nationalism and After*. In addition, they provide a revealing day-by-day application of Carr's principles to events and include some of his most incisive attempts to integrate ideas about foreign and domestic policy. Most importantly of all, they represent a sustained attempt by Carr to foster a coherent set of British policies including economic planning and a welfare state at home, post-war international co-operation in Western Europe, concessions to the Soviet Union in Eastern Europe, and prompt movement towards independence for British and European dependencies.

It was the first two of these four objectives that dominated Carr's

---

[32] PRO FO 371/24761 N6045/1224/59, Barrington-Ward to Laurence Collier, 28 July 1940. On the complexities underlying this bland statement, especially those concerning the relationship between Barrington-Ward and Carr, there is no better account than that provided by McLachlan, *In the Chair*, ch. 21.

[33] Archives of *The Times*.

[34] Additional corroboration for 1940 is to be found in a list of his writings kept by Carr which tallies precisely with the *Times* leader-diaries from June to August 1940: Carr Papers, Box 5, Birmingham University Library. For examples of Carr's occasional re-use of material from *The Times*, see below, ch. 5, n. 7.

Times leaders during 1940 and will therefore be considered at greater length during the remainder of this chapter.

Welfare and planning

Turning first to the campaign for economic planning and the creation of a welfare state, it may be helpful to consider what was being demanded before turning to the question of who was being addressed. While Carr made repeated pleas for a new social order at home, the brevity of the leader generally allowed him to avoid detailed specification of his demands. To the extent that they were spelt out they required the use of improved housing, transport, and public services to provide what he called a 'social minimum', supported by industrial regeneration and a thorough reform of agricultural production and supply.

Carr's post-war utopia was in many ways consistent with, perhaps even derivative from, the 1930s think-tank 'Political and Economic Planning'. Indeed, it may have been through Carr's association with this all-party group that its secretary David Owen became drawn into occasional leader writing for *The Times* from 1942, when he also took up the post of secretary to Stafford Cripps.[35] In Carr's vision, the state was to use planning law, selective provision of public housing, and an integrated public transport policy to ensure that industrial production and employment were widely dispersed across the country in ways that would allow the great mass of workers to live close to their jobs while enjoying easy access to the countryside. The inflated size of the metropolis would be dealt with by moving the seat of government to the Midlands. These initiatives in regional and industrial planning would be reinforced by enhanced provision of free education and health services to those least able to pay, by the further extension of the social wage through the subsidising of basic foodstuffs in line with a national nutrition policy, and by a progressive extension of the principle of state subsidy to embrace essential consumer goods and overseas aid.[36]

This focus on the responsibility of the community, acting through the agency of the state, for the welfare of individuals, could hardly be

---

[35] Paul Addison, *The Road to 1945: British Politics and the Second World War* ([London: Cape, 1975] London: Pimlico, 1994), pp. 188–9.
[36] Carr, *Conditions of Peace*, pp. 135–9.

discharged without extensive control of production. Pointing to 'the natural trend of modern industry towards monopoly' and the essentially public character of highly regulated private-sector service providers such as the railway companies or the banks that followed from this trend, Carr argued that formal nationalisation was hardly necessary. Having been imposed during the war, the much more extensive state regulation of industrial production, of the supply of investment capital, and of key prices including wage and interest rates must be retained in peacetime.[37] His vision was of 'a mixed economy in which essential services will be conducted in the form of autonomous units under government control, paying interest rather than profits on the capital invested in them, while luxury industries and services or new lines of production will continue to operate in the conditions of a more or less free market'.[38]

Supporting this mixed economy and its extensive welfare system, Carr envisaged policies for agricultural supply and trade which would continue to allow Britain to specialise in the advanced industrial activities which he considered essential to Great Power status. Since Britain lacked a sufficiently large domestic market and territory to support strategically essential industries or achieve autarky, it was vital – notwithstanding the difficulties of wartime supply – to pursue policies based on a relatively high level of international trade. In this context, the object of domestic agricultural policy would be to maintain a small and highly productive farm sector, specialising in perishable product and capable of rapid expansion in time of war. This could best be achieved through the use of income subsidies that were neutral in their effect on imports.

Fundamental to all these reforms were full employment and constitutional reform. Convinced that economic security was a prerequisite of political stability, Carr described full employment towards the end of the war as 'the master key to social justice in the modern industrial state'.[39] His argument had long been that unemployment could not be considered in isolation from the political order, its

---

[37] 'State and Industry', *The Times*, 6 December 1941, and *Conditions of Peace*, p. 78. On the public character of the largest corporations, see also John Maynard Keynes, *The End of Laissez-Faire* (London: Hogarth Press, 1926), pp. 42–5.

[38] Carr, *Conditions of Peace*, pp. 139–46.

[39] E. H. Carr, *Nationalism and After* (London: Macmillan, 1945), p. 68. See also 'Ordered Freedom', *The Times*, 9 May 1942; 'A Major Peace Aim', 23 January 1943; 'British Foreign Policy', 20 November 1943; 'Food, Work, and Homes', 24 November 1943.

prevalence in the inter-war years having been closely bound up with the Versailles settlement. Ill-judged application of the principle of self-determination had resulted in the creation of a profusion of competitive customs areas. Taken together with the reparations clauses of the treaty and the difficulties of economic readjustment in the belligerent countries, this had done much to break up the pre-war international economy and create the mass unemployment that had fed political extremism in Europe, ending only with the rearmament boom of the mid-1930s. 'Unemployment or fear of unemployment', he concluded, had been 'the most fertile cause of exclusion and discrimination in the modern world'.[40] Not only this: unemployment stood in the way of that full utilisation of all resources which Carr saw as a prerequisite for increased production and living standards, including the provision of social services, in the coming peace.

In short, foreign and domestic policy had become inextricably linked through the dual mechanisms of international economic interdependence and the demands made on an industrial society by total war. 'The streams of social and international policy have mingled', he declared.[41] Moreover, wartime conditions and precedents created the revolutionary conditions in which the log-jam of the inter-war years might be broken.[42] Bombing had 'given a new and brutal impulse to the process which [had] been for twenty years one of the main preoccupations of our social policy'.[43] War production had seen, he believed, a willingness of capital to sacrifice profits and of labour to relax trade demarcations that could be extended into the post-war

---

[40] Carr, *Nationalism and After*, p. 68.
[41] 'Planning for War and Peace', *The Times*, 5 August 1940. Cf. *Conditions of Peace*, p. 130: 'A successful foreign policy for Great Britain is now possible only on the basis of a substantially altered outlook which will inevitably reflect itself in every branch of domestic policy; and what we can achieve in Europe and the world will grow out of, and is in large measure dependent on, what we can achieve at home.' See also 'British Foreign Policy', *The Times*, 20 November 1943: 'An increasingly intimate link between domestic and foreign policy is a direct result of the technique of modern warfare, which makes national power . . . dependent . . . on the productive capacity of the nation as a whole.'
[42] *The Times*, 16 October 1940: 'War is not only confronting us with social problems which must be tackled at once, but is providing some of the conditions in which they can be met.' For the war as revolution, see Carr, *Conditions of Peace*, p. 130, and also 'Interdependence', *The Times*, 9 January 1941: 'The demands of war are revolutionizing ways of life and thought; and we shall carry these new ways with us to meet the demands of peace.'
[43] *The Times*, 5 October 1940.

period.[44] In general, Carr found that 'the intensification of the war effort and the increasingly complete mobilization of our resources render all the more imperative a far-reaching programme of social reconstruction in Great Britain'.[45]

A final yet fundamental aspect of Carr's programme of domestic reform was constitutional reform. How was the huge growth in state power which he foresaw and advocated to be reconciled with democracy? Carr argued that there was no choice but to acquiesce in the shift of power from legislature to executive and, above all, to the prime minister. However, this tendency could be balanced by the development of more effective scrutiny through specialised standing committees and the devolution of substantial powers to regional commissioners appointed by government.[46]

Carr saw in the system of regional government instituted in Britain during the war one more aspect of the general trend from *laissez-faire* to a more comprehensive state, 'called upon by common consent to protect, to adjust, and to regulate the interests of its citizens at almost every point'. 'The more far-reaching and the more ubiquitous the functions of the central government', he concluded, 'the more inevitable does it become to decentralize control in the interests of sound administration.'[47]

Social policy as propaganda

Underlying all Carr's thought about domestic policy was the belief that the war had brought an expansion of state power which must, at all costs, be projected forward into the coming peace if Britain were to achieve the ever-higher levels of production required for continued social order and effective foreign policy. Half a century later, his proposals may appear excessively centralist and interventionist. Because they represented a broad spectrum of elite opinion in the country and coincided in some respects with Labour Party policy, many were implemented in some form or other after 1945. Their practical weaknesses were to become steadily more apparent over the

---

[44] 'The Two Scourges', *The Times*, 5 December 1940. See also Carr's appeal for wartime co-operation between labour and capital to be extended into the coming peace: 'Prospects of Recovery', *The Times*, 18 March 1941.
[45] 'Looking Forward', *The Times*, 30 August 1940.
[46] Carr, *Conditions of Peace*, pp. 153–62.
[47] 'The Four Freedoms', *The Times*, 12 April 1941.

next thirty years, fuelling the neoliberal reaction that followed. But in the context of the early 1940s, when British victory was widely regarded as uncertain, their economic soundness was of less immediate concern than their effect as propaganda.

To whom were these appeals for reform directed? Carr addressed both the elite stratum of public opinion represented by the readership of *The Times* as a whole and the much smaller number of policy-makers, at home and abroad, who scrutinised the paper each day. Ostensibly directed at winning acceptance from a wide and influential swathe of British opinion for a 'peaceful revolution', the *Times* leading articles had also an aspect that was more covert and, hence, more realist.[48] As a member of the editorial team at *The Times* under Barrington-Ward, Carr was speaking directly to the governments of the United States, the Soviet Union, and Britain through a daily newspaper still regarded as the mouthpiece of a British government that, ironically, could no longer control it in wartime to quite the extent that it had done in the 1930s.[49]

The clearest example of this technique of double effect is undoubtedly 'The Two Scourges'. Published on 5 December 1940, this 'first leader' caused a considerable stir. Carr assigned equal status to unemployment and war. Both evils had to be dealt with if there was ever to be real security. Domestic economic and social reconstruction must therefore be thought through by the British government and publicly debated long before victory was in sight.

Substantial sections of the British Conservative Party were opposed in principle to the creation of a comprehensive welfare system and the extension of state economic planning. Others, while convinced that these steps might be necessary, thought their introduction for public debate premature and inopportune. Still others felt them to be consistent with one-country Toryism.

Personally, Churchill was deeply opposed to such measures. As far as possible he ignored them throughout the war, thereby contributing to Conservative electoral defeat in 1945.[50] Instead, he dedicated himself wholeheartedly but narrowly to military victory and the preservation of the British Empire. But it was quite otherwise with many in his government, notably his high-minded Anglo-Catholic

---

[48] The quoted phrase is that of Robert Barrington-Ward, editor of *The Times*: McDonald, *Struggles in War and Peace*, p. 98.

[49] Cockett, *Twilight of Truth*.

[50] Clive Ponting, *Churchill* (London: Sinclair-Stevenson, 1994), pp. 708–14.

foreign secretary, Halifax, who reported the support he had encountered for Bevin's economic and social proposals for Britain and post-war Europe from Woolton and 'a good many of us' at a meeting of non-Cabinet ministers held, at Churchill's suggestion, to discuss foreign policy issues. Halifax rounded off a letter to Duff Cooper at the MoI, reporting this meeting, with a strong statement of personal commitment. 'I am quite certain', he affirmed, 'that the human conscience in this country is not going to stand for a system that permits large numbers of unemployed, and that the masses of the population in foreign countries are also likely to be powerfully affected by whether or not we, with I hope the United States, are able to put up a counter plan in this economic field to Hitler's.'[51] Later in the war, Carr lunched with Beaverbrook, who 'described himself as a Left Conservative and said he agreed with most of the things *The Times* had been saying lately', but who 'appeared to share the P.M.'s opinion that it was useless to think about the future until the war is won'.[52]

Was Carr simply expressing a sincerely held welfarist view and participating in a domestic political debate? The origins of 'The Two Scourges' suggest that rather more was intended, and provide an insight into the rhetorical consciousness of the editorial team at *The Times*. The idea for the piece stemmed from a conversation between Lord Lothian, British ambassador to Washington, and Dawson, then still editor, in which the former claimed that the United States would never trust Britain fully as a democratic ally unless there were signs of a full employment policy for the post-war period. United States officials were already well on the way to a theory, later to be used to justify the creation of the Bretton Woods system, which attributed the war chiefly to the tendency of economic insecurity, mediated through unemployment, mass support for political extremism, and consequent changes in regime, to drive new populist administrations of the Right towards rearmament. They now had to be persuaded that Britain was committed to solving this problem. Carr came into Dawson's room during the conversation and Dawson suggested that he try a leader on this theme.

The aim of the piece was not, then, immediately or even principally to persuade the readership of *The Times*. It was written with an eye to

---

[51] INF1/862, Halifax to Cooper, 30 July 1940.
[52] News International, Archives of *The Times*, Carr's notes of conversation with Beaverbrook, 6 January 1943.

the arras: to those as yet uncommitted statesmen abroad who regarded *The Times* as the quasi-official British newspaper. Nor was this incident exceptional. Dawson and his successor Barrington-Ward were constantly aware of the propaganda impact of their newspaper. As early as July 1940, Barrington-Ward and Carr had come to a clear shared understanding of this task and of its delicacy. By and large, their views were shared by the co-chief proprietor, John Astor.[53] *The Times*, Barrington-Ward confided to his diary, 'almost alone in the press and certainly first, is trying to get the right "answer to Hitler" in a statement on our plans for war and peace to show that we are fighting for a new Europe not the old – a new Britain and not the old'. He continued: 'I wholly agree with Carr – planned consumption, abolition of unemployment and poverty, drastic educational reform, family allowances, economic organization of the Continent, etc., but all this needs the right presentation.'[54]

Abiding concern with opinion in the United States was most clearly evident in Carr's treatment of economic planning. Characteristically, he attempted to disarm by attributing his own ideas to those from whom he anticipated objections. The least word from Churchill on post-war planning was taken as endorsement of Carr's programme of reforms.[55] In much the same way, Carr seized whenever possible on the United States as the model for his package of economic and social policies, when he might almost as easily, had the occasion arisen, have worked from Italy or the Soviet Union. The populist element in the United States political tradition was appealed to as the model for a style of leadership able to overcome the power of vested interests and the machinations of political parties in order to represent 'the little man' and the nation at large by implementing revolutionary social and economic measures. Roosevelt's New Deal provided the model for economic planning defined as a 'method of eliminating the irrationalities of a largely unregulated economic system and of harnessing it to the purposes of a free self-governing community'.[56]

---

[53] McDonald, *Struggles in War and Peace*, p. 82.

[54] Ibid., p. 39.

[55] 'Looking Forward', *The Times*, 30 August 1940, and 'The Blockade and After', 3 December 1940. In much the same way, Carr seized on Churchill's admission that the effective exclusion of Russia from the 1919 settlement had been a disaster: 'Aid to Russia', *The Times*, 25 June 1941.

[56] 'Vital Democracy', *The Times*, 13 November 1940. The opportunity is not lost to flatter Churchill by recalling his repeated unwillingness to accept party discipline.

Pan-Americanism was offered as a working example of 'order rooted in conditions of freedom' when post-war European security and economic co-operation were referred to.[57] Later in the war, United States proposals for free trade were imperceptibly transformed by Carr into blueprints for managed liberalism.[58] Still at peace, United States isolationists were from time to time assured that they would not be caught up in the task of post-war European political reconstruction. (Though who can have been reassured by the assumption that this would be handled by the British?[59]) A more than polite welcome was extended to every move made by the United States in the direction of belligerency.[60]

Above all, at this point in the war, United States opinion had to be persuaded that Britain was more democratic than imperialist at heart. In much the same way, at a later stage in the war, Carr was to urge the British government, through the leader columns of *The Times*, to withdraw its support for the Greek Right in order to persuade Soviet leaders that Britain was not the 'reactionary, imperialist power' pictured by their ideologues.[61] Since each of Britain's leading allies was, in its different way, anti-colonialist, Britain was doubly obliged – like it or not – to forge a new identity in order to have any prospect of exercising legitimate power overseas in the post-war world. For sustained national power was every bit as important an objective for the ill-matched duo – Carr the advanced liberal and Barrington-Ward the deeply religious radical Tory – as was their explicit objective of social justice.

If they had the power to influence foreign perceptions of Britain, the editorial team also aspired to exert substantial influence over the British government. Barrington-Ward had access to Churchill himself, and was able to press him to consider post-war planning from an early point in the war in spite of his reluctance. Resistant not only on ideological grounds but because he expected to give way to younger

---

[57] 'Pan-Americanism', *The Times*, 23 July 1940.
[58] Carr applauds the principles of the Atlantic Charter before turning its provision for free trade inside out, pleading the superiority of security and social justice over aggregate wealth: *The Times*, 24 March 1942, 29 April 1943, and 26 January 1944.
[59] 'Looking Forward', *The Times*, 30 August 1940.
[60] 'Pan-Americanism', *The Times*, 23 July 1940 (on the US role in American hemispheric economic defence), and 'Interdependence', 9 January 1940 (on British cession of western hemisphere bases to the United States – 'a bridge built across the Atlantic [*sic*]').
[61] McDonald, *Struggles in War and Peace*, p. 118.

men after the war, Churchill preferred to concentrate on the conduct of the war. However, he succumbed to pressure in April 1942, accepting a memorandum in which Carr summarised the line advocated by *The Times*.[62] Partly in response to continued pressure from *The Times*, Churchill at last devoted an unprecedented broadcast to domestic policy issues on 21 March 1943, sketching a four-year reconstruction plan chiefly designed to keep Tory options open.[63] This gave powerful sanction to the emerging welfarist consensus already embodied in British war aims and so actively publicised in *The Times*.

Nationalism

A second major strand of policy pursued by Carr from the very earliest months of the war was of even less immediate concern to the British government than post-war social policy and economic planing and just as likely to alarm as to reassure neutral, Allied, and occupied European states. This was the question of post-war economic and political organisation in Europe, and the pressing need to overcome the aggressive nationalism that had plagued Europe since the end of the nineteenth century.

Here was an issue on which Carr had already adopted a position before the outbreak of war. *Nationalism*, described in its full title as 'A Report by a Study Group of Members of the Royal Institute of International Affairs', was not Carr's work, even though he was an active chairman of the group which drafted it. Though it has since become commonplace for social scientists to engage in group research and to publish jointly authored results, work of this kind was rare in the interwar period, and the Royal Institute of International Affairs was distinctive in actively fostering such an approach. It is not clear from the surviving correspondence quite how Carr came to be invited to chair a research group on 'Nationalism and Its Limitations'. Having accepted, he nominated his assistant at Aberystwyth, D. A. Routh, to be a junior 'working' member of the group.[64] Together, Routh and Michael Balfour, secretary to the group, appear to have provided continuity, conducted detailed research, and carried out a good deal

---

[62] News International, Archives of *The Times*, Barrington-Ward to Churchill, c. 1 April 1942, and Churchill to Barrington-Ward, 22 April 1942.

[63] McDonald, *Struggles in War and Peace*, pp. 100–1, 111.

[64] Archives of the RIIA, Records of the Nationalism Working Group, 9/12b, Carr to Balfour, 10 November 1936.

of the initial drafting, while other more senior members, who included N. F. Hall, G. M. Gathorne-Hardy, C. G. Vickers, T. H. Marshall, and Morris Ginsburg, provided memoranda for discussion at meetings of the group, which took place more or less monthly over a period of two years commencing in November 1936.

Any question of Carr attempting to dominate the group is easily dismissed.[65] Given his methodology, Carr could hardly have agreed with the naive and mechanistic view shared by Balfour and others in the group that a variety of distinct social science disciplines – anthropology, psychology, sociology – could each come up with its own independent and positive scientific results to be stirred into the pot. 'We have spent four months on the historical approach', Balfour confided to Morris Ginsburg, 'as a result of which we have gained a certain amount of information as to what Nationalism is and is not, but it was clear that there was a difference of opinion about the border-line. We have turned now to an abstract analysis of the group in order to clear this up, with the hope that sociology might have some established results in this direction which would help us. With that reinforcement we intend to go back to the historical analysis.'[66]

The report includes sections drafted by Carr and others that he seems scarcely to have touched.[67] It certainly entertains his expecta-

---

[65] The main interplay between the deliberations of the group and Carr's own work seems to have been with *The Twenty Years' Crisis*, which he was in midst of drafting. Carr seemed intent on exposing the falsehood of assumptions of harmony of interest, and on establishing the relativity of social truth, both key themes of his book. In discussion of rationality of state action, he asked whether what was rational from a Soviet point of view was also rational from a world point of view. 'Is it not being implied that national good necessarily coincides with international good? What proof is there that it does? From the international point of view, it would surely be necessary for certain nations to disappear' (Records of the Nationalism Working Group, 12/9a, Minutes of a Meeting of 15 November 1937, discussing a memorandum by Hall on economic advantages and disadvantages of nationalism). Again, in his very first letter about the study group, reacting to Balfour's first outline, Carr trots out one of the central themes of his attack he was to make on utopianism in *The Twenty Years' Crisis* : 'The odd thing about 1919', he mused, 'was that Wilson brought over from America, which was fifty years behind the times, the old idea of radical nationalism, which had been practically dead . . . and foisted it once more on Europe' (Archives of the RIIA, 12/9a, Carr to Balfour, 15 October 1936).

[66] Nationalism Working Group, 9/12b, Balfour to Ginsburg, 8 March 1937.

[67] For example, Nationalism Working Group, Carr to Balfour, 23 May 1938. 'Here are USA and Dominions. I'm afraid I've added a good deal to the US and partly re-written the Dominions.' Yet this was in the context of a great deal of circulation, re-drafting, and so on by many people, including an outer group of two dozen or so

tion that the world may be moving towards 'larger "multi-national" political and economic units', but argues that this will merely replicate the problem of nationalism at a higher level.[68] There is little hint of functionalist thought, the main emphasis of the report being placed instead on the analytical separation of nationalism from totalitarianism. Just as there had been benign, liberal nationalism in the past, so there could be a new and more benign place for nationalism in the post-war world. As Carr observed during one of the group's early meetings: 'That nationalism was desirable in the nineteenth century is not to my mind incompatible with its being undesirable today. Circumstances have changed.'[69] And this became the general view of the group, most clearly expressed in a letter from Gathorne-Hardy to Balfour, expressing agreement with a memorandum from Balfour. The main argument of this had been that the peculiarities of modern nationalism had more to do with modernity than with nationalism itself, and that it was insecurity above all that translated nationalism from a progressive to a retrogressive force. 'The key to the whole riddle, to my mind', wrote Gathorne-Hardy, 'is this existence of what amounts to a state of war, civil or international or both.'[70] A state of war transformed many things, nationalism being just one of them.

This line of argument did, of course, invite discussion of what forces might be expected to curb or transform nationalism, and some faint echo of Carr's emerging functionalist or 'international society' position may perhaps be detected in the discussion, summarised in chapter 17, of 'Sources of Resistance to Nationalist Policy'. However, this concentrates mainly on the twin ideologies of Christianity and Marxism and the so-called public conscience, after dismissing functional international organisations summarily on the ground that they do 'not normally arouse a loyalty strong enough to compete with that excited by the nation'.[71] Earlier, when the group had discussed the section on Austria-Hungary, Carr had made a bid for class as a social institution which cut sharply across nationality, but this idea found no place in the crucial chapter of the final report.

which included David Mitrany, Jacob Viner, Sir Alfred Zimmern, and Friedrich Hertz.

[68] *Nationalism: Its Nature and Consequences* (London: Oxford University Press for the Royal Institute of International Affairs, 1939), p. 339.

[69] Archives of the RIIA, 9/12a, Minutes of a Meeting of the Study Group, 12 April 1937.

[70] Ibid., 9/12b, Gathorne-Hardy to Balfour, 10 July 1937.

[71] Carr, *Nationalism and After*, p. 299.

The obsolescence of neutrality

Repeated references to the futility of neutrality and the need for post-war international co-operation in the 1940 *Times* leaders taken together with publication in pamphlet form of *The Future of Nations*, a section of his forthcoming work, *Conditions of Peace*, show the strength of Carr's concern to carry his opposition to the doctrines of modern nationalism to the widest possible audience.[72] Taken in conjunction with the *Times* leaders, *The Future of Nations* provided a trenchant critique of cultural nationalism as a foundation of independent statehood and a clear statement of Carr's initial wartime position on regional integration, especially as he hoped it might affect post-war Europe. This was confirmed early in 1945 by publication of *Nationalism and After*, little more than a pamphlet, with an unusually large print run of 20,000.

One tragedy of the Versailles settlement had been 'the creation of a multiplicity of smaller units at a moment when strategic and economic factors were demanding increased integration and the grouping of the world into fewer and larger political units'.[73] The question was of pressing concern. Carr was determined that the claims of linguistically or culturally identified national minorities should not stand in the way of a workable settlement following the Second World War.

The trouble was that small states were not viable in the modern world. Recent tendencies in technology, expressed both militarily and through markets, meant that the small size of the typical linguistic unit was no longer adequate for the provision of security and welfare. In the nineteenth century, a small power might still hope to mount a prolonged defence against a large power, imposing very substantial costs, as the Boers had done against the British. Tanks and air power had, he believed, made this impossible.[74] 'The next war', he suggested, 'will probably be fought in the main with airborne armies and with projectiles having a range of several hundred miles', adding that 'the whole conception of strategic frontiers may . . . be

---

[72] E. H. Carr, *The Future of Nations: Independence or Interdependence?*, *The Democratic Order*, no. 1 (London: Kegan Paul, 1941). See *Conditions of Peace*, ch. 3.

[73] Carr, *Future of Nations*, p. 26. Cf. 'The New Europe', *The Times*, 1 July 1940: 'Probably the gravest error of the last peace settlement was that it encouraged disintegration at a time when integration was already the crying need.'

[74] Carr, *Future of Nations*, p. 32. This obsolescence of neutrality was hammered home repeatedly in *The Times*. See also 1 July, 13 July, 30 August, 16 December 1940, 5 and 9 July, 26 August, 15 September, and 4 October 1941.

obsolescent'.[75] Neutrality was no longer a practical policy for small states, which were effectively bound to seek alliances with larger neighbouring states. Pondering the plight of Yugoslavia, Carr concluded:

> The moral implicit in the story is an old one – perhaps the primary political lesson of the war – that the smaller States must for the common security enjoy the protection and cooperation of the stronger. It is a fallacy to suppose that in modern warfare, where efficiency is built up almost entirely on industrial resources, even a combination of States not possessing such resources on any large scale can prove a match for a great power like Germany. In these circumstances salvation can only be found by the small country through cooperation with another Great Power possessing comparable resources. Nor can this collaboration be improvised from one week to the next. It must be prepared by a long process of planning for combined strategy, coordinated equipment, and unified command.[76]

Neutrality could no longer provide security for small states, but such was the pace of modern warfare that neither the old style of alliance nor the interwar approach to collective security could effectively replace it. 'Paper commitments of mutual assistance are valueless under the conditions of modern warfare unless they involve a pooling in advance of military resources and military equipment, and, above all, a common strategy, common loyalties, and a common outlook on the world.'[77]

The economic history of the interwar period had delivered a very similar message, Carr maintained. Fragmentation of markets in the interwar period had imposed costs on all, and these economic costs

[75] Carr, *Nationalism and After*, pp. 57–8. The paragraph beginning 'Two powerful arguments' was lifted more or less verbatim from 'Frontiers of Peace', *The Times*, 20 September 1944.

[76] 'Mr. Eden's Odyssey', *The Times*, 7 May 1941. See also 'The Small Nations', *The Times*, 16 December 1940.

[77] 'The Small Nations', *The Times*, 16 December 1940. See 'Interdependence', 9 January 1941, which dwells on military co-operation between Britain and France prior to the fall of France and contrasts it with British military co-operation with the Dominions. The same point about permanent military co-operation is made repeatedly in *The Times*. See 'The Key to the Balkans', 11 March 1941; 'A World Pattern', 15 September 1941; 'Norway Plays Her Part', 14 November 1941; 'Council of War', 24 December 1941; and 'Russia and Poland', 5 December 1941, the last of which jauntily hails military co-operation between the two Allies as 'a happy precedent for future Russo-Polish relations'.

had too often found expression in political extremism, fuelling further and equally self-defeating nationalist excesses.[78] The answer to Hitler's New Order therefore could not be a return to the old European patchwork, but rather to a 'new map . . . not . . . painted in quite so many contrasting and clashing colours' within which 'economic solidarity and a common economic policy will lay the foundations of political harmony'.[79] Out of both military and economic considerations, post-war planning would have to take account of 'the qualification which will have to be applied to the concept of neutrality in the crowded European continent'. Smaller European states might wish to 'paddle their own canoes', but would have to do so 'in convoy'.[80]

The metaphor poses two immediate questions: 'Who provides the escort?', and 'Where, in peacetime, is the enemy?' A first hint of the problems of leadership and rivalry in a world of multinational blocs was evident in the welcome accorded late in 1940 to an agreement on post-war political and economic co-operation between the Polish and Czech governments in exile. 'A first step towards a new order in Central Europe' to be achieved with British economic assistance, the new development was nevertheless to be seen in the context of 'the predominant interest which Soviet Russia can naturally claim in the settlement of the affairs of Eastern Europe'.[81]

European integration

Carr believed that the only practical response to the technologically driven redundancy of small states was a move to large multinational units. His preference was for a blend of functionally based economic and social organisation, intergovernmental macro-economic co-operation, and military forward planning, able to provide economic and military security and facilitate meaningful citizenship without suppressing cultural variety. He claimed that the respect of functional international organisations for individual needs and rights would provide the essential counterweight to the very large multi-ethnic states required for the purposes of economic organisation and military security. 'The existence of multi-national units of military and economic organization', he argued, 'does not stand in the way of the

---

[78] Carr, *Future of Nations*, p. 43.
[79] 'The Map of Europe', *The Times*, 2 September 1940.
[80] 'Looking Forward', *The Times*, 30 August 1940.
[81] 'Active Diplomacy', *The Times*, 12 December 1940.

maintenance, or indeed of the further extension, of national administrative and cultural units, thus encouraging a system of overlapping and interlocking loyalties which is in the last resort the sole alternative to sheer totalitarianism.'[82] There are strong hints here of the liberal negarchy proposed much more recently by Daniel Deudney.[83]

It is striking to see the extent to which this vision of the future was realised in the international regime of managed liberalism which prevailed between 1945 and 1974, with its 'systems of joint planning and organization between countries or groups of countries agreeing to pursue full employment policies in common, or to share in the economic development of backward areas . . . such regional policies [corresponding] in part, though not necessarily or exclusively, with the multi-national groupings of power'.[84] The great difference lay in the boundaries of the groups, which had placed Britain much closer to the United States than Carr had ever anticipated or desired.

Indeed, multinational groups of the sort Carr advocated remained uncertain and inchoate during the war, and necessarily so, since one of the aspects of the post-war order which the major Allies were most concerned to finesse was the balance between universalism and regionalism, concerted international management and spheres of influence.[85] Distinguishing the Americas and the Soviet Union as the clearest cases of emerging security communities, Carr urged Britain to maintain continued close relations with the self-governing Commonwealth, commending especially the functional and specific character of so many agreements between Britain and the Dominions in the past.[86] He also stressed the need to group British colonies into a much smaller number of associations to facilitate post-war programmes of economic and social development, anticipating ill-fated experiments with federation in Central Africa, East Africa, and the West Indies.[87]

---

[82] Carr, *Nationalism and After*, p. 59.
[83] Daniel Deudney, 'Nuclear Weapons and the Waning of the Real-State', *Daedalus*, 124:2, Spring 1995, pp. 209–31.
[84] Carr, *Nationalism and After*, p. 69.
[85] 'Common Counsel', *The Times*, 21 December 1944.
[86] A fine example of Carr's naivety was the effusive and incautious welcome accorded to Soviet constitutional proposals purportedly giving enhanced military and political autonomy to the component republics of the USSR, but surely designed rather more to maximise Soviet claims to voting power in the emerging UNO by mimicking the constitution but not the spirit of the British Commonwealth: 'The New Soviet Union', *The Times*, 3 February 1944.
[87] 'Colonial Reforms', *The Times*, 7 May 1942.

However, he firmly consistently rejected any outright British choice between maritime and Continental commitments.[88] In an interdependent world no political unit could be created, short of a worldwide empire, in which autarky could be reconciled with welfare and full employment, and if this were true for the Nazi New Order it was equally true for the British Commonwealth of nations.[89] It followed that there was no inconsistency between simultaneous British cooperation with the United States in the West and the Soviet Union in the East. Expecting the United States to set strict limits to its post-war commitments, Carr maintained that 'in Europe, Great Britain and Soviet Russia must become the main bulwarks of a peace which can be preserved, and can be made real, only through their joint endeavour'.[90]

Britain was well placed to take the lead in post-war economic organisation in Western Europe, and had three powerful motives for doing so.[91] First, Europe had become the centre of the very kind of pathological nationalism which must now be overcome. Indeed, future British security depended on its eradication. Secondly, Britain had long-established and considerable economic links with Continental Europe. Thirdly, Europe lacked an obvious leader to place it among the Great Powers in the era of the economic *Grossraum* and geopolitical 'hemisphere', however liberally defined, and . Carr thought it in the interest of Britain to provide that leadership.

Expecting responsibility for European welfare and security to be shared between Britain and the Soviet Union, Carr proposed links between Britain and Western Europe – 'military and economic rather than political in the narrower sense' – on the grounds that all these countries were united by common interest and by 'the same desire to find an answer based on principles which diverge both from the Soviet ideology of state monopoly and from the American ideology of unrestricted competition'.[92] A prudent British government was bound

---

[88] 'Mr. Eden's Mission', *The Times*, 29 December 1941. See also 'Pax Oceanica', 4 October 1941; 'The Western Powers', 11 November 1944; 'Common Counsel', 21 December 1944.

[89] 'The Expanding War', *The Times*, 5 July 1941. In the same vein Carr had argued, following the Willingdon Mission to South America, that closer inter-American relations need not clash with continued trade between Europe and Latin America: 'Good Will and Markets', *The Times*, 22 March 1941.

[90] 'Mr. Eden's Mission', *The Times*, 29 December 1941. See also, *inter alia*, 'Security in Europe', 10 March 1943, and 'Germany's Last Hope', 3 June 1943.

[91] Carr, *Nationalism and After*, p. 72.   [92] Ibid., p. 74.

to take this stance, he argued, because British industry could not afford to be excluded from European markets on which it had long depended and would depend even more in future as the Dominions continued to diversify their trade and develop their own industries.

In addition, the increasing size and economic weight of Germany had put paid to the old British policy of maintaining a balance of power in Continental Europe without heavy military commitment. But Carr expected the United States to fight shy of post-war European responsibilities.[93] He also calculated that neither France nor the Soviet Union was up to the job of matching German strength in the medium run, while no coalition of lesser powers could effectively balance Germany in a modern war. However, the policy of dividing or weakening Germany was absurd, wasteful, and impracticable, founded on a wholly mistaken notion of German national wickedness. It would bring about economic disaster and insecurity in Central Europe. In these circumstances, Britain, though weak, remained the strongest power in Western Europe and the only country able to counterpoise Soviet power by building a multinational grouping of states in the West to include a united and reformed German state. Britain must therefore somehow reconcile European responsibilities with strong political and commercial links to the Dominions and the United States. 'Her role must be to serve as a bridge between the "Western civilization" of Europe and the same "Western civilization" in its new homes in other continents.'[94] This was hardly a solution: more a restatement of the problem.

Carr began to spell out what all this might mean in a resounding leader on interdependence in January 1941, and sketched some more detailed implications for Western Europe in subsequent leaders, pulling the argument together in the closing chapter of *Conditions of Peace*. The starting point was wartime co-operation. The model was provided by the kinds of military co-operation that existed between Britain and the Dominions and which had been developing with Paris before the fall of France.[95] After the war, arrangements by which command of military forces was shared between two or more powers should be extended. The leasing of bases by one power to another should continue. So too should wartime arrangements for the

---

[93] Carr, *Conditions of Peace*, p. 206.   [94] Ibid.

[95] 'Interdependence', *The Times*, 9 January 1941.

purchase and distribution of strategic materials and for joint control of shipping.

For purposes of effective post-war relief it would be necessary to treat much of Europe as a single unit, with a single transport system under central control to ensure the smooth movement of emergency food supplies.[96] In addition, pan-European reconstruction and planning authorities would be required to take over whatever remained of Hitler's New Order together with the co-operative elements of Allied wartime control and the rudimentary elements of pre-war international economic management, forging them into a system capable of overcoming the deleterious effects of European territorial divisions. 'Frontiers have been swept away in Europe and a bridge built across the Atlantic', he declared. 'These things must not be undone.'[97] These early thoughts were developed further as the war progressed, with suggestions for common European policies on energy, industry, colonial development, and trade, as well as transport.[98]

Naturally, such arrangements would need to be backed by effective power, and Carr looked to the victorious Allies to provide this in the first instance, until the evident gains of integration brought legitimacy. Recognising the obstructive power of vested interests, he foresaw the possibility, in the longer term, of legitimising his New Europe by the federalist device of a 'direct appeal to the people themselves . . . rather than through any constitutional process of league or federation'.[99]

In general statements Carr showed a keen awareness of many of the nuances and pitfalls of any such scheme. He noted the risk of new multinational groupings becoming foci of loyalty to the point where they simply replicated past squabbles on a grander and still more destructive scale through 'a new imperialism which would only be the old nationalism writ large'.[100] Once again challenging the ontological realism of committed nationalists, he argued that individuals could determine themselves into different groups for different purposes, and that identity was not a natural attribute but a matter of individual choice within the constraints of experience.[101] Indeed, Carr

---

[96] 'United Europe', *The Times*, 25 September 1941.   [97] Ibid.
[98] 'Policies for Europe', *The Times*, 29 February 1944; 'The Western Powers', 11 November 1944.
[99] Carr, *Conditions of Peace*, p. 271.
[100] Carr, *Nationalism and After*, p. 66. For further warnings against the crystallisation of power, see pp. 53, 59, and 62.
[101] Carr, *Future of Nations*, p. 48.

went further, arguing that it was precisely a condition of a healthy and democratic society that individuals should adopt multiple roles in 'some such intertwined network of loyalties and interests . . . where no one institution – whether state, church, or trades union – makes an all-embracing demand on the allegiance of its members'. The best guarantee he could offer against the bleak and tyrannical tripolarity envisaged by George Orwell in *1984* was complexity. 'The complexity of human relations fortunately makes it natural and imperative for human beings to combine for various purposes in a variety of groups of varying size and comprehensiveness', he wrote, 'and this leaves abundant scope for the development of that community of national thought and feeling, of political and cultural tradition, which is the constructive side of nationalism.'[102]

The trouble started the moment examples were selected. One sign of the drift of history was the Soviet absorption of the Baltic states. 'Bitterly resented' by the older generation, this had been 'greeted with relief by the younger generation, which was convinced that only incorporation in some larger unit could restore prosperity to these little countries'.[103] In more general terms, Carr applauded reaction against the Versailles preoccupation with self-determination that had been evident throughout the former tsarist empire and welcomed the achievement of the Soviet state in creating a 'multinational state bound together by a tie of loyalty independent of, and indeed opposed to, national feeling'.[104]

Noting the persistent sense of distinctiveness felt by national minorities such as the Welsh, the Bretons, or the Flemings within established liberal democracies, Carr went on to maintain that a clear distinction could be maintained between the cultural nation and the political nation before concluding with a set of examples which suggest that history has still to make up its mind on this point. 'There is every reason to suppose', he confidently affirmed, 'that considerable numbers of Welshmen, Catalans, and Uzbeks have quite satisfactorily solved the problem of regarding themselves as good Welshmen,

---

[102] Ibid., p. 59. The balance of cultural independence and economic and military interdependence in post-war Europe was the subject of one of Carr's most careful and thoughtful leaders: 'Great and Small Nations', *The Times*, 23 March 1943.

[103] Carr, *Future of Nations*, p. 44. 'Russia on the Baltic', *The Times*, 25 July 1940, expresses almost identical sentiments, anticipating continued cultural autonomy under Soviet rule and hoping for the survival of small peasant holdings.

[104] Carr, *Future of Nations*, p. 25.

Catalans, and Uzbeks for some purposes and good British, Spanish, and Soviet citizens for others.'[105] Only marginally less uncomfortable than his Soviet examples are Carr's thoughts about the British Commonwealth or the pan-American state system as alternative models for post-war Europe. His is a world in which Afrikaners and Quebecois suffer no notable disadvantages and Latin America is broadly content with United States leadership and hemispheric defence.[106] It is in such judgements that Carr, from his standpoint in a privileged class of a satisfied power, comes closest to those hypocritical assumptions of harmony of interests against which he had warned so eloquently in *The Twenty Years' Crisis*. Yet even setting aside the frissons delivered by such cavalier interpretations of the politics of his own day, it is the collapse of the multinational state project, in Yugoslavia and Czechoslovakia as well as the Soviet Union, and the rekindling of divisive nationalisms at varying levels of intensity throughout Eurasia that place Carr's emphasis on the regional integration and the multinational state among the most topical and controversial aspects of his programme today. At the time, however, it was not the project as such so much as the question of leadership – whether British in the west or Soviet in the east of Europe – that caused greatest alarm. Indeed, it was to be on the linked issues of French attitudes to the European settlement and perceived Soviet influence in Germany and Western Europe that Carr would founder in the months following the war.

---

[105] Ibid., p. 50. See also Carr, *Conditions of Peace*, p. 63. Although Carr's position was to evolve during the war in some respects, this misplaced and ill-founded confidence persisted. In *Nationalism and After* he was to claim that 'In the British Commonwealth of Nations one may be an Englishman, Scot, or Welshman, a Frenchman or Dutchman, in the United States a German, Pole, or Italian, in the Soviet Union a Lithuanian, a Moldovan, or a Kazbek [*sic*] without finding any avenue of political and economic opportunity closed on that account, or any barrier placed on devotion to one's own language or national customs' (pp. 64–5).
[106] 'Pan-Americanism', *The Times*, 23 July 1940.

5   'An active danger'

Carr had done much between 1940 and 1942 to win elite support for a 'peaceful revolution' at home along lines similar to those finally adopted by the British Labour government after 1945. By contrast, his influence on foreign policy was to prove less palatable and less enduring. As concern about post-war Soviet power developed, his position on the USSR was rapidly labelled by critics as the mere transfer from Germany to the Soviet Union of a discredited and detested pre-war policy of appeasement. While this is an oversimplification, it was already clear by the end of 1940, even before the Soviet Union had entered the war, that Carr expected and accepted that post-war national self-determination in Eastern Europe would be heavily qualified by Soviet hegemony. Nor was the issue of post-war French attitudes to Carr's formula of Germany as the industrial dynamo within some form of Anglo-Soviet European condominium ever clearly anticipated.

Carr was first publicly denounced for his pro-Soviet line in June 1942 by Lord Elibank, speaking in the House of Lords, who pronounced him 'an active danger to this country'.[1] By 1943 the steady Leftward shift of *The Times* was generally admitted. At dinner one evening the Duke of Devonshire remarked to Barrington-Ward that he had 'still to call your paper publicly the journal of the London School of Economics'. David Bowes-Lyon, a director of *The Times*, chipped in: 'The *New York Times* calls it the final edition of the *Daily Worker*.'[2]

---

[1] Iverach McDonald, *The History of 'The Times'*, vol. V, *Struggles in War and Peace, 1939–1966* (London: Times Books, 1984), p. 105.

[2] The anecdote is related in Donald McLachlan, *In the Chair: Barrington-Ward of The Times, 1927–1948* (London: Weidenfeld & Nicolson, 1971), p. 206, n., citing Barrington-Ward's diary. The *Daily Worker* was the newspaper of the British Communist Party.

Many felt that the constant stress in *Times* leaders on the limited and non-ideological character of Soviet war aims and the strict parity between Britain's relations with the USA and the Soviet Union went well beyond anything that might be required to reassure Stalin.[3] At least one Foreign Office official had come to the conclusion that it was 'important to get Mr. Carr out of Printing House Square' because of his line on the Soviet Union.[4] English men and women who scarcely knew Carr's name seem nevertheless to have begun to mistrust the anonymous author of leaders which some regarded as the work of a crypto-Communist and a traitor to his country. Middle-class breakfast tables had been violated, their morning tea turned to gall.

This chapter seeks to identify those aspects of the foreign policy advanced by *The Times* that caused most offence and to chart the consequent decline of its influence on foreign policy. It also poses the distinct but related question of how exceptional, if at all, was the friendliness shown by *The Times* to the Soviet Union, which remained, after all, a major ally. Before attempting these tasks, discussion returns briefly to the question of Carr's personal responsibility for the line taken by *The Times*.

The extent of Carr's responsibility

It has already been made clear that Carr on occasion assisted the British government by accepting inspired articles and by submitting *Times* copy for comment. Furthermore, of ten offensive leaders that have left most trace in the records of the Foreign Office, just half appear to have been written by Carr, only one of them dating from before 1943. Moreover, since the smouldering objection in the Foreign Office, though fanned to life by specific editorials, was increasingly similar to the general policy with which Carr was so closely associated, this often led to any leader exhibiting pro-Soviet tendencies being automatically, and sometimes mistakenly, assumed to have

---

[3] The following are among the most notable of Carr's pro-Soviet leaders of the period 1942–4: 'Britain, Russia, and America', *The Times*, 7 March 1942; 'Security in Europe', 10 March 1943; 'Great and Small Nations', 23 March 1943; 'End of the Comintern', 24 May 1943; 'Germany's Last Hope', 3 June 1943; 'The New Soviet Union', 3 February 1944; 'The Terms of Peace', 2 October 1944; 'Russia, Britain, and Europe', 6 November 1944; 'Common Counsel', 21 December 1944.
[4] PRO FO371/56866 N3041/3041/38, W. Risdale, Minute, 12 March 1943.

been drafted by him.[5] This is why the extent of Carr's responsibility for the 'Carr line' needs to be addressed.

Some years ago Alan Foster wrote a perceptive article on the attitude of *The Times* towards the USSR in which he argued persuasively for the existence of a coherent underlying philosophy of international relations behind the apparent vacillations of the great newspaper.[6] Curiously, Foster reserved treatment of the personal role of Carr to the conclusion, attributed no specific leaders to Carr, and attempted no comparison of the 'underlying philosophy' of *The Times* with the published and attributable views of its assistant editor. Was Foster right to accept the anonymity of the leader writer and the collective responsibility of the team? Given the detailed account of the paper's history since provided by Iverach McDonald, it would be ingenuous to continue to do so. Of the twelve wartime *Times* leaders cited by Foster, no less than nine were allocated to Carr. More generally, rejection of ideology in foreign policy in favour of interest and an insistence on the progressive character of the war – identified by Foster as aspects of the philosophy of international relations underlying the *Times* leaders – were as much features of work published in Carr's name as of the collective view adopted by the newspaper he served. Yet no reference is made to any of Carr's publications, even though these occasionally incorporate whole paragraphs first published in *The Times*.[7] Instead, Foster follows his brief discussion of the role played by Carr with the rather lame disclaimer that 'the tone of any great newspaper . . . is something that cannot entirely be established by any one man', before going on to discuss the pro-Soviet positions of Ralph Parker and Lewis Namier.

It is probable that Foster simply did not know of the key to the allocation of leader topics retained in the archives of *The Times*, and that an elderly Carr, interviewed by Foster, had either forgotten or did

---

[5] McDonald, *Struggles in War and Peace*, p. 139, notes that Donald McLachlan (*In the Chair*, pp. 245–6) compounded Whitehall's error with respect to a leader of 9 March 1946 written by Rushbrook Williams. When McDonald in his turn tried to sum up the 'Carr line' only two of the three leaders he cited were from Carr's pen (p. 135 – the exception being 14 July 1946).

[6] Alan Foster, 'The Times and Appeasement: The Second Phase', in Walter Laqueur, ed., *The Second World War: Essays in Military and Political History* (London: Sage, 1982), pp. 275–99.

[7] Cf. p. 53 of Carr, *Conditions of Peace* (London: Macmillan, 1942), and 'Hazards of Neutrality', *The Times*, 13 July 1940, or pp. 57–8 of *Nationalism and After* (London: Macmillan, 1945), first printed in *The Times*, 20 September 1944.

not care to enlighten him. The effect has been to allow what may well have been the most sustained and radical intervention into foreign policy formation by a British academic to remain hidden from the great majority of those who still read Carr's classic introduction to international relations for its theoretical insights.

It is perfectly true that there was shared responsibility for the pro-Soviet line followed by *The Times*, which often took the form of Barrington-Ward toning down Carr's work. It is also true that Barrington-Ward stuck to the 'Carr line' in substance even after Carr's resignation and that other members of the team on occasion produced leaders that were taken to be by Carr. But Barrington-Ward generously and accurately conceded that the vigour and originality of the 'Carr line' were indeed Carr's own.[8]

Cultivating friends and dividing enemies

Among the hundreds of editorials on foreign policy matters written by Carr during the war, many were simply routine and uncontroversial. Having first delivered himself of the gospel of economic planning, co-operation, and welfarism through the 1940s leaders, Carr settled, in many of his 1940 and 1941 leaders, to a task not much different from the one he had undertaken at the Ministry of Information. A succession of articles, clearly addressed as much to foreign as to home readers, emphasised the strength of the British position, drew attention to British values and war aims, applauded resistance to Axis expansionism among neutrals, and tried to drive wedges between states sympathetic to or allied with Germany.

As Hitler's land forces swept all before him, Carr painted a picture of a world-wide conflict which made German conquests in Europe seem relatively inconsequential.[9] France might fall, but French Equatorial Africa and the Cameroons, beyond the control of the Vichy regime, provided 'a solid belt of territory' capable of resisting further Axis aggression.[10] The very completeness of German victory in Europe was put to work in Britain's favour as Carr contrasted the centralised, contiguous, and autarkic Nazi ideal with the British empire of 'discontinuous territories dispersed, under diverse forms of

---

8 McDonald, *Struggles in War and Peace*, pp. 134–5.
9 'A World War', *The Times*, 20 August 1940.
10 'France Old and New', *The Times*, 11 September 1940.

political organization, but firmly upholding the ideal of freedom and resistance to domination, all over the world': this, in a leader welcoming United States occupation of Iceland, a small neutral country.[11]

When Hitler advanced into the Balkans, Yugoslavia, Greece, and Turkey were fulsomely praised and Soviet nerves tweaked.[12] As Vichy France became ever more subservient to German policy, Carr played on French national pride with reminders of 1870 and commentary on 'Bourbon' aspects of the new regime, while applauding the Free French forces and sowing seeds of doubt about Italian expansionism in North Africa.[13] When three Italian destroyers went down protecting a German military convoy en route for North Africa, Carr ingenuously inquired 'whether . . . Hitler deliberately sacrificed the Italian Navy . . . in furtherance of his own North African plans'.[14] As Germany turned on the Soviet Union, Carr was quick to exploit Japanese embarrassment and concern.[15] Conversely, United States occupation of Iceland became the occasion for a hyperbolic statement of Western values while the Anglo-Soviet occupation of Iran in August 1941 would be accompanied by extensive soothing of Turkish and Arab opinion.[16]

This patently instrumental scatter-gun technique allowed Carr to praise Stalin one day and Franco a few days later.[17] Nor was anything close to a consistently pro-Soviet line to be observed in the early months of the war: though he defended Soviet incorporation of the Baltic republics in July 1940, Carr was distinctly acerbic in his comments on Soviet gains from non-belligerency the following month.[18] Indeed, if Carr showed any consistency during the crucial period of British isolation that separated the fall of France from the German attack on the USSR, it was in favour of the United States, not

---

[11] 'The Bridgehead', *The Times*, 9 July 1941.
[12] 'The Balkan Cauldron', *The Times*, 3 July 1940, 28 February, and 7 May 1941.
[13] 'Hitler over France', 'Made in Germany', and 'From Vichy to Versailles', *The Times*, 9, 11, 16 July 1940; 'The Defence of France', 5 June 1941; also 'France Old and New' and 'Italy's Quest for Spoils', 11 and 27 September 1940.
[14] 'The Sea and the Desert', *The Times*, 22 April 1941.
[15] 'Aid to Russia', *The Times*, 26 June 1940.
[16] 'The Bridgehead', *The Times*, 9 July 1941; 'Action in Iran', 26 August 1941.
[17] 'The Spanish Outlook', *The Times*, 15 August 1940; 'Russia on the Baltic', 25 July 1940.
[18] 'Russia on the Baltic', *The Times*, 25 July 1940; 'No Change in Moscow', 3 August 1940.

the Soviet Union. The North Americans were defended against charges of neoimperialism in Latin America, their values praised, and their every step in the direction of belligerency welcomed.[19]

Renouncing imperialism

The same practical propaganda objectives that shaped Carr's treatment of independent European, Asian, and American powers were also evident in his much less frequent references to dependent territories. The restoration of Haile Selassie to the imperial throne of Abyssinia had, so readers of *The Times* were asked to believe, restored the faith of Africans everywhere in Great Britain 'as a champion of justice for the African peoples'.[20] Anxious to legitimise the occupation of Syria and Lebanon, Britain and Free France hurriedly recognised their independence. Carr, no friend to small nations, duly concluded that 'the forces now entering Syria come therefore as liberators', salving his conscience with a blissfully tactless nod in the direction of a pan-Arab federation.[21] Germany was consistently presented as an imperialist force in the Middle East and North Africa; Britain, by contrast, as the protector of Arab independence.[22]

While the dependent empire was never among his chief concerns, Carr turned to it from time to time with a qualified version of his social gospel. There must be more systematic economic development of the colonies, not simply as sources of raw materials but as markets.[23] Education must be improved and the excessively rigid social and racial barriers of the past broken down.[24] Constitutional reform to facilitate post-war reform should take the form of the creation of larger groupings of territories. By the end of 1942, with a

---

[19] 'Solidarity at Havana', *The Times*, 1 August 1940; 'A World War', 20 August 1940; 'The American Spirit', 26 April 1941; 'The Expanding War', 5 July 1941; 'Studying America', 17 June 1941.

[20] 'Return of an Emperor', *The Times*, 5 May 1941.

[21] 'Liberating Syria', *The Times*, 9 June 1941, and 'Independent Syria', 30 September 1941.

[22] 'Mr. Eden Looks Forward', *The Times*, 5 May 1941, and passim.

[23] 'The Colonial Future', *The Times*, 14 March 1942, stresses the future of the colonies as markets. See also 'Colonial Reforms', 7 May 1942, and 'Partnership in Empire', 23 June 1942.

[24] 'The Colonial Future' (on social and racial stratification), *The Times*, 14 March 1942; 'Partnership in Empire' (on education), 23 June 1942.

very clear eye to North American opinion, Carr was describing the Empire as 'a self-liquidating concern'.[25]

In India, too, *The Times* was keen to clear Britain of the charge of imperialism, arguing for the release of political prisoners and issuing a prompt call for the formation of 'a fully representative Cabinet, commanding the widest popular support' following Pearl Harbor, and arguing that 'the fullest and most unreserved participation of Indians in the work of defending India . . . will provide the strongest argument for the independence of India . . . in the future'.[26] The 1942 mission of Sir Stafford Cripps and the goal of full and prompt independence at the conclusion of hostilities were enthusiastically welcomed, but the extremity of the Japanese military threat and the fragility of Indian political support for the war were such that the tone of Carr's leaders throughout the middle passage of the war was uncharacteristically cautious.[27]

The Soviet alliance

Amid the plainly instrumental and occasionally inconsistent man-oeuvrings willingly undertaken by *The Times* in support of a belea-guered nation during the first phase of the war, the early Soviet leaders hardly merited comment. When German and Finnish troops moved against Russia on 22 June 1941, Carr was quick to welcome a new ally, but then so were the great majority of his beleaguered nation. Hailing the preliminary Anglo-Soviet agreement of July as 'tantamount to an alliance', Carr set out to sweep away the misgivings of the Right.[28] The Soviet Union, he contended, was to be distin-guished from Nazi Germany. It had not based its economy on arms production and it was not so distant from Britain ideologically as to rule out convergence around the ideal of co-operation between culturally distinct nations in an extensive security complex coupled with shared commitment to some form of marriage between economic planning and political liberty.[29]

[25] 'A Colonial Debate', *The Times*, 21 November 1942.
[26] 'Fresh Start in India', *The Times*, 23 December 1941.
[27] 'New Hope for India', *The Times*, 12 March 1942; 'The India Plan', 30 March 1942; 'Retrieving a Setback', 13 April 1942; 'The Goal Ahead', 4 May 1942; 'The Indian Arrests', 10 August 1942; 'Initiative in India', 6 October 1942.
[28] 'Britain and Russia', *The Times*, 14 July 1941.
[29] 'Russia's War', *The Times*, 19 July 1941, and 'Britain and Russia', 7 November 1941.

But the ground bass was there from the start, even though it only gradually became insistent, and finally intolerable, to many of the listeners. The clearest early statement came at the start of August in 'Peace and Power'. Post-war leadership in Eastern Europe, Carr proposed, 'can fall only to Germany or to Russia. Neither Great Britain nor the United States can exercise, or will agree to exercise, any predominant role in these regions . . . There can be no doubt that British and Russian – and, it may be added, American – interests alike demand that Russian influence in Eastern Europe should not be eclipsed by that of Germany.'[30] By the year's end hypothesis had become orthodoxy. Commenting on Anthony Eden's visit to Moscow, Carr took it for granted that 'in Europe, Great Britain and Soviet Russia must become the main bulwarks of a peace which can be preserved, and can be made real, only through their joint endeavour'.[31]

As the war progressed, *The Times* began to be distinguished above all else by this attitude towards the Soviet Union. Carr and Barrington-Ward had explicitly agreed as early as 1942 that at the end of the war Britain would be too weak to prevent the Soviet Union from dominating, if not occupying, the whole of Eastern Europe at least as far west as Berlin. Still anticipating an early United States withdrawal from Europe and fearful of reviving the alliance between Germany and the USSR by ill-judged and ineffectual opposition to Soviet plans, Carr urged that Britain should accept this extension of Soviet influence while striving to maintain a united and prosperous Germany within an integrated post-war Europe.[32]

A number of practical corollaries followed. Most immediately, the need for good relations with the USSR in the post-war world required that Stalin's demands for a second front to relieve pressure on his forces be promptly met. Later, Britain would have to acquiesce in rough Soviet treatment of Eastern Europe. In the longer run, Carr argued, the British government would have to set limits to its relationship with the United States and take the lead in West European political and economic co-operation. 'It would be the height of unwisdom to assume', he thundered in May 1945, 'that an alliance of the English-speaking world, even if it were to find favour with American opinion, could form by itself the all-sufficient pillar of

---

[30] 'Peace and Power', *The Times*, 1 August 1941.
[31] 'Mr. Eden's Mission', *The Times*, 29 December 1942.
[32] McDonald, *Struggles in War and Peace*, pp. 104–7.

world security and render superfluous any other foundation for British policy in Europe.'[33]

All this was consistent with and perhaps the only means to the preservation of British power in the longer run. For Carr's consistent objective was for there to be *three* superpowers in the post-war world: the USA, the USSR, and the British Commonwealth.[34] But it was already considered unbalanced and harmful by some officials in the Foreign Office in 1943, when W. Risdale minuted that 'the leaders [on Soviet and East European affairs] which appear in *The Times* cause more harm than do Mr. Parker's articles', adding that 'those leaders are nearly always the work of Mr. Carr, and it is much more important to get Mr. Carr out of Printing House Square than it is to get Mr. Parker out of Moscow'.[35]

The post-war settlement

Just as there was an ideological element in the opposition he encountered over his support of the Soviet Union, so too there was in Carr's own position.[36] But the same debate about the place of Britain in the post-war international system could also be argued through in strictly non-ideological terms, as Carr generally preferred to do. The starting point was the relative power of the British state, and the central tenet of Carr's position was that Britain could maintain parity with the United States and the Soviet Union only if the solidarity of the 'Big Three' were maintained. This was because future British power depended crucially on economic success and growth.[37] 'If Britain is to continue to play her old part in the world, domestic

---

[33] 'Conditions of Confidence', *The Times*, 23 May 1945, quoted by McDonald, *Struggles in War and Peace*, p. 135.

[34] See W. T. R. Fox's 'E. H. Carr and Political Realism: Vision and Revision', *Review of International Studies*, 11:1, January 1985, n. 4, and the same author's *The Superpowers: The United States, Britain, and the Soviet Union – Their Responsibility for Peace* (New Haven, CT: Yale University Institute of International Studies, 1944), therein referred to. Maintenance of Britain as one of three pre-eminent world powers was the central plank of Carr's programme, returned to again and again in the leader columns of *The Times*. Examples include 'Great and Small Nations', 23 March 1943; 'Concerted Policy', 29 July 1943; 'Security and Power', 25 September 1944; and 'Conditions of Confidence', 23 May 1945. There are many others.

[35] PRO FO371/56866 N3041/3041/38.

[36] Timothy Dunne, 'International Relations Theory in Britain: The Invention of an International Society Tradition', University of Oxford, DPhil., 1993, p. 33.

[37] 'Peace, Trade, and Output', *The Times*, 26 October 1946.

reconstruction must be pressed forward', he insisted. 'For power abroad depends on a healthy economy at home.'[38] A strong economy, in turn, depended on maintaining close trading links and good relations both with Europe and with the English-speaking world. Completing the circle, these links required a balance of maritime and Continental commitments which could not be maintained in the face of sustained hostility from either the United States or the Soviet Union.[39] 'Neither the security nor the economic well-being of Great Britain is compatible with a one-sided policy', he insisted.[40]

Any split would force Britain to choose sides and adopt a role subordinate to one or other of its wartime Allies. Though he did not concede it publicly until March 1946, Carr understood very well the extent of British financial and military weakness relative to the USA and the USSR.[41] Fortunately, the general interest, too, required unity, because no two powers, acting in concert, had sufficient authority to impose an enduring general settlement and guarantee world security.[42] Moreover, Three Power hegemony could be justified on moral grounds, since no other country besides Britain, the USA, and the USSR had made a comparable contribution to victory.[43]

A number of consequences seemed to Carr to follow from his basic position. First of all, relations with the United States, while amicable, must on no account give any ground for fear of an emerging alliance from which the Soviet Union might be excluded.

Secondly, German unity must be rapidly restored before the division of the country into zones created new bones of contention between the Allies.[44] The continued division of Germany, he observed in July 1946, would mean in effect the division of Europe.[45]

---

[38] 'After the Debate', *The Times*, 8 February 1946.
[39] 'The Three-Power Pattern', *The Times*, 4 December 1945. See also 'Agenda for Moscow', 11 December 1945; 'UNO', 8 January 1946; 'After the Debate', 8 February 1946; 'Britain and the World', 22 February 1946.
[40] 'The British Role', *The Times*, 25 September 1946.
[41] 'British Foreign Policy', *The Times*, 7 March 1946.
[42] 'Policy and the Atom', *The Times*, 8 November 1945; see also 'Italian Colonies', 21 September 1945, and 'A Failure to Retrieve', 3 October 1945.
[43] 'After the Setback', *The Times*, 4 October 1945.
[44] 'A Call for Unity', *The Times*, 25 October 1945. See also 'The German Deadlock', 11 March 1946: continued division of Germany threatened to provoke 'dissensions and rivalries between the allies by inviting constant and competitive intervention'. Deploring the divergence already evident between the zones of occupation, he hoped in vain for a belated solution from the imminent Four Power Conference.
[45] 'The Peace Conference', *The Times*, 29 July 1946.

On this subject Carr consistently maintained the line he had adopted during the war, arguing that, 'whatever the safeguards which may still be needed, it is difficult to believe that either economic or political reconstruction can be achieved without the establishment of central agencies of administration run by Germans and comprehending the whole of Germany'.[46] Political unity was the prerequisite for effective German participation in forms of European economic integration which Carr believed essential to broader British and European interests.[47]

A third consequence of Carr's endorsement of a Three Power settlement concerned the atom bomb. It was a source of puzzlement and dismay to Barrington-Ward that Carr, deputising for him on the day in question, failed to get out an editorial on the first atomic attack on Japan into *The Times* on the morning of 7 August 1945.[48] He put this down to a lack of journalistic imagination. It may have been quite the contrary: that Carr grasped the implications of the new weapon all too well, and they gave him pause. For years he had claimed that modern weapons made the position of small powers untenable and the condition of neutrality perilous. He argued from this to the need for more or less formal groupings of states on the model of the inter-American system or the Soviet Union. The implication of an intercontinental attack of such destructiveness was that no state, be it ever so extensive, could now offer the level of security that had been provided, only a hundred years before, by a couple of hundred thousand square miles of contiguous territory.

Nuclear one-worldism – in which the territorial state system no longer provided security – was a logical extension of Carr's position, but an extension he was slow to explore.[49] Instead, he took refuge in idealism, urging that in order to avoid an ephemeral and fortuitous United States technological advantage becoming the source of insecurity and suspicion between the Big Three, control of atomic weapons should forthwith be handed over to the United Nations Security Council. While it is easy to endorse Carr's prophecy that 'the

[46] 'A Call for Unity', *The Times*, 25 October 1945.
[47] 'German Unity', *The Times*, 13 November 1945. See also 'Harnessing German Industry', 5 November 1945.
[48] McDonald, *Struggles in War and Peace*, pp. 144–5.
[49] Daniel Deudney, 'Nuclear Weapons and the Waning of the Real-State', *Daedalus*, 124:2, Spring 1995, pp. 209–31.

'An active danger'

withholding of these . . . secrets . . . may prove to be an advantage dearly bought in terms of future insecurity and suspicion' and possible that he may have been justified in his belief that the effective pooling of atomic weapons would have paved the way to the settlement of other issues, there is not the least inkling in any of Carr's leaders on the subject of any plausible reason why the United States might have wished to exchange the certainty of its current monopoly for the chance of better relations in the long run.[50]

Carr's persistent emphasis on the continued co-operation of the Big Three had further implications for British foreign policy. France – and British relations with France – must be marginalised.[51] One reason for this was that France would not willingly concede the political unification and rapid economic recovery of Germany which he regarded as essential in order to relieve Britain of the costs of feeding its military zone and reassure the Soviet Union about the intentions of the Western powers.[52] Another reason was that no fourth power must be permitted to claim superpower status.

A fifth corollary of Carr's insistence on Three Power hegemony was that the United Nations Organization, useful though it might be, must be subordinated to the Big Three, whose political differences ought not to be paraded in public in New York, but settled quietly at summit or ministerial level. Carr accepted that the UNO possessed certain political and technical advantages over its predecessor, the League of Nations, but characteristically argued that its success must depend on 'the concentration of effective power which it is likely to represent'. This, in turn, depended on unanimity of the Big Three.[53] When the Persian government appealed to the Security Council over continued interference in Azerbaijan and the failure to withdraw Soviet troops, the USSR responded by making allegedly analogous appeals concerning British troops in Greece and Indonesia. Carr voiced strong

---

[50] 'The Atom and After', *The Times*, 23 November 1945. See also 'The Explosive Atom', 31 October 1945; 'Policy and the Atom', 8 November 1945; 'Peace and the Atom', 16 November 1945; 'Agenda for Moscow', 11 December 1945.

[51] 'Agenda for Moscow', *The Times*, 11 December 1945, has strong anti-French implications. For a comprehensive indictment, see 'General de Gaulle's Challenge', *The Times*, 22 January 1946.

[52] On French intransigence and Carr's remedy, see 'Agenda for Moscow', *The Times*, 11 December 1945, and 'Control over Germany', 12 December 1945.

[53] 'UNO', *The Times*, 8 January 1946; 'Mr. Bevin's Speech', 18 January 1946. See also 'The United Nations', 4 November 1946.

opposition to the Soviet decision to bring to the UN differences which, he felt, would be better and sooner settled behind closed doors.[54]

Finally, if there must – as Carr reluctantly conceded – be more or less exclusive spheres of influence in the post-war world rather than a multilateral settlement jointly concluded and guaranteed by the Big Three, then regional integration and other forms of international co-operation must be conducted in the least provocative way possible.[55] Though the advantages of wartime military co-operation should not be squandered, Carr was now less anxious to stress the importance of joint military planning, standardisation of weapons, and shared bases than he had been during and before the war and rather more inclined to emphasise economic co-operation instead.[56] It was important to soothe Soviet fears about the nature of Western co-operation by showing it to be non-aggressive. This, he claimed, could best be done by closer economic and financial association with West European states, even if it entailed some loss of sovereignty.[57] A similar line was taken in January 1946, for example, when Carr welcomed an Anglo-Greek financial and economic accord in an editorial that emphasised economic recovery as the path to political stability and urged bulk purchase by Britain of Greek tobacco and currants.[58] Also consistent with this non-aggressive style of international co-operation was the enthusiastic welcome accorded by Carr to Bevin's revival in February 1946 of proposals for economic reorganisation of the countries of the Middle East and 'the strengthening of direct economic links between them'.[59] Finally, it also accounts for the enthusiastic reception accorded to the announcement of Marshall Aid in June 1947, an initiative which Carr optimistically commended to the Soviet Union,

---

[54] 'UNO and the Powers', *The Times*, 6 February 1946. Carr described the Soviet move as 'a reprisal'. Two days later he returned to the same theme, advising that differences between the Big Three would 'be settled not by resounding declarations of principle but by the quiet conciliation of particular interests, not by public recrimination, but by amicable private discussion': 'After the Debate', *The Times*, 8 February 1946. See also 'Procedures for Persia', 21 January 1946, and 'The Soviet Appeals', 23 January 1946.

[55] 'A Failure to Retrieve', *The Times*, 3 October 1945; 'Mr. Bevin's Review', 5 June 1946. See also 'Britain and the World', 22 February 1946. The same argument against public diplomacy is extended to peace negotiations in 'Publicity and Peace', 17 October 1946.

[56] 'British Foreign Policy', *The Times*, 7 March 1946.

[57] 'Mr. Bevin's Review', *The Times*, 24 November 1945.

[58] 'Recovery in Greece', *The Times*, 26 January 1946.

[59] 'After the Debate', *The Times*, 8 February 1946.

registering it as a conciliatory step back by the United States from the hard-line economic liberal ideology that had seemed to debar European economic integration and a clear signal that Europe need not after all be divided into hostile camps.[60]

Under attack

Though much of what Carr wrote in *The Times* during the closing months of the war and the first year of peace was well within the permitted bounds of public debate and loyal opposition, the persistent trickle of pro-Soviet leaders became steadily more evident and finally drew fire as the Anglo-Soviet alliance of 1942 started to unravel. By mid-December 1944 the position adopted by *The Times* on Greece had attracted hostile attention from Churchill. Following a Communist insurrection in Greece on 3 December 1944, Carr and Barrington-Ward opposed the despatch of British troops to support the incumbent Right-wing government. Jock Colville, one of Churchill's private secretaries, wrote to the MoI to complain of a leading article by Carr, asking Brendan Bracken to speak about it to Barrington-Ward.[61] A further leading article of 1 January 1945 by Carr finally goaded Churchill into a public denunciation of *The Times* in the House of Commons, which was met with 'the loudest, largest, and most vicious – even savage! – cheer that I have heard in the House', Barrington-Ward noted ruefully, 'a vent for the pent-up passions of three years, a protest against all that has, rightly or wrongly, enraged the Tories in the paper during that time'.[62]

Yet following Churchill's outburst, relations between *The Times* and the British government, and with them Carr's position, might have been expected to improve. Barrington-Ward was comforted and his resolve stiffened by the support of a number of well-placed acquaintances and friends who thought Churchill's behaviour excessively authoritarian. Encouraging hints of support were received from Max Beaverbrook and Brendan Bracken, who claimed to have restrained Churchill from further excess by reminding him of 'the whole record of *The Times* and its fine work in this war'. John Astor, as proprietor, had been re-reading the leaders that had given offence and found

---

[60] 'Europe's Opportunity', *The Times*, 19 June 1947. Carr was, of course, to be disappointed in his desire for Soviet co-operation.

[61] PRO FO371/43709 R21228/73/19.

[62] McDonald, *Struggles in War and Peace*, p. 122.

them 'quite soberly expressed, offering advice rather than censure'. Barrington-Ward himself re-read the Greek leaders and was 'once more impressed by their balance and moderation'. Though the majority of the letters arising from the incident were hostile, the margin was tolerably narrow.[63] It still seemed to Barrington-Ward that by standing firm *The Times* could continue in peacetime to advance British interests through the dual policy of economic growth and Soviet alliance which it had set out so trenchantly during the war. Indeed, this was a position to which Barrington-Ward would remain committed as late as January 1947, some months after Carr's departure. '*The Times* ought to have great chances in 1947', he confided to his diary. 'In particular we can help by swelling the demand . . . for production at home (all else hangs upon that) and by promoting a firm but realistically based understanding with Russia, without which there cannot be peace.'[64]

To the consistent support of his editor, Carr could add, following the general election of July 1945, a Labour government that might have been expected to be more in tune with *The Times* than its predecessor. Yet as time went by the Foreign Office became less and less patient and by March 1946 the new Labour foreign secretary, Ernest Bevin, was every bit as hostile as Churchill had been two years before.

By stating the realities of the British position as baldly as he did in what the Soviet leadership continued to regard as an official newspaper, Carr appeared to Whitehall officials to have effectively undermined the negotiating position of British diplomats. They might with some justice have thrown back in his face Carr's pre-war comments about the abortive 1939 discussions for an Anglo-Soviet agreement, during which constant media attention had placed the British government 'in the position of a man trying to strike a bargain with an astute negotiator while his nagging wife adjures him, in audible asides, to concede without scrutiny any and every demand made by the other party'.[65] The Foreign Office protested, and four months before Carr's departure the political bankruptcy of his partnership with Barrington-Ward was made all too clear when the latter was summoned to the

---

[63] Ibid., pp. 123–5, quoting Barrington-Ward's diary.
[64] Ibid., p. 127, quoting Barrington-Ward's diary entry for 1 January 1947.
[65] Carr, *Britain*, p. 12.

Foreign Office in March 1946 and subjected to a tirade from the Labour foreign secretary, Ernest Bevin.

Barrington-Ward later noted down the essential points of Bevin's repetitive and emotional attack: *'The Times* did great harm. It was taken abroad for a national newspaper. He was going to tell the House of Commons that it was not, and that it was pro-Russian and not pro-British. I had a lot of pink intelligentsia down there and he didn't believe I was in control.'[66] As Britain slipped steadily into the embrace of the United States, this mud stuck. Rebecca West, a representative member of the British pre-war Left intelligentsia, 'stunned fellow guests at a dinner party [in New York early in 1947] by asserting that *The Times* of London was now a Communist party organ'. Taken by her biographer as evidence of near pathological obsession with Communist infiltration, this was in effect no more than an echo of the view that had first been expressed some four years before by David Bowes Lyon, and which had since become conventional, of *The Times* as the 'thrupenny *Daily Worker'*.[67]

In July 1946 Carr resigned his post at *The Times* to devote himself to the projected history of the Soviet Union, though he continued for a time to contribute leaders. It would be surprising if the decision had not been prompted at least in part by the realisation, not yet fully shared by Barrington-Ward, that the paper had been fatally wrong-footed and its ability to influence foreign policy effectively terminated by the onset of the Cold War. How had this debacle come about?

The eclipse of *The Times*

One reason why Foster understated the extent of Carr's personal responsibility for the foreign policy line adopted by *The Times* may have been that many of its component elements were quite widely held. Carr's support for the Soviet Union – though not his specific justification of it – was common enough in wartime Britain. Foster himself noted Ralph Parker, *Times* correspondent in Moscow during the war, whose ready apologies for Stalinist excesses appalled Arthur Koestler, and the very different case of Lewis Namier, who argued,

---

[66] McDonald, *Struggles in War and Peace*, pp. 139–40.
[67] Victoria Glendinning, *Rebecca West: A Life* (London: Weidenfeld & Nicolson, 1987), p. 188.

like Carr, that Polish self-determination could not be allowed to stand in the way of good Anglo-Soviet relations in the post-war world.[68]

Ralph Parker was not himself a member of the Communist Party, though his secretary was.[69] Communist penetration was more advanced in other sections of the British media. Readjustment of public attitudes towards the USSR in the weeks following Hitler's June 1941 invasion fell largely to Peter Smollett, as head of the Russian Department of the MoI, and Guy Burgess at the BBC, both later to be identified as Soviet agents.[70] Carr was doubtless happy to oblige his former MoI colleague when asked to supply a leader celebrating the twenty-fourth anniversary of the October Revolution in 1941.[71] There is some irony in the fact that his pro-Soviet line, on this occasion at least, came in direct response to a government request. But to regard Carr, on this evidence, as Smollett's 'creature' is to fall prey to far too conspiratorial a view of British support for the Soviet Union at this time.[72] There was no single source of pro-Soviet views, nor were they wholly orchestrated from Moscow. On the contrary, Graham Ross has shown the extent to which senior figures within the Foreign Office shared Carr's position. As late as 1944, in marked contradistinction to the chiefs of staff, the Foreign Office was optimistic about post-war Anglo-Soviet relations. Ross notes 'how much store the Foreign Office was still setting on maintaining co-operation with Russia and how little faith it still had in the United States as a post-war collaborator in Europe'.[73] During 1944, the predominant view in the Foreign office also favoured a West European grouping to control German recovery if, as expected, the United States withdrew into relative isolation.[74] This was also Carr's position.

If Carr's pro-Soviet and integrationist attitudes on the European settlement were unexceptional in themselves, why did they lead him,

[68] Foster, '*The Times* and Appeasement', p. 294.

[69] PRO FO371/56866 N3041/38.

[70] W. J. West, *The Truth about Hollis* (London: Duckworth, 1989), p. 66.

[71] Ibid., p. 67. Cf. 'Britain and Russia', *The Times*, 7 November 1941.

[72] W. J. West, *Hollis*, p. 107. Carr was under fire from Right and Left. In March 1943 Yalman, the Polish ambassador in Turkey, accused him of acting for the same British anti-Bolshevik faction that had used *The Times* to promote appeasement before the war: PRO FO371/37467 R3427/55/44.

[73] Graham Ross, 'Foreign Office Attitudes to the Soviet Union, 1941–1945', in Laqueur, *Second World War*, p. 266.

[74] Sean Greenwood, 'Ernest Bevin, France, and "Western Union": August 1945–February 1946', *European History Quarterly*, 14:3, 1984, p. 320.

and *The Times*, into the wilderness? This outcome may partly be explained by the quasi-official status of *The Times*, the excessive coherence and consistency of the general philosophy of international relations that underpinned Carr's leaders, and the force with which they were expressed. In part, it had to do with specific content and policy-making context. But above all it was the timing of some of the more trenchant leaders on European affairs in relation to the unfolding conflict between leading politicians and officials of the victorious Allied states that sank Carr. He held on too long.

The *coup de grâce* would be delivered by Ernest Bevin, yet the views of the Labour foreign secretary on European integration and the place of Britain in the post-war settlement during his early months in office were not dissimilar from those expressed by Carr. Sean Greenwood has argued persuasively that Bevin was initially content with the idea of a European union as a 'Third Force' on a par with the USA and the USSR, even arguing, as Carr did, that it should initially be based upon functional co-operation on economic and social issues in order to avoid the provocation that a more formal security arrangement might offer to the Soviet Union.[75] Initially moved to use British military control of the Ruhr as a springboard to European economic co-operation, Bevin had moved by the end of 1946 to acceptance of a divided Germany.[76]

The reason for this was that the practicability of a 'Third Force' policy depended on close co-operation between Britain and France, and this proved to be unobtainable. As early as September 1945 the French blocked an agreement at the first post-war Council of Foreign Ministers to provide for a central German post-war administration. Carr felt that French concerns about a united Germany could be dealt with by imposing international control over the Ruhr.[77] But the decisive moment for Bevin came in the new year when de Gaulle, barely two months in office, announced his resignation from the presidency. French intransigence might be overcome, but political chaos and economic collapse were a different matter. Much influenced by the gloomy prognostications reaching him from the Paris embassy, Bevin foresaw the Channel ports 'virtually in Russian hands'. He

---

[75] Ibid., pp. 323–5. See also 'Mr. Bevin's Review', *The Times*, 24 November 1945.
[76] Sean Greenwood, 'Bevin, the Ruhr, and the Division of Germany: August 1945–December 1946', *Historical Journal*, 29:1, 1986, p. 203.
[77] 'Agenda for Moscow', *The Times*, 11 December 1945; 'Control over Germany', 15 December 1945.

concluded that the project for European economic and social co-operation, and with it the concept of a British-led 'Third Force', was not longer viable. As mistrust between the wartime Big Three deepened, he felt bound to align Britain with the United States.

Not so Carr. Late in February, admitting clearly for the first time the incipient breakdown of the wartime alliance but presumably taking a more sanguine view of the French crisis, he was still arguing that for Britain to deviate from strict even-handedness between them would inevitably result in subordination to the United States or the Soviet Union. The only option for Britain remained the simultaneous strengthening of ties with the Commonwealth and Europe.[78] Early the next month he responded to the Fulton speech in which Churchill advocated Anglo-United States military alliance and spoke of an 'iron curtain' descending across Europe, by deploring its excessively ideological tone and seizing upon every available straw of conciliation towards the USSR in Churchill's text.[79] A few days later a frank and well-balanced summary of the events that had led to the breakdown of the wartime alliance concluded with a plea to the Soviet Union to honour its agreement to withdraw from Persia.[80] Vapid assertions of an underlying common interest in peace of precisely the kind he had condemned in the early chapters of *The Twenty Years' Crisis* weakened Carr's peroration and can have been no more convincing when repeated a few days later.[81]

Once Bevin made up his mind, during the early weeks of 1946, that Soviet designs constituted a serious and imminent threat to British security, the unfolding of the Cold War was only a matter of time, and the foreign policy that Carr had nurtured with such care throughout the war was doomed. Carr cannot be accused of failing to realise the dangers of confrontation or to foresee the implications of Cold War for British power. It was his all too accurate foresight as much as any ideological preference for centralism and planning that led Carr to his passionate attachment to the ideal of a Three Power Concert. In June 1943 he had warned that 'were a rift to occur after the war between Russia, Britain, and America, were mutual suspicion and mistrust to prevail over mutual sympathy and understanding, then any policy for Europe as a whole would be bankrupt from the start. Other countries,

[78] 'Policy in the Making', *The Times*, 21 February 1946.
[79] 'Mr. Churchill's Speech', *The Times*, 6 March 1946.
[80] 'The Three Powers', *The Times*, 14 March 1946.
[81] 'The Common Interest', *The Times*, 19 March 1946.

enrolling themselves as clients of one or other group, would provide fresh causes of friction by the introduction of their own lesser jealousies and animosities. Germany, from her central vantage point, would quickly regain her freedom of manoeuvre.'[82] Three months later, dismissing as illusory the belief that an Anglo-American alliance could provide 'a self-sufficient guarantee of world peace', he warned that 'its fallacy consisted in ignoring . . . which it would provoke among other nations, and especially in Europe . . . It would make the British Isles a remote, exposed and not easily defensible outpost of the English-speaking world.'[83]

If Carr foresaw the costs of failure with clarity, he also appreciated the intellectual nature of the problem of Great Power co-operation and offered a technical solution. At the risk of anachronism, it may be helpful to think of the wartime alliance as a three-player game of prisoners' dilemma: logically, if inelegantly, this must be termed 'Prisoners' Trilemma'. If the Big Three were able to maintain co-operative relations with each another until the war was won and a new world order firmly established, then this outcome would yield the maximum available joint gains from the game. But the structure of the game made it improbable that the players would succeed in achieving maximum joint gains.

In the standard game of prisoners' dilemma, the problem consists in the knowledge, common to the two prisoners, that either can secure his own immediate release by denouncing the other, who will in consequence suffer sustained imprisonment. The two prisoners are unable to communicate with each other. If each remains silent, both will be released after a short period for lack of evidence. This solution represents the best joint outcome. However, each knows that the other can achieve a superior individual outcome by defection if and only if he is the first to defect.

The most likely outcome on a single play is almost certainly defection, but some years ago Robert Axelrod provided a plausible account of how, in repeated plays of the game, the pattern of co-operation and defection could be used to signal willingness to co-operate. Moreover, he established that the best way to maximise joint gains in an iterated game of prisoners' dilemma was through a 'tit-for-tat' strategy in which the defection of an opponent was promptly

---

[82] 'Germany's Last Hope', *The Times*, 3 June 1943.
[83] 'Foundations of Peace', *The Times*, 30 September 1943.

punished by defection in the next play of the game followed by an immediate return to co-operation.[84]

In the three-player game as experienced by the major wartime Allies, when stripped to its essentials, the worst outcome for each was isolation in the face of an exclusive combination of the other two. Britain feared marginalisation by an anti-imperialist consensus between its two mighty Allies. The United States feared the emergence, whether through social revolution in France and Italy or the deliberate policy of the British Labour government, of a Western Europe ideologically and militarily aligned with the Soviet Union. The Soviet Union feared what rapidly came to pass: isolation in the face of an Anglo-European security system based on close and exclusive military and economic co-operation between the United States and Britain. In these circumstances, defection could take two forms: unilateral action on matters of common concern without consultation or, more damagingly, co-operation with one of the other players against the third.

Though he did not express it in precisely these terms, Carr perfectly realised that the delicate balance of the wartime alliance was vulnerable to cumulative misunderstanding over innumerable issues. He also showed at least an intuitive grasp of Axelrod's solution through his insistence on repeated private consultation between the leaders of the powers. In prisoners' dilemma, linguistic communication between the players is not possible. Axelrod's breakthrough consisted in demonstrating that in the iterated game the moves themselves provided a means of communication, rather in the manner that varying forms of deployment in war constitute a coded language that may result either in the escalation or the humanisation of conflict.

It might seem that the analogy between prisoners' dilemma and international relations breaks down because states possess, in diplomacy, a means of effective communication. But Carr's point was that the public and official utterances of states were often ineffective because they performed so many simultaneous incidental purposes, speaking as much to domestic constituencies or third parties as to their purported recipients. Hence his insistence, as the war moved into its final phase towards the end of 1943, on the extension to the Soviet Union of 'the machinery of constant discussion at many levels, through which . . . so many Anglo-American differences have been

---

[84] Robert Axelrod, *The Evolution of Cooperation* (New York: Basic Books, 1984).

amiably ironed out'.[85] Hence the vehemence with which he deplored the lack of a 'regular process of consultation at every level' between the Big Three, attributing to this the marked deterioration in their mutual relations already evident at the end of 1944.[86] Hence also his repeated attacks on public debate of sensitive differences between the Big Three at the United Nations, to which he strongly preferred quiet consultation between the interested parties.[87]

Yet however accurate in foreseeing the looming Cold War and however ingenious in devising and advocating preventative stratagems, Carr was slow to appreciate the practical implications for policy once the game was lost. Things might have worked out differently; Bevin might have stood his ground and resisted what looks very much like panic in the early months of 1946. But he did not, and one symptom of the panic was the way in which he rounded on *The Times.* Thereafter, Carr's chances of exerting any profound influence on affairs were negligible. In these changed circumstances, three examples illustrate the naivety – very possibly false – with which he continued to flog his dead horses around Printing House Square during the remainder of 1946 and into 1947 after the showdown with Bevin. They are the November 1946 Labour back-bench revolt over foreign policy, the early 1947 discussions about the future of the Anglo-Soviet treaty of 1942, and the announcement of Marshall Aid in June 1947.

Since Bevin's change of heart early in 1946 and the failure of the Labour leadership to dissociate themselves convincingly from Churchill's Fulton speech, the Left of the party had been seeking an opportunity to clarify and affirm a distinctive line on British foreign policy. Proposing an amendment to the king's speech, signed by fifty-seven Labour back-benchers, on 12 November 1946, Richard Crossman called on the leadership to take the lead in forming a 'Third Force' to provide 'a democratic and constructive Socialist alternative to an otherwise inevitable conflict between American capitalism and Russian communism'.[88] Attlee vigorously attacked the Third Force proposal in the House of Commons, later threatening its advocates

---

[85] 'Framework of Peace', *The Times*, 2 November 1943.
[86] 'Common Counsel', *The Times*, 21 December 1944.
[87] 'After the Debate', *The Times*, 6 February 1946; 'Publicity and Peace', 17 October 1946.
[88] Crossman, quoted in Wayne Knight, 'Labourite Britain: America's "Sure Friend"? – The Anglo-Soviet Treaty Issue, 1947', *Diplomatic History*, 7:4, 1983, p. 267.

with expulsion from the party and forcing an apology from Crossman.[89] Carr further compromised himself by rallying in support of a cause already lost. Four days after its parliamentary defeat he wrote in support of the revolt as being expressive of 'a wider, more national, and more commendable faith in the possibility and desirability of a foreign policy independent of both "Communist Russia and capitalist America"'.[90] It was all very well to quote Smuts and Anthony Eden in support. He might just as well have quoted Bevin's own views of the previous year. The game had moved on.

One consequence of the breakdown of Three Power co-operation which Carr did not fully grasp was that advocacy of co-operation of the kind that had earlier been calculated to avoid the breakdown became, after the event, manipulable by one side or the other. Thus Stalin's friendly overtures to Britain at the beginning of 1947 were rightly or wrongly perceived as a mischievous attempt to sow dissension between Britain and the United States. Arising out of a meeting between Stalin and Field Marshall Montgomery in Moscow in January 1947, Anglo-Soviet exchanges concerning the status of the 1942 treaty following the defeat of Germany were seen at the Foreign Office as a crude and transparent attempt to lure Britain into a sweeping defensive military alliance that would cloud or even disrupt relations between Britain and the United States, perhaps by forcing Bevin out of office.[91] Carr's effusive response to the Anglo-Soviet exchange of notes, with its restatements of the old Third Force view and its attempt to distance Britain from United States policies, could not possibly influence a British government already so clearly committed to the United States, and could only encourage a pointless prolongation of the charade by misleading Soviet readers.[92]

Last came Carr's hope that Marshall Aid, announced in June 1947, by opening the possibility for discriminatory economic co-operation in Europe, was intended by the United States and would be perceived in the Soviet Union as a step back from doctrinaire economic liberalism meriting an equally conciliatory response that would allow it to facilitate agreements between East and West European nations and a consequent lifting of the Iron Curtain.[93] Carr's former colleagues at

[89] Ibid., p. 269.
[90] 'A British Policy', *The Times*, 16 November 1946.
[91] Knight, 'Labourite Britain', pp. 275–7.
[92] 'Reaffirming the Alliance', *The Times*, 1 February 1947.
[93] 'Europe's Opportunity', *The Times*, 19 June 1947.

the Foreign Office would have required no hindsight to recognise this editorial as the merest wishful thinking given the general context of Great Power relations. Three years into his history of the Soviet revolution, a less and less frequent visitor to Printing House Square, Carr was no longer in touch.

6 Carr's debt to Mannheim

Mannheim and the sociology of knowledge

Now that his extended engagement in the British policy-making process has been examined, it is time to return to the more abstract and theoretical features that account for the durability of Carr's work on international relations. These have already been touched upon in chapters 1 and 3. A more comprehensive and critical survey occupies chapter 7. But first it will be necessary to reach an assessment of the extent and the implications of Carr's reading of Karl Mannheim for his thought about social science in general, and, more particularly, for his realist critique of utopianism and his views on economic and social planning.

In his preface to the first edition of *The Twenty Years' Crisis*, Carr issued a blanket acknowledgement of the published work of others before naming two books: *Ideology and Utopia* by Karl Mannheim and *Moral Man and Immoral Society* by Reinhold Niebuhr. These, as he put it, 'though not specifically concerned with international relations, seem to me to have illuminated some of the fundamental problems of politics'.[1] An obvious reason for examining Carr's debt to Mannheim is that it may help establish just what he believed 'the fundamental problems of politics' to be. So it does; and a major conclusion is that its rootedness in Mannheim's ideas enables one more easily to detect a coherence of method and policy recommendation and to delineate the relationship between domestic and international issues in Carr's work.

---

[1] E. H. Carr, *The Twenty Years' Crisis, 1919–1939: An Introduction to the Study of International Relations* (London: Macmillan, 1939), p. x.

It would be wrong to emphasise what might be judged a marginal comment without a little more justification. Mannheim deserves consideration by students of international relations chiefly because he provided Carr with the dialectical structure of *The Twenty Years' Crisis* and a distinctively post-positivist social scientific methodology that would mark him off from the dominant positivism of the Anglo-Saxon world of his day. Far from being a methodologically unsophisticated historian, a traditionalist displaced by post-war behaviourism as it colonised international relations, Carr was a social scientist in a tradition that had already proclaimed the redundancy of behaviourism.[2] But in the eyes of those of his critics who realised this, the connection with Mannheim proved to be for Carr the methodological equivalent of his wartime policy towards the Soviet Union. Each was conceived of as a Centrist stance, capable of commanding the assent of substantial sections of the British policy-making community and administrative elites. Each was transformed by the onset of the Cold War into an apparent commitment to the Left, rendering Carr vulnerable and depriving him of such influence as he had once possessed. The association with Mannheim therefore helps explain Carr's ultimate failure and account for the strange readings of his work that prevailed until quite recently.[3] Carr's debt to Niebuhr, such as it is, told in the opposite direction, for the theologian, whose work is in any case far less systematic than that of Mannheim, was to become one of the leading sources of inspiration for post-war United States realism.

Carr's reading of *Ideology and Utopia* merits close attention.[4] After a spell as professor at Heidelberg, Mannheim had moved to the new Institut für Sozialforschung as one of two professors in what was soon

[2] Karl Mannheim, *Ideology and Utopia: An Introduction to the Sociology of Knowledge* (London: Kegan Paul, 1936), pp. 39–42.

[3] A brilliant anticipation of the more recent reinterpretation of Carr is to be found in Graham Evans, 'E. H. Carr and International Relations', *British Journal of International Studies*, 1:2, July 1975, pp. 77–97. W. T. R. Fox, 'E. H. Carr and Political Realism: Vision and Revision', *Review of International Studies*, 11:1, January 1985, pp. 1–16, is excellent, as are Ken Booth's 'Security in Anarchy: Utopian Realism in Theory and Practice', *International Affairs*, 67:3, July 1991, pp. 527–45, and Paul Howe's 'The Utopian Realism of E. H. Carr', *Review of International Studies*, 20:3, July 1994, pp. 277–97, which very successfully extends the contemporary reading of Carr beyond *The Twenty Years' Crisis* and advances the claim that Carr's thought is coherent, but says little about its sources.

[4] So, less obviously, does Karl Popper's treatment of *Man and Society*. Mannheim, *Ideology and Utopia*; Mannheim, *Man and Society in an Age of Reconstruction: Studies in Modern Social Structure* (London: Kegan Paul, 1940).

to become known as the Frankfurt School. Its director Paul Horkheimer, and other figures such as Herbert Marcuse and Theodor Adorno, were to develop, in critical theory, a distinctive approach within the Marxist tradition. Mannheim himself was no Marxist, but his sociology of knowledge was sufficiently sophisticated to be regarded as a threat by Marxist contemporaries and to draw their fire. Horkheimer attacked *Ideology and Utopia* within a year of publication. Marcuse, sympathetic at first, soon became more critical. Adorno stoked the fire with a 1953 critique of *Man and Society in an Age of Reconstruction*. In the meantime, Karl Popper, who had set out in his early years within the same broad German-speaking radical milieu as Mannheim, Hilferding, and their Marxist critics, had diverged sharply from this circle, so that the intellectual Cold War of the later 1950s and 1960s found Mannheim caught between the two: simultaneously condemned as arch-historicist by Popper and dismissed as irretrievably bourgeois by the Marxists.

All this lay ahead when Carr first came across Mannheim, probably through the English translation of *Ideology and Utopia*, published in 1936. Acceptance of the sociology of knowledge, as of Marxism, has some of the characteristics of religious experience, and Carr displayed the full enthusiasm of an acolyte in *The Twenty Years' Crisis*. Characteristically, however, Carr bent Mannheim to his own will, twisting the structure of his argument in unexpected ways.

The case that Mannheim puts forward is neither simple nor elegantly expressed, but its main outline is clear enough. The first step is to expose the incoherence of naive empiricism. Is it possible that all knowledge could be derived by an individual from experience of the world through the senses? No, replies Mannheim, because the stream of raw sense data would not constitute meaningful knowledge until it was organised.

Part of the process of rational organisation of knowledge might be universal. Kant's purpose in the first critique had been to delineate this sphere, though later philosophers were to challenge the universality even of mathematics and formal logic.[5] Yet even if a Kantean

---

[5] David Bloor, *Knowledge and Social Imagery* (London: Routledge & Kegan Paul, 1976); Ludwig Wittgenstein, *Remarks on the Foundations of Mathematics* (Oxford: Blackwell, 1956), and the discussion by B. Stroud, 'Wittgenstein and Logical Necessity', *Philosophical Review*, 74, 1965, pp. 504–18; Peter Winch, 'Understanding a Primitive Society', *American Philosophy Quarterly*, 1:4, October 1964, pp. 307–24, reprinted in Winch, *Ethics and Action* (London: Routledge & Kegan Paul, 1972).

compromise between empiricism and idealism were conceded, it could still be argued that many of the concepts employed in practical reason – that is, reasoning about moral and political affairs – grew out of the distinctive experience and activities of each social group and were embodied in its practices and language. Such cultural artefacts were likely to vary over time, across different language groups, between national societies, and even between classes. Indeed, the categories used to describe intentional action are doubly cultural, depending on custom and consent for their reproduction both in discourse and in political practice, and therefore demanding that the social scientist adopt a hermeneutic methodology.

It would be anachronistic to attribute every step in this greatly truncated argument to Mannheim. However, its methodological and political implications are at least broadly consistent with his work. Indeed, the methodological implication for sociological inquiry, and for a science of international relations of the kind that Carr sought to found, was to be nicely summed up in *Man and Society*. Mannheim claimed that an empirical science of society which avoided empiricism was possible provided his view of the relationship between fact and theory was accepted. One might start from either, 'but whatever procedure [is chosen], facts and structure are continuously related to each other and facts only become more than data if their function in the whole mechanism is adequately realized, for it is the total structure of society alone which reveals the real function and meaning of the parts'.[6]

The argument appears to be that fact and theory, like participation and understanding, are mutually constitutive. So for Mannheim, the individual had meaning only through membership of society. 'We belong to a group', he claimed, 'not only because we are born into it, not merely because we profess to belong to it, nor finally because we give it our loyalty and allegiance, but primarily because we see the world and certain things in the world the way it does . . . In every concept, in every concrete meaning, there is contained a crystallization of the experiences of a certain group.'[7]

If all this were as Mannheim and his followers supposed, how

---

[6] Mannheim, *Man and Society*, p. 26.
[7] Mannheim, *Ideology and Utopia*, p. 19. Applied to the international anarchy, the argument adumbrated here is not the structuralism of Kenneth Waltz, but something closer to the pragmatic structural-realist approach to international relations developed by Buzan and his co-authors: Barry Buzan, Charles Jones, and Richard Little, *The Logic*

could empiricism and its individualist account of knowledge ever have gained currency? How, more specifically, did the application to social science of a positivist methodology parasitic on empiricist epistemology take hold? Mannheim offers a conjectural history as his solution to the puzzle. Emphasis on private property and autonomous individual decision-making, coupled with the anonymous and quantifiable character of market exchange, led the bourgeoisie as a class to see knowledge itself as a form of property emerging from individual labour and able, like property, to be appropriated, accumulated, and freely traded by individuals. Seen from within this group, 'society appeared as if it were only an incalculably complex multiplicity of spontaneous individual acts of doing and knowing'.[8]

As this individualistic theory of knowledge gained ground it influenced all aspects of life. Under its sway political discussion and philosophy became more abstract and rational. Yet this could not change the essentially conflictual nature of politics, and Mannheim found it 'difficult to decide . . . whether the sublimation or substitution of discussion for the older weapon of conflict, the direct use of force and oppression, really constituted a fundamental improvement in human life'.[9] Here is a nostalgic romanticism worthy of Sir Walter Scott himself, in whose novels the spirit of the laws was so often safer in the hands of those whose business was coercion than of those responsible for upholding it.[10] Carr, by contrast, was much more decided. The main policy thrust of *The Twenty Years' Crisis* was that this transformation of consciousness did indeed mark an improvement, facilitating the resolution of international conflicts through

---

of Anarchy: From Neorealism to Structural Realism (New York: Columbia University Press, 1993).

[8] Mannheim, *Ideology and Utopia*, p. 29.   [9] Ibid., p. 34.

[10] In *Old Mortality*, Major Bellenden, about to plead to Claverhouse on behalf of Morton (a confused renegade in the tradition of Waverley), muses: 'I never knew a real soldier that was not a frank-hearted, honest fellow; and I think the execution of the laws . . . may be a thousand times better intrusted with them than with peddling lawyers and thick-skulled gentlemen.' Earlier, Morton had reasoned along similar lines: 'in a time when justice is, in all its branches, so completely corrupted, I would rather lose my life by open military violence, than be conjured out of it by hocuspocus of some arbitrary lawyer' (Sir Walter Scott, *Old Mortality* (Edinburgh: Black, 1878), I, pp. 198 and 188). The international politics of Sir Walter Scott is a largely unexplored continent. For an erudite introduction, see Karl Kroeber, 'Frictional Fiction: Walter Scott in the Light of von Clausewitz's *On War'*, in James Pipkin, ed., *English and German Romanticism: Cross-Currents and Controversies* (Heidelberg: Carl Winter, 1985), pp. 251–73.

negotiation backed by the threat of force rather than by prompt resort to force. This somewhat idealistic conviction provided Carr with a strong motive for obscuring the bleaker side of the argument as developed by Mannheim. Castigated for his supposed worship of power, Carr turns out on closer examination to be vulnerable chiefly for having placed excessive reliance on reason and the possibilities of conciliation.

The darker thinking behind Mannheim's ambivalence towards public reason was that political theory and supposedly rational political discourse in the modern age seemed to him to be every bit as polarised and intransigent as two opposing armies. Those with a strong interest in maintaining the status quo espoused theories which obscured or marginalised negative features of society; by contrast, those who wished to change society saw only its faults. Mannheim referred to these opposing world views as ideology and utopia respectively. Each obscured the real condition of society and neither was capable of inspiring effective political action.

The structure of Mannheim's argument was to expose these anti-phonal positions by applying the critical sociology of knowledge to each. The hinge of the argument was that any positive policy recommendations had then to be built on some foundation capable of transcending the critical conclusion that all knowledge was socially constructed; and it was to be this re-grounding of practical political action, whether in changed human consciousness or in prevailing social trends, that was to cause most trouble both for Mannheim himself and for his disciple, Carr.

Awareness of the role played by interest in the supposedly rational formation of general philosophies of politics seemed at first to confer great advantages. To unmask the irrational and interested base of bourgeois thought had been a great achievement of Marxism. But by the early twentieth century everybody was doing it. 'In the measure that the various groups sought to destroy their adversaries' confidence in their thinking by this most modern intellectual weapon of radical unmasking, they also destroyed, as all positions gradually came to be subjected to analysis, man's confidence in human thought in general.'[11] Most of all, Mannheim's critical argument is reflexive. It is not hard to provide a conjectural history of the emergence of the

---

[11] Mannheim, *Ideology and Utopia*, p. 37. The argument recurs in the much-cited passage at the end of Carr's chapter on 'The Limitations of Realism': Carr, *Crisis*, p. 119.

sociology of knowledge that parodies Mannheim's own account of the rise of methodological individualism.

This first phase of the argument developed by Mannheim appeared to lead to relativism and reflexivity and thence to scepticism and irrationalism. It infuriated Marxists who wished to contrast the false consciousness of the bourgeois and the untutored proletarian with the true consciousness of the revolutionary and the party. But its impact was wider, since, together with Freudianism, it threatened to undermine any use of reason as a basis for political action by effectively denying all rationalisations of deliberate actions. These now turned out to have been determined by class struggle or the unconscious. To all who accepted these deterministic accounts of rationality, the intellectual world seemed to be divided neatly in two. On one side stood those who held firmly to the nineteenth century, closing their minds to the sociology of knowledge because they were convinced that it opened the door to irrationalism and nihilism.[12] Ranked against them, in this romantic version of the modern predicament, were those – including Mannheim and Carr – who were ready to step through and mount fresh defences of reason on the unsteady ground of the twentieth century, working under the bright though flickering arc lights of Nietzsche, Freud, Marx, and Darwin.[13]

Ideology, utopia, and two varieties of realism

In *The Twenty Years' Crisis*, Carr adopted the main argument of *Ideology and Utopia* but twisted its rhetorical structure almost out of recognition. What Mannheim had termed 'ideology' was renamed 'utopianism' by Carr. This was a rationalisation, by those in power, of

---

[12] P. F. Strawson once summed up this position nicely, when exploring the implications of assuming determinism to be true. 'A sustained objectivity of inter-personal attitude, and the human isolation which that would entail, does not seem to be something of which human beings would be capable, even if some general truth were a theoretical ground for it': Strawson, 'Freedom and Resentment', in Strawson, ed., *Studies in the Philosophy of Thought and Action* (London: Oxford University Press, 1968), p. 82.

[13] Carr is quite explicit about this in *The New Society* (London: Macmillan, 1951). See especially p. 106: 'To unmask the irrational by stripping from it its hypocritical fig leaf of false reason is a salutary and necessary task. But this does not entail a panic flight from reason into the anti-rationalism of Kierkegaard and Dostoevsky or into the irrationalism of Nietzsche; on the contrary, it is an essential part of the movement towards understanding and overcoming the irrational. Reason is an imperfect instrument: it is good to recognize and study its imperfections.'

their privileged position. The supposedly beneficent social outcomes of self-regulating social systems like the market or the balance of power were taken as evidence of fundamental harmony of interests, while unequal distribution of gains as between established and new actors was played down. It was an approach to politics whose adherents were happy to employ legal and institutional innovation to preserve the status quo, sincerely believing that by promoting the League of Nations they were putting forward plans for radical change and social reform. But in practice it amounted to an attempt to sustain existing structures of power, and an ineffectual one at that.

What Carr termed 'realism', however, was not the equally interested though diametrically opposed rationalisation of political change that Mannheim had called 'utopia'. Instead, it was the critical technique of the sociology of knowledge, culled from Mannheim, by which Carr was able to demonstrate the interested or socially relative character of utopianism.

Rhetorically, this twist was of vital importance to Carr, who wished to set up, and then discredit for their extremism, two positions misleadingly labelled Left and Right in the early chapters of his book. As was shown in chapter 3, his aim was to position his own substantive policy positions in the later chapters as moderate compromises. Carr may best be termed a compensatory liberal. Since his policy aim was to win over the elites of a nation in which the preponderance of power lay with middle-aged male members of the British Conservative Party who regarded themselves as moderate fellows, he needed to lay down heavy smoke before starting his manoeuvre. Table 6.1 shows, in summary fashion, the way he set about this.

The first step was to argue that what Carr termed utopianism, as expressed in the League of Nations, was essentially conservative in spite of its avowed concern to achieve radical change by instituting a system of collective security. The Anglo-Saxon powers maintained that all nations had a common interest in peace. Yet others could immediately object that the clock had been stopped at that point in the game when Britain, the United States, and France had achieved their major objectives, and had done so by warfare. It was obvious that these were the states that had the most to lose from any future war, while others, notably Italy, Germany, and Japan, might hope to gain and could hardly therefore be expected to acquiesce in decisions of the League.

In the same way, a system of free trade between nations might

Table 6.1 *Differing uses of terms common to Carr and Mannheim*

	Conservative /status quo	Radical /revisionist	Critical /meta-ideological
Mannheim	Ideology	Utopia	Sociology of knowledge
Carr	Utopianism	Parts III and IV of *Crisis*	Realism

provide gains for all, but nothing in economic theory guaranteed equitable distribution of these gains. Once again, it was the wealthiest and best-established trading nations that stood to gain most from an open system. Others were quick to object that, in the first place, Britain and the United States had employed monopoly, coercion, and protectionism to attain their dominant positions in world trade and, secondly, that these policies offered the best opportunity for new-comers to catch up the leaders. Comparative advantage, the linchpin of Ricardian trade theory, was not a natural endowment. The competitive advantages of nations had been more or less deliberately constructed over the centuries. Economic liberalism provided a rationalisation for policies which, like the League, sought to stop the clock at the moment that suited those currently ahead of the game. Once again, there was no good reason for newly industrialising states to accept the current state of things.

In both economic and political affairs, new states had therefore no reason to accept British or United States claims that the League, or economic liberalism, was the practical expression of an underlying harmony of interests between nations. And by the mid-1930s their reasonable refusal had effectively destroyed the institutions of cosmopolitanism. Seeking a fundamental explanation of this observed breakdown of liberalism, Carr turned to what he called realism. Superficially, his account is of the *Realpolitik* school, with its emphasis on conflict and its identification of morality with power. It appears, no less than the utopianism he had just described, to be analogous with Mannheim's 'ideology': a rationalisation of power and the status quo, but this time a rationalisation distinguished from liberal cosmopolitanism by its complete lack of hypocrisy.

Carr claimed to find the foundations of this realism in Machiavelli and Hobbes.[14] By way of the German idealists and Marx, he

[14] Carr, *Crisis*, pp. 81–3.

approached the modern period, firmly attaching to Marxism and Nazism that kind of rigid historicism that unhesitatingly crowns the victor before clothing him in the borrowed robes of Enlightenment belief in progress. Then came a sudden lurch. *Modern* realism was distinguished from the *Realpolitik* tradition, German idealism, geopolitics, and the historical school. As a creation of the previous fifty years, modern realism turned out to be identical in all essentials with the sociology of knowledge. 'The outstanding achievement of modern realism', he contended, had been 'to demonstrate that the intellectual theories and ethical standards of utopianism, far from being the expression of absolute and a priori principles, are historically conditioned, being both products of circumstances and interests and weapons framed for the furtherance of interests.'[15] Theories, he asserts, are almost always responses to events rather than pre-existing grounds of political behaviour. But realism, of course, is just as much socially conditioned, and just as much the reflection of particular interests, as utopianism.

In sliding from an account of the *Realpolitik* tradition to one of the sociology of knowledge, and bringing both under the term 'realism', Carr departs from the symmetry of Mannheim. He uses 'realism' to cover elements of the conservative ideology that Mannheim labels 'ideology', but much more as a label for the sociology of knowledge by which Mannheim had sought to transcend the sterile opposition of ideology and utopia. In short, the realism and utopianism of part II of *The Twenty Years' Crisis* are not neatly counterpoised rationalisations of conservatism and radical change in the rather simple way that a very different ideology and utopia had been for Mannheim. Instead, they provide a rhetorical structure calculated to allow Carr to voice what, in Mannheim's terms, must be termed his own finessing of ideology and utopia, in the guise of a moderate blend of power and morality.

How did Carr get away with this? The trick lay in his use of repeated dichotomies, especially in the early chapters of the book. Utopia was hitched up to free will, theory, the intellectual, the Left, and the primacy of value; realism to determinism, practical politics, the bureaucrat, the Right, and the primacy of fact. Carr promised to create a science and to offer policy recommendations formed by a compromise between the two extremes.

[15] Ibid., p. 87.

But surely the intention was that, even when utopianism had been discredited as a conservative position posing as radicalism, the reader would somehow miss the fact that both utopianism and realism, as forms of conservatism, might just as well be placed on the Right, since Carr's own avowedly Centrist compromise was, in some respects, well to the Left of either. It takes only a moment to realise that the opposition of utopia and realism in international relations – a plausible enough expression of some of those neat dichotomies when the United States of Woodrow Wilson is pitted, albeit anachronistically, against the Germany of Adolf Hitler – starts to look decidedly pale when supposedly Leftist, theoretical, and intellectual 1930s France and Britain are contrasted with the fantasy of a Rightist, un-doctrinaire, and intellectual Soviet Union as, respectively, status quo and revisionist, utopian and realist in temper.

So Carr's tactic was to allow the utopianism of his political opponents and the critical technique of sociology of knowledge to exhaust each other, allowing him to slip into the abandoned fortress of utopianism by the postern gate and deploy its considerable rhetorical artillery in the cause of those radical social and political changes by which alone, he believed, the conservative and statist objective of maintaining British power in the world might be upheld.

It has already been observed that Carr was very much more optimistic than Mannheim about the prospects of sublimating conflict between opposing interests. In foreign policy terms, under the slogan 'negotiation backed by force', this substitution of reason for coercion took practical form as the leading general policy recommendation of *The Twenty Years' Crisis*, intended to justify Neville Chamberlain's policy of appeasing the revisionist powers of the day by measured concessions. In later works it would be used to commend revision of the terms of formal empire, regional integration under British leadership in Western Europe, and Soviet hegemony in Eastern and Central Europe.[16] In relation to domestic policy it was to be used to advocate adoption of Keynesian macro-economic policy, national planning, and the creation of a comprehensive welfare state.

It is certainly possible to present this package of ideas and policy as yet a third form of conservatism, since its avowed intent was to adapt to change in a manner that avoided social revolution while maintaining Britain as one of a diminished number of Great Powers. But on

[16] Ibid., ch. 13.

this measure, any policy short of anarchism must be judged conservative. Readers of *The Times* in the 1940s were in no doubt. Seeing the
radicalism of Carr's means much more clearly than the conservatism
of his ends, they began to perceive him as the Red Professor of
Printing House Square.

Carr on methodology and planning

If Carr leaned heavily on Mannheim for the rhetorical structure of the
book in which he presented the first mature formulation of his cocktail
of appeasement and welfare, he owed an even greater, though less
clearly acknowledged, debt in the fields of methodology and social
planning. Here, five corollaries of Mannheimean sociology of knowledge demand attention: the malleability of human nature, the social
construction of formal classifications of knowledge, the historically
relative character of the division between domestic and international
politics, the necessity of democratic planning, and the means by
which relativism might be overcome and policy firmly re-grounded.

Classical realists such as Hans Morgenthau or Herbert Butterfield,
who may be dubbed 'human nature realists' or 'continuity realists',
would often be referred to by their behaviourist successors as having
been excessively historical in approach. The irony is that, by fixing the
parameters of social change, they themselves developed a model of
the social and political world which was essentially ahistorical
because synchronic. Events followed one another during one long
moment in which the important things – human nature, natural law,
divine providence – remained fixed. It is little wonder, then, that Karl
Popper should have reacted so strongly against Mannheim. Popper
supposed that, when Mannheim discussed changes in values and
personality, he must be proposing deliberate change, in response to
structural constraints, of what were either to be regarded as natural
points of reference or, if malleable, as strictly the moral preserve of the
individual. Having set out to construct a world fit for men and
women, Mannheim appeared bent on fitting men and women for the
world he planned.[17]

Mannheim, by contrast, started from a diachronic approach to
history in which nothing about humankind except, perhaps, its

---

[17] Mannheim, *Man and Society*, pp. 201 and 204; Karl Popper, *The Poverty of Historicism*
(London: Routledge & Kegan Paul, 1957), p. 70.

biology was regarded as fixed over historical time. Social turbulence stemming from technological and environmental change was constant and to be expected. Human nature was not a constant factor untouched by such pressures; nor could any monopoly of initiating changes in human nature be reserved to individual moral agents. The newly emerging compromise, for Mannheim, was that, having once developed a historical consciousness of their condition, individuals might now cautiously seek to participate rather than merely acquiesce in the process of social change.

From the perspective of the academic discipline of international relations, the first conclusion to emerge from this consideration of Mannheim and Carr is therefore that Carr, as a realist, is to be sharply distinguished from the 'human nature' or 'continuity' realists with whom he is often classified. His attempt to found a new social *science* was just that. He set out to found international relations as a critical and profoundly historical social science of the kind envisaged by Mannheim. The first chapter of *The Twenty Years' Crisis* is no mere warming-up exercise, but was intended to be read with care and taken seriously as a methodological manifesto.

One implication of this adoption of Mannheim's critical sociology was that Carr was alive to the idea that the formerly fixed parameters of a field of inquiry might need to be revised and extended in response to historical change: hence the opposition to the conventional differences between economics and politics which was to make Carr favoured reading among pioneers of the new sub-field of international political economy from the 1970s, and which clearly derived from Mannheim's earlier attack on the bourgeois division of the social sciences.

In a world of global economy and total war, the methodological sovereignties of the political and the economic realms, just as much as those of small states, were an anachronism. Carr had argued persuasively in *The Twenty Years' Crisis* for the unity of state power and the fungibility of its various manifestations: economic power, military power, and power over opinion. Working on this assumption in the wartime leading articles he wrote for *The Times*, Carr repeatedly juxtaposed economic, political, and military expressions of a single theme to drive home the methodological point in a manner that strongly recalled the insistence of Mannheim on the redundancy of the old division of labour in the social sciences. On regionalism, for example, he argued for European partnership based on prior military planning and integration, standardised equipment, and common strategic planning, before tossing out, in a final paragraph, a proposal for economic integration.[18]

In a similar manner, the analogous or even interlaced character of arguments about foreign policy and domestic social policy was continually stressed, not least by the rhetorical structure of the leaders. This was most obvious in 'The Two Scourges', where Carr maintained that 'to abolish war means to create an international order in which good faith will be observed, and in which the unchecked pursuit of national interest will be tempered by consciousness of loyalty to some wider community [while] to abolish unemployment means to create a social order in which the ideals of nineteenth-century democracy are extended from the political to the social and the economic sphere'.[19] But it was evident also in the mixing of foreign and domestic and of economic and political items in a list of priorities for 1941 and in the call, a few days later, for 'the same readiness on the part of the individual to place himself and his possessions at the service of the community, and on the part of the nation to take its place in a wider community of nations'.[20]

More substantially, Carr constantly pursued the practical argument, calculated just as much as progressive social policies to appeal to United States decision-makers, that regional integration within a multilateralist economic framework offered the best hope of an enduring peace, since it had been precisely the neglect of economic integration and the consequent collapse of multilateralism that had proved the undoing of the Versailles settlement. This, once again, brought constant juxtapositions of foreign and domestic policy issues. No post-war international political settlement could endure that was not supported by sound economic and social foundations. Sovereignty ought not to be allowed to stand in the way of this. British prosperity required a recovery of European markets and living standards that could scarcely be achieved without integration.

This second methodological observation, of the inseparability of domestic and foreign policy, leads easily to consideration of Carr on

[18] 'The Small Nations', *The Times*, 16 December 1940. This is expanded in Carr, *Conditions of Peace* (London: Macmillan, 1942), ch. 10. For Carr's cautiously phrased vision of British leadership in Western Europe, see ch. 9 of the same work.

[19] 'The Two Scourges', *The Times*, 5 December 1940.

[20] 'The War in the New Year', *The Times*, 1 January 1941; 'Interdependence', 9 January 1941.

welfare and planning. The argument is that academic international relations, by sticking so firmly to *The Twenty Years' Crisis* as the recommended Carr text, has obscured one of the strongest methodological points that Carr wished to make: that in an age of mass democracy the old separation of foreign and domestic policy, no less than the separation of economics and politics or insistence on the fixed character of human nature and knowledge, was redundant. The collapse of each of these axioms of nineteenth-century liberalism could be represented as a challenge to modern consciousness, to be met either by digging in and defending a synchronic approach, by abandoning oneself to irrationalism, or by seeking to re-construct reason in the uncertain stream of post-modern understanding. Defence, surrender, or affirmation: the choice was less a moral than an existential one; and, every time, Carr was for affirmation. 'Planning', for him, was nothing less than the practical application of this methodological principle.[21]

Nothing illustrates the implications of this decision for the relationship between social policy and international relations more clearly than the genesis of the leading article Carr wrote for *The Times* in December 1940 under the headline, 'The Two Scourges'. The article placed unemployment alongside war. Both needed to be solved if there were to be any real security. The frankly instrumental origins of this leader were recounted in chapter 4. Lord Lothian, as ambassador in Washington, was troubled by United States scepticism about Britain's democratic credentials. Carr had come into Geoffrey Dawson's office while Lord Lothian was explaining his concern, and Dawson suggested that Carr try a leader calculated to reassure the North Americans, and the result was 'The Two Scourges'.

Here was a classic piece of Mannheimean reasoning. Attempts to construct an international political order after the First World War had failed because they ignored the damage that had been inflicted on the underlying social and economic order. The economic crisis at the start of the 1930s had not been promptly solved, as it might easily have been, because of stubborn insistence on national sovereignty, leading to destructive policies of economic nationalism. The frontiers around

---

[21] Carr's view of planning anticipated Mannheim's. In *Man and Society in an Age of Reconstruction*, democratic planning is alleged to consist in developing 'a just and effective balance between competition and regulation' (pp. 6–8), an essentially adaptive or strategic process to be sharply distinguished from 'establishment', or the attempt to work to a blueprint of an ideal society.

disciplines and the frontiers around states, both inherited from the bourgeois epoch, had blocked the path to a liberal solution and left the way open to totalitarianism.

The answer lay in a threefold expansion of the parameters of the problem. The boundary between political and economic analysis must be set aside, national sovereignty relaxed, and democratic planning accepted as readily in peacetime as in war. In what might have served equally well as a call for the invention of either development studies or international studies, Mannheim drew attention to the inadequacy of the conventional social sciences when called to deal with trans-boundary problems. '*The most essential aim of this book*', he wrote in *Man and Society*, 'is to show that the claims to absolutism of this type of [discipline-bound] thinking have been invalidated by the tasks set by the social process and that the transition to interdependent thinking has become a necessity [emphasis added].' Interdependent thinking consisted in 'bringing together everything which is required to explain a concrete situation, whether the themes selected fall within one or several fields of the already existing special sciences.' 'The division of labour', he concluded, 'will be determined by problem-units which will be concrete analyses of situation and structure.'[22] There could hardly be a better statement of the necessarily interdisciplinary and issue-focused character of international studies as it was to be conceived in the 1970s.

The task Carr set himself after leaving the Foreign Office had been nothing less than to educate elite opinion in this new connectedness of formerly discrete disciplines, classes, and sovereign powers. In the closing chapters of *The Twenty Years' Crisis*, in *Nationalism and After*, in *Conditions of Peace* and *The New Society*, but above all in his *Times* leaders, Carr disclosed a distinctive programme of compensatory liberalism and sought to persuade the decision-makers of Britain of its merits.

It remains to press home the claim that the link between foreign and domestic policy in Carr's realism was more than coincidental, deriving substantially from Mannheim, and to examine Carr's solution to the problem of relativism. The most economical way to achieve this will be to concentrate on the *Times* leaders, *Conditions of Peace*, and *The New Society*.[23] This is not because these works bristle with references

---

[22] Mannheim, *Man and Society*, p. 229.
[23] Carr, *Conditions of Peace*; Carr, *New Society*.

to Mannheim. Quite the contrary. But they do postdate *Man and Society* and provide the clearest statements of Carr's views on planning and social policy and their relation to foreign policy while at the same time offering strong indications of how Carr believed policy might be grounded.

The most characteristically Mannheimean move in the reconstruction leaders that Carr contributed to *The Times* in the second half of 1940 and early 1941 was his insistence that the war marked a revolutionary social transformation of the same order as the transition from feudalism to modernity achieved by the armies of Napoleon.[24] War acted as the catalyst of social change.[25] The influence of Mannheim is evident also in the repeated attacks on both national and disciplinary frontiers. The argument is always that radical social change means that existing social institutions and intellectual habits have to be revised. Institutional design and social thought are, effectively, the slaves of historical change.

There followed, from this revolutionary moment, the need for planning in the special transitional and provisional sense given to the term by Mannheim. The easiest way of grasping what Mannheim meant by democratic planning is to examine the distinction he drew between 'establishing' and 'planning'. To establish a new bank or a school meant starting from scratch with a clear idea of what the finished institution should look like. 'Establishment proceeds from a fixed and finished scheme which exists in the mind of the founders before it is carried out', Mannheim explained. 'The problem of execution is no more than the problem of adequate means.'[26] Planning, by contrast, was *not* an end-driven attempt to do this for the whole of society at once.[27] Instead, it was to be conceived of as an essentially strategic, permanently provisional, transitional process. If the nation were compared to a system of air transport, planning would be neither the aircraft, nor the routes, but the air-traffic controllers, who alone could enable the system to adapt to changes in its normal parameters resulting from extreme weather conditions, unexpectedly high traffic levels, or technological change. Planning, for Mannheim, was a conscious attempt to discover and utilise the least costly passage from one condition of equilibrium in a system to the next.

---

[24] 'Interdependence', *The Times*, 9 January 1941.
[25] 'Planning for War and Peace', *The Times*, 5 August 1940.
[26] Mannheim, *Man and Society*, p. 192.   [27] Ibid., p. 191.

More needs to be said about Mannheim's concept of planning, some of it critical. But his declared intention to produce a democratic form of planning and his rejection of end-driven 'establishment' already suggest that there may be good grounds for appeal against the judgement of Karl Popper, which rubbed off on Carr as well as Mannheim. Popper saw in *Man and Society* 'the most elaborate exposition of a holistic and historicist programme' available, and therefore singled it out as the principal target of *The Poverty of Historicism*.[28] Yet, looking back on the furious polemic Popper launched against Mannheim, the most striking feature is the extent to which the two men seem, in retrospect, to have been in agreement about planning.

Both agreed that there were no laws of social or historical development to be discovered that could act as a basis for prediction.[29] In spite of this, some measure of planning was not only possible but also unavoidable in an industrial mass society.[30] Both agreed that social engineering might reasonably be used to attain specific objectives. Indeed, Popper, later to figure among the favourite political theorists of Keith Joseph and Margaret Thatcher, offered, with approval, some examples of objectives appropriate to 'a systematic fight against definite wrongs, against concrete forms of injustice or exploitation'. These included counter-cyclical policy, securing a more equitable distribution of income, and ameliorating 'avoidable suffering such as poverty or unemployment'.[31] Both agreed that the planning process held great dangers. At least four were identified in very similar terms by the two, supposedly opposed theorists. The first of these was the tendency, among planners, to confuse an abstraction or model with society itself, and to make the mistake of thinking that society in all its complexity could be grasped intellectually in very much the same holistic manner in which Gestalt psychology taught that an image or a melody could be grasped.[32] Not so. 'The structure of all the social and historical events of an epoch is', Mannheim explained, 'too intricate to be understood at a

---

[28] Popper, *Poverty*, p. 67.
[29] Ibid., p. 45. Cf. Mannheim, *Man and Society*, p. 149, where attention is drawn to the constraint placed on planning by a limited 'radius of foresight', by which he meant 'the length of the causal chain which can be more or less accurately forecast'.
[30] Popper, *Poverty*, pp. 46, 60; Mannheim, *Man and Society*, p. 193.
[31] Popper, *Poverty*, p. 91; also pp. 59 and 68.
[32] Ibid., pp. 76–83. The reference to Gestalt is on p. 78. Cf. Mannheim, *Man and Society*, p. 30.

glance. Nor is it directly perceptible.'[33] Society could be scientifically studied only through processes of abstraction.

A second agreed danger was the observed tendency for planners to become obsessed with current trends to the point where the conditions underlying them and the possibilities of their reversal were forgotten.[34] Mannheim lambasted the approach to planning that would 'describe dogmatically what will happen in terms of its own wishes [and which] then, on the basis of this as yet unrealised future condition . . . undertakes to give meaning to what is still in process of development.' 'Events', he continued, 'are accordingly interpreted in terms of this anticipated future.'[35]

Besides this concerted condemnation of specious prediction, the two men were also opposed to any idea of planning as the realisation of a preconceived plan or blueprint.[36] Mannheim's attitude on this point has already been recorded. He drew a sharp distinction between establishment, planning, and administration. Planning was not establishment writ impossibly large. Nor was it a permanent process of administration. It is a point that bears repetition because, of all objections to socialist planning, this was perhaps the one most often heard during the middle years of the century. 'Socialists almost always create their Utopia in theory and then attempt to work backwards from it', commented one British civil servant in 1940. 'It is wiser to struggle forward, with a definite objective in view, but prepared to adapt that objective as obstacles on the way and the conditions prevailing at the end may necessitate. *Idées fixes* are always dangerous when they relate to the future, because it is past human ingenuity to guide the course of events.'[37] But this was common ground between Mannheim and Popper.

Finally, Popper and Mannheim both accepted that overambitious holistic planning would lead to a flood of unintended consequences, with which it was beyond the power of the planners to deal.[38] Mannheim drew attention to the need for planning to respect the 'radius of action', which he defined as 'the extent of the causal

---

[33] Mannheim, *Man and Society*, p. 184. [34] Popper, *Poverty*, p. 129.
[35] Mannheim, *Man and Society*, p. 189. [36] Popper, *Poverty*, pp. 67, 84.
[37] J. Colville, *The Fringes of Power: 10 Downing Street Diaries, 1939–1955* (New York: W. W. Norton & Co., 1985), p. 142: diary for 29 May 1940. Colville was one of Winston Churchill's private secretaries.
[38] Popper, *Poverty*, pp. 68–9.

sequences directly brought about by our initial activity and remaining more or less under our control'.[39]

For his part, Carr argued that the best intellectual justification for economic planning lay in the tendency of capitalist competition to produce concentration and oligopoly, which offered 'most of the abuses of monopoly without its efficiency'. But he recognised that, as a matter of fact, it had been the impracticability and inhumanity of allowing markets to cope with the massive adjustments required by depression and war that had moved democratic states to adopt planning. 'There is nothing alarming, and certainly nothing incompatible with freedom, in the current catchword of "planning"', Carr declared, before adding a characteristically Mannheimean touch. 'The free man', he argued, 'is not one who refuses to look ahead, but one who organizes to make freedom secure.'[40] There followed demands for post-war reconstruction and for reformed policies on housing, nutrition, education, and social security.

All these themes were to be spelt out in more detail in *Conditions of Peace* and *The New Society* and have been examined at length in chapter 4. The point of returning to them is to draw attention to the ample evidence in his spontaneous journalistic outpourings of 1940–1 to identify Carr not only with the sociology of knowledge developed by Mannheim in *Ideology and Utopia*, but also the distinctive attitudes towards social planning of *Man and Society*. His objective was to create an integrated social science, at once liberal and critical, fully aware of the circumstances of its own genesis, that would deal as readily with domestic as with international issues and pay little heed to the conventional boundaries between economics, sociology, and political science. In practical terms, he believed that the revolution through which he was living challenged the frontiers of states and the traditional divisions between domestic and external policy. In consequence, he argued for an extension of democracy from the political sphere to the economic and social, and for a reconstruction of capitalism in which trade would flow readily within integrated multicultural groupings of states that avoided autarky in their mutual relations, while accepting the need for a measure of restriction to protect social order against the Promethean energy of the market.

But if many of his ideas, and much of their strength, derived from the critical methodology and the systematic character imparted by

---

[39] Mannheim, *Man and Society*, pp. 149–50.   [40] Carr, *New Society*, p. 26.

Karl Mannheim, crucial weaknesses nevertheless remained. If all values were socially conditioned, how could planning – albeit transitory and strategic – be justified? If the answer was that planning did no more than anticipate a technologically driven world that was coming into being willy-nilly and facilitate conformity to it, it could be objected that planning might as easily be used to resist changes for the worse as to hasten those for the better. Carr himself had, after all, promoted democratic planning as a form of resistance against Hitler's New Order. How, without sneaking universalist values back in, was one to tell the difference between those impending social realities with which one ought and ought not to conform?

It was the inclination of Mannheim to ignore this question of moral judgement and ground policy-making in the supposed drift of events that most aroused the opposition of Karl Popper, becoming, under the title 'historicism', the essential point that divided him from Mannheim.[41] Having once selected Mannheim as his target, Popper was inclined, like any polemicist, to exaggerate the range of their disagreement. In practical terms, they were agreed on a broad social democratic adoption of planning to avert the worst consequences of an unregulated market through counter-cyclical macro-economic policies, income redistribution, and the alleviation of poverty and unemployment.[42] But once the many points of agreement are discounted, what seems to have offended Popper most in Mannheim's approach to planning was its passivity or acquiescence rather than its ambition.

'The essential attitude of the planning age', Mannheim had declared, 'inherits something of the humility of the religious mind in that it does not pretend to act as a creator of [fundamental] forces, but rather as a strategist, who only watches over the factors at work in society in order to detect . . . new possibilities . . . and to reinforce them at those points where vital decisions must be made.'[43] Given the anti-empiricist basis of Mannheimean thought, this acceptance of fundamental social tendencies as a guide to policy represented less a

---

[41] Mannheim on planning is the chief butt of Popper's *Poverty of Historicism*; Mannheim's historicism receives close attention in the second volume of *The Open Society*. Popper's critique would have been read by many British intellectuals of the 1950s and 1960s as applying *pari passu* to Carr, who conceded as much by attempting a reply in *What is History?* Popper, *Poverty*; Popper, *The Open Society and Its Enemies* (London: Routledge & Kegan Paul, 1945); Carr, *What Is History?* (London: Macmillan, 1962; 2nd edn, Penguin, 1987).

[42] Popper, *Poverty*, p. 91; also pp. 59 and 68.   [43] Mannheim, *Man and Society*, p. 190.

readmission of any form of materialism than of socially constructed and interested forms of interpretation as the grounds for political action. Just who was to decide which tendencies in contemporary history were fundamental and which ephemeral? While the anonymous operation of the market provides part of the answer, it still leaves a residual set of political problems arising from market failure and the legal and political foundations required by markets.

Carr had little hesitation in selecting the fundamental tendencies. He was sure about a tendency towards larger states or groupings of states driven both by the military and economic considerations, and confident that the appropriate response was acquiescence, most notably in the emergence of spheres of influence for the superpowers. But it was one thing to accept on tactical grounds the futility of alienating the Soviet Union by ineffective protests about the rights of East European states, quite another to rationalise that policy as part of a world-wide and irreversible trend towards larger states.

If the answer to the question of how to ground policy once the ideological masks had been removed were, more plausibly, to be that democratic planning simply reflected new interests thrown up by the world revolution of which totalitarianism, war, and depression had been symptoms, then Carr might surely have been rather more explicit about just what and who these interests were. Why should realist concession to a changing distribution of power stop short at readmitting the Soviet Union and a consolidated Western Europe to a world of three Great Powers? Did the arguments of *The Twenty Years' Crisis* not apply equally to China, or by 1947 to India, as his *Times* leaders strongly implied? Was Carr's desire to close the potentially disruptive gap between capability and status motivated primarily by acceptance of the justice of claims made by revisionist powers or by fear of the consequences of ignoring their claims? Correspondingly, reformist social policies engineered by a liberal elite might ameliorate the condition of the poor, ensure social order, and avert future wars, but it was far from obvious that Carr intended any substantial empowerment of the working class. On the contrary, his most consistent motive seems to have been maintenance of the power of the British state, whose servant he had been for almost twenty years. In the end, his proved to be a political realism far less radical in its implications than his individualist opponents claimed. If Carr realised fully the extent of his own elitism and the surreptitious universalism it implied, he must also have reasoned that to expose and work through the pattern of emergent social interests at any length would undermine the practical progress of his policy recommendations. But to concede that effective political action sets limits to the radical unmasking of interest demanded by the sociology of knowledge is surely to admit a major internal inconsistency in the intellectual foundations of social democracy. A generation later, we are once again having to face the consequences of coyness about the universalist claims that underlie ostensibly pluralist forms of Western liberalism and the elitism without which a democratic welfare state can hardly be sustained.

7 Carr's distinctive realism

The charge sheet

Carr took constant pains to situate himself precisely halfway between utopianism and realism. However, this strategy has generally been regarded as little more than a flourish, and Carr has consistently been taken for a political realist. William Fox, subtle and knowledgeable in his treatment of Carr, unhesitatingly referred to 'Carr's realist vision' and his 'version of realist doctrine'.[1] Earlier critics like Hugh Trevor-Roper were never in any doubt that Carr was a realist.[2] In works on foreign policy, nationalism, and international relations written during the ten years that followed his departure from the British Foreign Office in 1936, Carr constantly laid emphasis on power and poured scorn on assumptions of harmony of interest. Yet while realism became associated after 1945 with the political Right in Britain and North America, and a hawkish resolve to resist Soviet aggression, Carr has been very clearly shown to be a man of the Left. Though, like many other Britons of his generation, he was less a Marxist socialist than a compensatory liberal, his sympathy with the Soviet experiment went beyond anything justified by his *Realpolitik* analysis of the importance to Britain of good relations with the Soviet Union. Nor was Carr a warmonger. Quite the contrary: up to the very eve of war in 1939 he continued to advocate appeasement.

Carr was a realist of some kind or other, yet he eludes easy textbook classification. To make matters worse, *The Twenty Years' Crisis*, the

---

[1] William T. R. Fox, 'E. H. Carr and Political Realism: Vision and Revision', *Review of International Studies*, 11: 1, January 1985, pp. 1 and 7.
[2] Ved Mehta, *Fly and the Fly-Bottle: Encounters with British Intellectuals* (London: Weidenfeld & Nicolson, 1963), p. 111.

single work by which he has most frequently been introduced to generations of international relations students, is probably the least realist of his works. Close examination in chapters 3 and 6 has shown it to be too rich and flamboyant, too clever by half, too revealing, and too ambitious ever to have been a wholly effective political instrument, even if it had been published before war broke out. The fate of this less than consistent realist was almost inevitably to be misrepresented. Carr saturated his best works in kerosene. Opponents had only to toss a match to start the conflagration.

In the search for an explanation of the strength of feeling against Carr that developed from the mid-1940s, it helps to distinguish impatience with his elaborate and elitist manner, his frequent, seemingly opportunistic inconsistencies and ambiguities, his lapses into geopolitics and determinism, and his alien social-constructivist methodology from more straightforward dislike of his specific policy proposals. The two certainly fed on one another, but they remain analytically and perhaps even socially distinct. The second kind of criticism was clearest in the growing resistance of readership and politicians to his *Times* leaders and has been considered at length in chapter 5. The first and more profound, which provides the point of departure for this chapter, was most evident in the responses of intellectuals to his longer published works.[3] Even here, some criticisms were frankly superficial. Carr's use of stalking horses lent itself to misinterpretation, whether it was the caricature utopianism and realism of the early chapters of *The Twenty Years' Crisis* or his seeming pro-fascism of the late 1930s, crudely calculated to win support for concessions to all revisionist powers, regardless of ideology.

The prompt reaction of Susan Stebbing, a philosophically sophisticated reviewer of *The Twenty Years' Crisis*, is instructive. She proceeded to beat Carr about the head with views not so very different from those he had himself reached by the end of the book, seeming to assume he was actually committed to the version of realism advanced in chapter 5 but effectively demolished in chapter 6.[4] Another early critic, Czeslaw Poznanski, attacked *Conditions of Peace* for setting economic rationality above nationality as the criterion for political

---

[3] An interesting cross-over publication is the pamphlet, *What Is Democracy?* (London: National Peace Council, n.d. [1946]), which reprints reactions to Carr's 1946 Cust Lecture by eminent intellectuals including Harold Laski, Salvador de Madariaga, and Bertrand Russell which first appeared in the *Manchester Guardian*.

[4] Susan Stebbing, *Ideals and Illusions* (London: C. A. Watts, 1941).

self-determination, and *The Twenty Years' Crisis* for its advocacy of appeasement. He concluded by accusing Carr of a wholly unprincipled view of foreign policy, but never took issue with the sustained attempt made in the later chapters of *The Twenty Years' Crisis* to establish a moral basis for foreign policy.[5] Such attacks on Carr were plausible only because of the all too lifelike features of his men of straw.

More perceptive critics judged the danger from Carr to lie rather more in his social scientific methodology than advocacy of any specific policy. After 1945 judgements of Carr from intellectuals, when they rose above the commonplace and simplistic attacks on appeasement, crypto-Communism, and the like, almost invariably attacked the relativism and determinism that were held to lie at the heart of Carr's method. Hans Morgenthau was among the first and most astute. In a faithful and fair review article of 1948 he argued that the root of Carr's problem lay in moral relativism. 'Mr. Carr has no transcendent point of view from which to survey the political scene' and for this reason had become 'a utopian of power', mistaking pre-eminent will for right, both in his judgements of politicians and in the exercise of his own literary skills, it may be said. Rightly recognising Carr as the political romantic he was, Morgenthau concluded that while 'it is a dangerous thing to be a Machiavelli . . . it is a disastrous thing to be a Machiavelli without *virtú*'.[6] All this, of course, could be of little comfort to any who perceived themselves to be living 'after virtue', after the collapse of faith in the moral integrity of that great modernist hope, the Soviet state.

For Hugh Trevor-Roper, determinism was the prime offence. He seized gleefully on what he took to be Carr's volte-face, from pro-Nazi appeaser in 1939 to Leninist historian in the 1950s. In a vituperative review of *What Is History?* published in *Encounter*, he noted Carr's realism and recalled his past support for appeasement before referring sarcastically to the supposed change of mind about the realities of power which had made Carr 'the Red Professor of Printing House Square' during the Second World War. Moving on to Carr's work on the Soviet Union, Trevor-Roper accused Carr of a more fundamental crime: of writing determinist history, a victor's

---

[5] Czeslaw Poznanski, *The Rights of Nations* (London: Routledge, 1942), pp. v–vi.
[6] Hans J. Morgenthau, *The Restoration of American Politics* (Chicago: University of Chicago Press, 1962), p. 43.

history in which he allowed 'no voice . . . to Lenin's opponents'. Just as 'the Nazi success-story' which Trevor-Roper suggests Carr might easily have written in the 1930s 'has ended in discredit and failure', so now, it is implied, the final failure of the Soviet state would demonstrate the intolerance of the history Carr really did write. 'No historian since the crudest ages of clerical bigotry', Trevor-Roper concluded, 'has treated evidence with such dogmatic ruthlessness as this.'[7] The change of mind, in short, was proof of the folly of Carr's advocacy of swimming with the tide of history. Tides went in and out; and beside the tides there were strong and unpredictable eddies in historical waters.

These criticisms hardly do justice to Carr. They serve as a reminder of the 'Carr problem' identified in chapter 1. More important, they are accurate in identifying methodology, rather than policy, as the central area of contention. The first objective of this concluding chapter is therefore to abstract the social scientific method employed by Carr from the tactical and policy considerations that have been to the fore in earlier chapters. Next comes an exposition of the chief tensions or contradictions to which this method leads, and Carr's dialectical progression through them. A brief consideration of Carr as a political romantic is followed by a more practical critique of his style of pragmatic realism in relation to contemporary issues. The chapter, and the book, then concludes by appealing for a pragmatic approach to international relations – as much pre-modern as post-modern – that squarely faces the limits to reason and the ineradicable play of contingency, violence, will, and deceit.

Pragmatic realism

It has been argued in chapter 6 that the point of departure for any treatment of Carr as social scientist has, without doubt, to be the social constructivist methodology he adapted from Karl Mannheim. Evident in his critiques of utopianism and naive realism, constitutive of his version of modern realism, this critical method led Carr to repeated denials of continuity and constancy in a number of spheres. Human nature was not fixed, but subject to change in response to varying material and social circumstances. The nation was not a natural

---

[7] Hugh Trevor-Roper, 'E. H. Carr's Success Story', *Encounter* (1962), quoted by Mehta, *Fly and the Fly-Bottle*, p. 112.

group, but a historical one, varying in character and significance over time and from one region to another. Changing material conditions explained why nationalism had once been an adequate basis for statehood but was now to be viewed with contempt. Outside Western Europe, neither language nor any other objective feature could be relied upon to indicate political loyalty.[8] Accordingly there was no rational means to decide what organic entity possessed rights to statehood and self-determination.

From this it followed that national interest, though a convenient short-hand term, was too mercurial to provide a secure or principled basis for foreign policy.[9] Nor was ideology any better. The deeply opposed world views of Left and Right offered no independent foundation for principled foreign policy. Capitalist Germany and Communist Russia, united by weakness, had clung together in spite of their differences in the 1920s. Revolutionary Soviet foreign policy expressed through the Comintern was a spent force by 1924. Shared predicament, which is not at all the same thing as common interest, had created 'a topsy-turvy world in which the German Right toyed with Bolshevism and world revolution, and German Social-Democrats looked for salvation to American capitalism'.[10]

Every bit as much as human nature or nationality, language, too, was socially constructed. Meanings were no more stable than social institutions or their interests. 'Words', Carr observed, 'are often misleading in politics because their meanings change.'[11] Diplomacy and propaganda, viewed as the systematic manipulation of meanings, were consequently vital resources of state, for there were times when the appearance of strength could multiply coercive power, avoid a decisive test, or legitimise a reform. 'Few statesmen', he confidently proclaimed, in what might almost have been a personal manifesto, 'fail in an emergency to recognize a duty to lie for their country.'[12]

The practical implications of the sociology of knowledge for Carr had been to obliterate many of the certainties of Enlightenment

---

[8] E. H. Carr, *The Future of Nations: Independence or Interdependence?*, The Democratic Order, No. 1 (London: Kegan Paul, 1941).

[9] Carr, *Britain: A Study of Foreign Policy from the Versailles Treaty to the Outbreak of War* (Ambassadors at Large: Studies in the Foreign Policies of the Leading Powers, general ed., E. H. Carr; London: Longman Green, 1939), p. 2.

[10] Carr, *German–Soviet Relations Between the Two World Wars, 1919–1939* (The Albert Shaw Lectures on Diplomatic History, 1951; Baltimore: Johns Hopkins Press, 1951), p. 2; see also p. 65, on the impact of Rapallo.

[11] Carr, *Britain*, p. 3.   [12] Carr, *German–Soviet Relations*, p. 89.

rationality. Whether in relation to politics as practice or politics as science, fact, law, certainty, and reason were often trumped by appearance, discretion, contingency, and delusion. How could a good man practice politics in such an uncertain world? Aristotelean in spirit, Carr's answer may be summed up in two words: 'pragmatism' and 'democracy'.

What Carr meant by 'pragmatism' may best be understood through his specific applications of the concept to foreign policy, domestic social and economic planning, and the academic study of politics. Pragmatism in international politics was unavoidable. No prior legislation or rehearsal could substitute for deliberation and prudent decision-making because the ends of policy could not be specified. He argued that 'foreign policy is not, as some people imagine, the discovery and application of appropriate means to achieve known ends. It involves the discovery and formulation of ends and means and the adaptation of both to the circumstances of the moment.'[13]

To explain what pragmatic foreign policy-making meant, Carr resorted to the concepts of freedom and deferral, compromise, and bargaining. The pragmatic policy-maker avoided any restriction of freedom by prior commitments. The wisdom and morality of going to war or entering into an international agreement would depend on circumstances at the time. These could not be foreseen. Any prior commitment was therefore conditional and provisional, and therefore hardly a commitment at all.[14] Better by far to retain freedom of choice to the last possible moment by deferring decisions until they could be made in the light of the fullest possible knowledge.

Pragmatism took on two additional guises in *The Twenty Years' Crisis*. Most obviously, it took the form of the grand compromise between power and morality unveiled in part III of the book. Quoting Niebuhr, Carr concluded that 'politics will, to the end of history, be an area where conscience and power meet, where the ethical and coercive factors of human life will interpenetrate and work out their tentative and uneasy compromises'.[15] Elsewhere in *Crisis*, Carr offered a third expression of pragmatism through discussion of the concept of

---

[13] Carr, *Britain*, pp. 1–2.
[14] Carr, 'Public Opinion as a Safeguard of Peace', *International Affairs*, 15:6, November–December 1936, pp. 846–62. See ch. 2 in this volume.
[15] Reinhold Niebuhr, *Moral Man and Immoral Society* (New York: Scribner's, 1932), p. 4, quoted by Carr, *The Twenty Years' Crisis, 1919–1939: An Introduction to the Study of International Relations* (London: Macmillan, 1939), p. 130.

bargaining as a substitute for warfare, drawing on the analogy between international negotiations backed by the threat of force and collective bargaining between labour and employers, backed by the threats of lock-out and strike, in a liberal world where industrial relations were not regarded as a matter for state intervention.

When writing of domestic policy, Carr articulated his political pragmatism primarily through discussion of planning. Carr perfectly understood the distinction drawn by Karl Mannheim between 'establishment' and 'planning'. Moreover, he shared Mannheim's enthusiasm for the latter as a flexible and responsive process, though, as always, there would be inconsistencies in his application of the idea, which often veered towards excessive centralism. Pragmatic planning relied on limited and provisional predictions subject to constant revision. Where possible it utilised existing practice, as Carr did in his own proposals for post-war European integration, which built upon the extensive systems of joint military planning and economic co-operation that had grown up during the war. In short, Mannheimean planning, as adopted by Carr, was analogous to the concept of 'process utopia' as defined by Levitas and elaborated by Ken Booth in his seminal essay on Carr: 'benign and reformist steps to make a better world somewhat more probable for future generations'. It was to be contrasted with the unwisdom of 'end-point utopias', which 'look towards a future blueprint, such as world government, when history virtually comes to a stop'.[16]

To freedom, deferral, compromise, bargaining, negotiation, and planning must be added democracy, as the key synonym of pragmatism in Carr's personal lexicon. The appeal to democracy was partly propagandist. At the Ministry of Information he had argued that foreigners must be persuaded that a British victory was not only possible but also desirable. To achieve this end, British propaganda would have to stress the democratic political culture of Britain, the reality of self-government within the Commonwealth, and the commitment of Britain to international co-operation and peaceful settlement of disputes.

But pragmatism demanded that Britain not only seem democratic but be democratic. This was because democracy, under Carr's own

---

[16] Ken Booth, 'Security in Anarchy: Utopian Realism in Theory and Practice', *International Affairs*, 67:3, July 1991, pp. 536–7. Booth cites Ruth Levitas, *The Concept of Utopia* (New York: Philip Allan, 1990).

somewhat eccentric definition, was the prerequisite of any tolerable exercise of hegemonic power. Only with democratic government could a world system of large multinational states operate without collapsing into international conflict and domestic tyranny.

If there is a debt to Kant in this vision of a necessarily simultaneous solution of the problems of domestic and international politics, Carr is disinclined to acknowledge it. Nor, like Kant, is Carr disposed to spell out the vision in much detail. There was, however, a hint of what he understands by it in the closing pages of *The Twenty Years' Crisis*, which opted for a future *pax Americana* in preference to German or Japanese hegemony. The argument was that only within Anglo-American culture had there been sufficient entrenchment of consent and conciliation to provide ruling elites accustomed to compromise and concession and prepared to apply these virtues in their foreign policy. However, it was in his *Study of Foreign Policy* and a post-war lecture on democracy in international affairs that Carr provided the most complete statements of his grounding of pragmatism in democratic political culture.[17]

This turns out to consist in a portrait of democracy all too reminiscent, in its emphasis on compromise, governability, and order, of the arguments in favour of peace that Carr had ascribed to hypocritical status quo powers in *The Twenty Years' Crisis*. It is hard to see much light between the two. When the 'thinking Englishman' strives for the focal point of his feeling of national identity he finds it not in monarchy, countryside, blood, or language, but in a distinctive shared sense of democracy as 'give-and-take', mutual respect of majority and minorities, equipoise between obligation and privilege and between community and individual, and an ingrained preference for consensus over coercion. Democracy does not seek converts abroad and is consistent neither with willing resort to war nor with the conduct of war, which requires the suspension of some of its dearest values and institutions. Yet, Carr concludes, with its back to the wall, democracy is more resilient than totalitarianism because consent enables it to mobilise citizens and resources more completely and effectively, because the reluctance with which it goes to war provides a moral advantage, and because its culture of self-criticism makes it supremely

---

[17] Carr, *Britain*; Carr, 'Democracy in International Affairs', Cust Foundation Lecture, 1945, University of Nottingham, delivered 9 November 1945 (published by the University).

adaptable to new circumstances.[18] There is little room in this vision of democracy for radical dissent or mass participation. Indeed, when Carr does discuss participation and direct democracy it is to assure his readers of their consistency with highly centralised wartime government or to suggest that tighter Whitehall control of local government would increase local democracy.[19]

Completed in July 1939, hastily revised during the first days of war two months later, and published with a glowing preface by the incumbent foreign secretary which generously identified Carr closely with the Department of State on which he had turned his back three years before, this passage encapsulates many of the problems typically posed by Carr's texts. It is grossly manipulative, needing only recital by Olivier against a score by Walton to release floods of patriotic tears. (Sadly Branagh takes much the same attitude to the 'big' speeches in Shakespeare, the camera pulling back remorselessly to reveal a vast Norwegian host looking for all the world like sticks in the snow, as the music wells up to compensate for the image and obscure the words.)

This passage is clearly an instrument of British propaganda, endorsed by Lord Halifax and closely anticipating the wartime policy statement that Carr would shortly draft at the Ministry of Information. As a definition of democracy it makes academic hair stand on end, having much more to do with the pragmatic conduct of affairs by a governing elite of 'thinking Englishmen' than with representation, elections, the testing of public opinion, or other mundane details.

This is democracy by the grace of the state, and its étatist focus was to become still sharper in response to war and to the Soviet system which Carr, mistakenly, thought likely to prove superior in economic performance to Western capitalism. By 1945 British readers were being nudged in the direction of accepting a more communitarian view of democracy, finding freedom in the Hegelian formula of 'the knowledge and willing acceptance of the laws of necessity', affirming the superiority of democratic procedures over any contrary expression of the majority, and acquiescing in the ultimate superiority of the state over the rule of law. The danger for the English-speaking democracies, Carr blithely advised, was that 'with the traditional encouragement which they give to the extremer forms of individual and national self-determination, they may prove less flexible than Soviet democracy

---

[18] Carr, *Britain*, pp. 3–8.
[19] Carr, *The Soviet Impact on the Western World* (London: Macmillan, 1946), p. 18.

and less easy to reconcile with the degree of political and economic planning which the modern world requires'.[20]

Pragmatism elides into democracy, but democracy then collapses into elitist state socialism of the most centralist and hollow variety based in an unjustified faith in the historically progressive character of the state and the superiority of central economic planning. This tendency in Carr's 1945 Cust lecture provoked prompt and vigorous response in the pages of the *Manchester Guardian*, Salvador de Madariaga placing willing and informed consent at the heart of democracy, Lord Lindsay plumping for extensive and inclusive national debate, an anonymous leader writer choosing toleration, D. W. Brogan opting for scepticism, freedom, and deferral, and all, in company with Harold Laski and Bertrand Russell, expressing grave reserve about Soviet democracy and Carr's advocacy of it.[21]

Part of the trouble was that Carr was a child of his time, but part – as witnessed by the level of dissent among his contemporaries – stemmed from tensions within his chosen and distinctive critical method and between that method and the practical imperatives of wartime propaganda. Carr's way of steering through these tensions was to resort once again to the idea of pragmatism. In the same way that he believed that the practice of politics to be pragmatic, Carr held that its scientific study could be reduced neither to the accumulation of facts nor to the application of timeless and universal theory. Fact without theory made no sense. Theory, being socially determined, necessarily embodied will and purpose in the selection and interpretation of fact.

As early as 1936 Carr had argued that no formulaic or mechanistic explanation of war could be looked for that pinned the blame squarely on human nature, class, or demography and thereby legitimised the appropriate practical remedy.[22] Citing Kant and Mannheim, Carr had opted instead for a view of social science in which fact and theory, analysis and purpose, were mutually constitutive.[23] It was more than

[20] Carr, 'Democracy in International Affairs'. The quotations are drawn from pp. 13 and 19.
[21] *What Is Democracy?*. The pamphlet reprints articles originally published in the *Manchester Guardian* during March and April 1946.
[22] Carr, 'Public Opinion'. As might be expected, Carr's thoughts on democracy drew fire. See *What Is Democracy?*. Parts of Carr's Nottingham lecture found a wider audience the next year in the first chapter of Carr, *Soviet Impact*.
[23] Carr, *Crisis*, p. 5. See Karl Mannheim, *Man and Society in an Age of Reconstruction: Studies in Modern Social Structure* (London: Kegan Paul, 1940), p. 26, quoted pp. 000–00 above.

coincidental that both the conduct and the study of politics were pragmatic in character, for the two were inseparable. 'Political thought is itself a form of political action. Political science is the science not only of what is, but of what ought to be.'[24]

The play of inconsistency

It is no exaggeration to say that Carr was both a post-positivist and critical social scientist and a post-modern statesman. It would, however, be an exaggeration to claim that he performed either of these roles with any measure of consistency or enduring success. Shortly I will argue that inconsistency was a characteristically romantic device which Carr more or less deliberately deployed to keep seemingly irreconcilable elements in his programme in play, but that he was too much a captive of the Enlightenment to pull the trick off. Instead, each dichotomy tended to collapse through the privileging of one of its terms.

Four such dichotomies stand out, and their dialectical progression will briefly be considered before an attempt is made to characterise them collectively as the expression of a certain kind of political romanticism. They are the tensions between structure and agency, idealism and nihilism, coercion and voluntarism, and persuasion and truth. The argument is that, for Carr, an inextinguishable flame of idealism justified faith in agency which, in turn, justified resort to coercion and to its rhetorical analogue, persuasion.

Fully aware of the dangers of historical prediction, constantly warning the reader of the malleability of social institutions and language, Carr nevertheless made predictions which rested explicitly on assumptions about the supposed continuity of underlying structures beneath the flow of events. Perhaps more tellingly, he often betrayed belief in such structures through his inadvertent choice of phrase or image. Agency was implicitly denied when Carr wrote of a world that had 'moved on', as though it were a train with no driver, leaving the small national state exposed as 'an anomaly and an anachronism'.[25] Elsewhere Carr confidently declared that 'we know

---

[24] Carr, *Crisis*, p. 7.

[25] Carr, *Nationalism and After* (London: Macmillan, 1945), p. 37. I once rode on a train with no driver: a less terrifying experience than one might expect. The driver and guard had dismounted to remove a dead donkey from the track when a failure of the brakes allowed the train to move off on down the incline. Passing through Gerrards

the direction in which the world is moving, and in which we must move with it or perish'.[26]

Three particular predictions stand out. Carr was sure that technological change and the operation of world markets meant that the game was up with small nation-states. 'Few positive forecasts about the shape of the world after the war can be made with any confidence', Carr thundered in 1945, in his best *Times* leader style, 'but two negative predictions may claim some degree of certainty. We shall not again see a Europe of twenty, and a world of more than sixty, "independent sovereign states".'[27] Instead, the world would be organised through multinational groupings of states for which the Western hemisphere, the Soviet Union, and the British Commonwealth were the models. If a materialist vision of history provided this prophecy, a geopolitical understanding of space supplied its corollary. Though it was not the whole story, propinquity was decisive in the formation of such groupings, leading to the assumption of a prompt post-war United States withdrawal from European affairs and providing natural legitimacy for the leadership of Britain and the Soviet Union in Western and Eastern Europe respectively. Carr was equally certain of a third historical reality: that the rise and fall of states and the consequent clash between satisfied and revisionist powers was an enduring characteristic of international politics far more basic than ideology or nationality.[28]

Yet the whole practical thrust of Carr's work was to deny this third, almost geological truth and its implied denial of agency by forging policies that would allow Britain to buck the trend, retain its position as a major power alongside the USA and the Soviet Union, and so evade national decline. Fully conversant with the dilemmas of Marxist theory of history and the reflexive character of Mannheim's sociology of knowledge, Carr was cautious and measured when voicing the customary caveats about the ability of humanity to shape its own history and of the intellectual to rise above social conditioning,

Cross it startled waiting commuters by failing to stop. They were relieved when the train, encountering an upward slope, reversed direction and seemed to return for them. Instead, it passed through the station before momentarily coming to a halt once more, allowing those responsible to regain control. As for those of us on board, immersed in our newspapers, we learned of the incident the next day in the press.

[26] Carr, *Conditions of Peace* (London: Macmillan, 1942), p. 129.

[27] Carr, *Nationalism and After*, pp. 51 and 37; and see Carr, *Future of Nations*, p. 50.

[28] E. H. Carr, 'Europe and the Spanish War', *Fortnightly*, 141 (new series), January–June 1937, p. 26.

but the whole of his work from the day he left the Foreign Office to the day he left *The Times* breathed supreme confidence that agency – through propaganda, through organisation, and through planning – could make a decisive difference to the outcome of the war and the peace that followed. Having no option but to endure history, mankind could choose between alternative inexorable tendencies. Destiny could be eluded and national senility indefinitely deferred. Historical tendencies, indeed, might be orderly and remorseless in themselves but would not reliably deliver social or political order. Quite the contrary: 'Unless plans are laid in advance, chaos will be the inevitable result.'[29]

What permitted Carr to privilege agency over structure in this way was a strong modernist faith in what may be termed 'the virtue of agency' coupled with a naive theory of the state. Recall for a moment an older meaning of the word 'virtue'. To the medieval mind the virtue of a substance was the quality that enabled it to achieve its end. In men and women, virtues provided the power to act rightly, in accord with natural law, but this was a special case of a more general understanding of the world in which herbs, drugs, minerals, or other inanimate bodies were enabled by their virtues to act efficaciously in the cure of specific ailments or the performance of particular functions. When pressed, Carr believed that mankind was virtuous in both senses, being able both to transform structures, rather than merely suffer or reproduce them, and likely to do so in progressive and justifiable ways. This made him ultimately proof against the nihilist tendency in Central and East European thought with which he had become familiar as a young man.

In this second sense, the virtue of agency rested in the hands of the state and its servants, the governing elite and the intelligentsia, to which he himself belonged. Well read in the texts that had done most to upset modernity, Carr was willing towards the end of his life to suggest, with disarming candour, that the greatest single source of inconsistency in his work was an inextinguishable modernist belief in progress which held him back from the bleaker kind of post-modernist nihilism. Characteristically and consistently, he attributed this meliorist bias to his own social background. He just couldn't help himself; even being aware of the problem did not help very much.[30]

---

[29] Carr, *Conditions of Peace*, p. 134.
[30] Carr, *What Is History?* (2nd edn; London: Penguin, 1987), p. 6.

When summoned to justify his optimism he gestured in the direction of his Edwardian childhood and passed on. The response of unrepentant modernism to revelation of its own nakedness is more often irony than shame.

Human nature might be malleable, but the scope and tendency of change was constrained by its inherent utopianism. Shot through with images of growth and maturity, Carr's works breathe a patriarchal assurance that trial and error will yield maturity, good will, competence, and progressive enlightenment.[31] 'Faith in some sort of progress still clings to me', he confessed to Ved Mehta at the beginning of the 1960s.[32] Nothing in Carr's work can help explain the Holocaust as anything more than social atavism. Half a century later, in the face of persistent and widespread ethnic and religiously motivated violence, this modernist excuse has worn thin.

Worse, Carr extended his faith in utopianism from the individual to the state. Well aware of Niebuhr's warnings about 'immoral society' and fully conscious of the fiction involved in any personification of the state, Carr nevertheless happily acquiesced in the shift of power from legislature to executive and from local to central government. Part of his confidence in the state arose from a belief in its progressive denationalisation. The experience of the inter-war years had turned him against any idea of the state as guarantor of the rights of national collectivities. Instead, the state was to be a secular guarantor of individual rights that laid plans for the common good. But it is hard to resist the conclusion that his optimism about the ability of the state to reconcile these two objectives owed much to his reception of the legitimising ideology of discipline and public-spiritedness shared by the British diplomatic and civil services.[33] Pinning his faith on technocratic elites and meritocracy, Carr seems never fully to have appreciated the potential of the state for tyranny. While appreciating the importance of separation of powers in his more functionalist moments, he underestimated the importance of other forms of democratic and constitutional constraint and of a robust civil society in averting political corruption.

Carr's treatment of Walter Rathenau provides a clue. Son of the founder of the industrial giant, AEG, Rathenau had been responsible

[31] This is precisely Kant's theory of universal history.
[32] Mehta, *Fly and the Fly-Bottle*, p. 150.
[33] On Carr's elitism, see Kenneth W. Thompson, *Morality and Foreign Policy* (Baton Rouge and London: Louisiana State University Press, 1980), p. 137.

for raw materials division of German Ministry of War during the First World War. A Jew, equally at home in the worlds of government and industry, he opposed Bolshevism, yet was fascinated by the Russian revolution. Sending a young aide to Russia as early as 1919 to study Lenin's system, Rathenau organised a study commission on Russia composed of German industrialists in 1920. He thought a return to capitalism in Russia impossible. Marxism and the Russian workers had proved to be effective forces of destruction, but they could do no more than destroy. Only a 'spiritual aristocracy' could rebuild. Rathenau propounded a gospel of 'constructive socialism'. In this spirit he fostered the flow of German technicians to the young Soviet Union.[34] When writing for *The Times*, Carr addressed governments at home and abroad, but seems to have conceived of his readers as composing just such a spiritual aristocracy: the revolutionary cadres of Political and Economic Planning on whose management of the British state must depend victory and post-war reconstruction.

From belief in agency and the innate goodwill of his own kind, it was a short step to the justification of coercion as a means of applying technically superior political solutions in the belief that, once imposed, they would acquire legitimacy through growing awareness of their practical benefits. Thus, European integration was to be imposed on small allies and a defeated Germany at the conclusion of the war in the hope that 'we may find that we have constructed something which mankind will come gradually to recognise as indispensable to its future well-being and which can some day be given . . . wider geographical extension and constitutional forms'.[35]

From this acceptance of coercion in practical politics the resolution of a fourth opposition, between persuasion and truth, followed simply by analogy. The rhetorical equivalent of coercive institution is the founding lie. In *Nationalism and After*, Carr recalls the benefits that accrued in the nineteenth century from the liberal doctrine of the separation of the political and economic spheres. There had in fact been nothing natural about the Gold Standard; it had been the product of human agency, mostly British. But the fiction of its anonymous and non-political character had made it acceptable, and this had been to the general good.

In much the same way, Carr perfectly well saw that functional

---

[34] Carr, *German–Soviet Relations*, p. 20.
[35] Carr, *Conditions of Peace*, p. 273.

international organisations supervising trade in primary commodities, health regulations, legal traffic in narcotic drugs, and the like – forms of organisation which he believed to be essential elements of a stable post-war international order, bridging regional multinational group-ings which might otherwise degenerate into mutually hostile autarkic blocs – were bound to infringe on the sovereignty of states. Carr's conclusion nicely re-states the doctrine of the founding lie. Since it is also one of the more subtle statements of his view of international society it is quoted here in full:

> It would be simple to-day – as it would have been simple in the nineteenth century if anyone had thought it worth while – to point to the fictitious elements in the separation of non-political from political authority, and to demonstrate that political power, however dis-guised and diffused, is a presupposition that lies behind any auth-ority, however non-political in name. Nevertheless the world to-day, like the world of the nineteenth century, may have to put up with a certain salutary make-believe if it can find no way of consciously and deliberately effecting an international separation of powers. In the national community the concentration of all authority in a single central organ means an intolerable and unmitigated totalitarianism: local loyalties, as well as loyalties to institutions, professions and groups must find their place in any healthy society. The international community if it is to flourish must admit something of the same multiplicity of authorities and diversity of loyalties.[36]

There is a sense in which social scientific writing is always a lie: there is always more information to be had, there are always more views to be canvassed, more theories considered. In one of the first articles on international affairs published under his own name after leaving the Foreign Office, Carr had playfully expounded rival British (idealist) and French (realist) interpretations of the League, before turning to a third possibility, 'the League as it will appear to the historian' or 'the League as it has actually functioned since 1920'. But here, he ruefully admitted, was the heart of the problem. 'It is easy enough to say with reasonable accuracy what the League means to the Idealists and what it means to the French. But what the League has in fact been can be almost endlessly debated.'[37]

The academic typically meets such difficulties by delay and

---

[36] Carr, *Nationalism and After*, p. 49.
[37] Carr, 'The Future of the League – Idealism or Reality?', *Fortnightly*, 140 (new series), July–December 1936, pp. 386 and 391.

qualification. The journalist performs a leap of faith: convinced of the argument as the deadline approaches; equally sure that time will dissolve that certainty; unworried by the trail of petty inconsistencies. It must already be clear to the reader of this book that Carr, up to 1946, was much more journalist, propagandist, and publicist than scholar, antiquarian, or historian. He regarded himself as an intellectual, and increasingly a 'dissident intellectual'.[38] Yet he always remained enough of a scholar to admit the malleability of historical interpretation, to draw attention to the founding lie, to warn the enemy he was on his way.

From the moment he left the Foreign Office to the end of his service at *The Times* in 1946 Carr never desisted from his attempts to influence public policy. Recognising that the functions of language were both expressive and persuasive, he remained close enough to his own parody of realism to opt for persuasion as the more urgent task, but too much the liberal ever entirely to conceal the means of persuasion from his readers. This tender-heartedness certainly divides Carr from what may be termed 'opaque' realists: those who believe it permissible wholly to conceal the rhetorical techniques by which they pursue their ends. It places him instead, along with Richard Rorty, in the company of those 'transparent' or 'utopian' realists of a democratic and ironic cast of mind – patient, piecemeal, and accepting of contingency – who figure that the trip will not have been worth taking if half the passengers end up not knowing how they got there.

Romantic realism

To read the successive collapse of the central dichotomies in Carr's work in the manner attempted here may be thought unfair. Careful readers of his work will observe that Carr sees the dangers at every turn along the course that has just been charted and is for ever at the pumps working to keep the craft afloat; but he is reluctant to abandon any of the cargo as it slides across the deck, even though it includes a wild variety of mutually incompatible postures and convictions, stratagems and projects, some of which threaten combustion on contact.

Knowing this, Carr resorts to defensive notions of compromise, duality, and the productive tension of opposites in an attempt to lash

---

[38] Carr, *What is History?* (2nd edn), p. 6.

down the most dangerous items while filling the threadbare spinnaker of British imperial power with a voluminous and sustained national conversation. This desire to hold on to opposites, to prolong the voyage, and to resist resolution may be termed political romanticism. It is not compatible with pragmatism.

The trouble with talk of political romanticism is that the term has a difficult and dirty history. It has been synonymous with revolution to one writer and reaction to the next. A good part of the reason why Carr intrigues, and finally deserves to be called a romantic, is that it is quite easy to place him in either of these opposed camps. Admiring the Soviet ally and favouring social revolution at home, he pursued an essentially conservative purpose: the preservation of British power and the extension of British political culture through meritocratic forms of government. He supped with a very long spoon, commending far-reaching changes in the lives of others while leaving his own daily round and that of the mandarin class to which he belonged quite undisturbed. His vision was therefore romantic in the double sense of being built from the tension of irreconcilable desires and constituted by a subjective aestheticisation of everyday events.

The early pages of Carl Schmitt's classic treatment can hardly be bettered for their critical account of the confusion that has resulted, in European thought, from competing definitions of romanticism. Schmitt finds a unity among very differently disposed romantics which is very close to the idea advanced here.[39] His tightest definition of romanticism is 'subjectified occasionalism'. 'The romantic subject', Schmitt alleges, 'treats the world as an occasion and an opportunity for his romantic productivity.'[40] The key to Carr's view of international relations may be found as much in the reader of Dostoievsky, Herzen, Marx, and Bakunin as in the professional diplomat, and rather more in the biographer than the later academic historian.

---

[39] Carl Schmitt, *Political Romanticism* (Cambridge, MA: MIT Press, 1986). I became aware of the significance of Schmitt's work only lately, through Chantal Mouffe, *The Return of the Political* (London: Verso, 1993). My own route to an understanding of political romanticism was a very different one, depending much more on Hispanic reception of French ideas than on the German tradition. I am grateful to Chantal Mouffe for persuading me that it would be confusing to describe Carr as a romantic pragmatist, since this effectively constituted a contradiction in terms. Better to locate the contradiction where it belongs: in Carr himself.

[40] Schmitt, *Political Romanticism*, p. 17.

Identifying romanticism as belonging to the last of four distinct forms of reaction against eighteenth-century rationalism, Schmitt opens his account of the structure of the romantic spirit by referring to the tendency of this fourth 'emotional-aesthetic reaction', rather than set up a philosophical system, to transform 'the oppositions it sees into an aesthetically balanced harmony.' 'In other words', he continues, 'it does not produce a unity from . . . dualism, it reduces . . . oppositions to aesthetic or emotional contrasts in order to fuse them.' 'The origin of romantic irony', he concludes, 'lies in this suspension of every decision, and especially in the vestige of rationalism that it reserves for itself in spite of its thoroughly irrational bearing.'[41]

This captures an important aspect of Carr's work, but immediately requires the qualification that Carr, more than most exemplars of Schmitt's ideal type of the political romantic, holds on to that 'vestige of rationalism' through his persistent realist focus on policy- and decision-making. He can entertain an audience for years with the fantasy of a multi-ethnic state which respects cultural difference, but has in the end to decide whether Soviet hegemony in post-war Eastern Europe will fit the bill or not. In the decision, either way, lie seeds that will choke the fantasy.

To call Carr a political romantic in this particular sense, far from singling him out from his contemporaries, places him among the modern host of politicians who have aestheticised politics, not simply in speech and writing, but through the institution of new regimes and institutions, weaving intellectual threads spun out of the fleece of mundane politics back into the coat of the old wolf. Those fancy constitutions and ingenious partitions whether in Cyprus or Ireland, Yugoslavia or Central Africa, Uruguay or Germany, those dreams of order and progress, breathe occasionalism even as they declare their rationalist modernity through a brutal stripping-down of the awkward and complex lumpiness of the world in the name of a succession of sleek structuralist social theories, from market liberalism to Marxist socialism and onwards to the progressively more desperate populist and totalitarian creeds of the twentieth century.

The implosion of political romanticism cannot be indefinitely averted because the irreducible core of politics is about making decisions that cannot be deferred and deliberated upon for ever and because solutions to practical political problems that rely on

---

[41] Ibid., pp. 55–6.

representation and aesthetic appeal to cloak deferral have limited purchase on the loyalties of the general run of people. A truly pragmatic form of political realism, of the kind to which Carr aspired, may therefore best be described as an engagement in what happens at the end of the romantic conversation, when the irreducible element of conflict has finally to be faced and resolved.

8 Conclusion

This survey of the contribution of E. H. Carr to international relations has introduced readers to a much broader range of his work than is usually read or easily obtainable. It has, in particular, drawn attention to the leading articles Carr wrote at *The Times* between 1940 and 1947. Throughout the period from 1936 to 1946, during which Carr wrote his major works on international relations, the determination of foreign policy was of far more pressing concern to Carr than the formulation of an academic science of international relations. Because of this, and because of the influence on Carr of the social constructivist methodology of Karl Mannheim, emphasis has been placed throughout on the policy context of works which came in later years to be valued chiefly for their theoretical insight. This has exposed the relationship between policy objectives and the means of persuasion available to Carr, directing attention to his self-consciously manipulative rhetorical technique and to the journalistic haste and political opportunism of much of his work.

Examining the predicament which Carr faced has brought into sharp focus some patterns and inconsistencies in his work. Above all, Carr set out between 1936 and 1946 to extend the reach of the state far more thoroughly than ever before into British economic and social life, with the clear intention of engineering a material recovery that would allow the status of Britain as a Great Power to be maintained. This overriding political aim required that Britain first resist the military challenge posed by the Axis and subsequently play a full part in building a Concert of victorious Allies sufficiently cohesive to avert the bipolar conflict between the United States and the Soviet Union which he thought bound to relegate Britain to a subordinate position in world politics.

In pursuit of this aim of continued British power, Carr was consistent in favouring collective security, first through a more effective League of Nations and later through a United Nations Organization based on the Three Power Concert of the United States, the Soviet Union, and Britain. He regarded this as the only way of preserving Britain's Great Power status. Accordingly, his core project was at once realist, in its stress on the state and the conflictual nature of international relations, and utopian, in Carr's critical sense of the term, in its devotion to preserving the position of a satisfied power by appeals to the general interest in international co-operation and peace.

The same ambivalence that characterised Carr's core policy aim may also be detected in the means he adopted in pursuit of it. The desperation of Britain's plight led Carr to adopt propaganda techniques that were highly realist, in the sense of being unscrupulously instrumental and often inconsistent, in pursuit of short-term objectives. Just as he pulled out every stop to build a Concert of Great Powers of which Britain might remain a member, so, at home, he strained to reinforce the emerging consensus of Labour, Liberal, and Left Conservative opinion around policies of social and economic reform, the restriction of military commitment to allies and dependencies, and the Anglo-Soviet condominium in Europe which he regarded as the pivot of Britain's political future. Yet however realist Carr's propagandist rhetoric may appear in matters of detail, it was deeply idealist in its faith in the power of words to shape perceptions and guide political action. Key decision-makers, including Churchill and Bevin, not to mention Stalin, proved obdurately resistant to the considerable charms of his prose.

The same fundamental ambivalence between idealistic political commitment and realist analysis and method helps account for further inconsistencies. I have gone so far as to characterise this ambivalence or appetite for tensions between incompatible opposites as political romanticism. The idealist in Carr actually believed in economic planning and the Soviet formulations of democracy on grounds of social justice and not just as the surest means to British recovery and world power. They were not means adopted for their mere effectiveness by a pragmatic realist in pursuit of state power. The hollow romanticism of Carr's purported pragmatism was therefore fatally exposed when its recognisably liberal foundation – the happy coincidence of private desire and public interest – collapsed with the onset of the Cold War.

Similar difficulties attend another leading feature of Carr's pragmatic realism: his attempt to balance the social need for large states with the individual need for identity. Carr consistently held that economic and military security could be guaranteed only by large multinational groupings of states. The extensive markets needed to support rising living standards and full employment could not otherwise be developed and stabilised. Security, equally, required continuous military collaboration and planning under modern conditions. Effective armies could no longer be thrown together at the whim of princes.

Against the degeneration of such groupings and of relations between them, the only effective defence was frequent and private discussion of their differences by political leaders of the highest rank, a process out of tune with his earlier condemnation of secret diplomacy. Besides, Carr recognised that such groupings might easily approach 'a size which cannot be exceeded without provoking a recrudescence of disintegrative tendencies', and that the only remedy to this lay in toleration of the local, national, and religious communities with which citizens most readily identified. His pragmatism was also at odds with the necessarily fixed character of the commitments involved in prior military collaboration.

These tensions in Carr's thought and political practice provoke thought about current international relations. The last ten years have seen the bipolar settlement of the 1940s dismantled, posing a set of problems not dissimilar to those faced by Carr and his contemporaries. The large multinational state was tried with mixed success. It failed most obviously where it was used to achieve relative autarky or became the legitimating device for a hegemonic and privileged political party, ethnic group, or religion. The appearance and duration of its success throughout much of the Third World rested on an enforcement of post-colonial settlements through international law, economic and military assistance, and intervention, which was in turn motivated by Cold War rivalries between the powers. Its longevity in the First and Second Worlds may be attributed to their prolonged suspension in the formaldehyde of the Cold War.

But for the anti-politics of the Cold War, the British case, which Carr knew to be delicately balanced between maritime and Continental solutions, might speedily have been resolved on his prescription, and in spite of his protestations to the contrary, in favour of

Europe.[1] Instead, a bipolar world allowed Britain to continue to fudge the issue and aggravate the problem. No sooner had the British dismantled their Empire and joined the European Community than waves of British corporate capital, seeking security from a turbulent decade, began to break upon the shores of North America, while government, in the concluding phase of the Cold War, bound itself ever more tightly to the United States.

The consequent tension between Atlanticist and European stances brought a succession of ministerial resignations and would continue to divide the Conservative Party. However the terms of the British debate about Europe are more commonly reminiscent of Carr's romantic preoccupation with the tension between security and identity *within* multinational groupings than with the particular problem of British orientation, which in any case matters less now that the country is no longer a major force in world politics.

Indeed, continuing debate about British geopolitical and corporate orientation has served principally to preserve Gaullist doubts elsewhere in Europe about the extent of British commitment to the emerging Union, placing one more obstacle in the way of a positive British contribution to the far more relevant internal debate about European political development. This debate continues to be conducted within Britain in terms of a crude opposition of national sovereignty and foreign tyranny, community versus bureaucracy, which seldom pauses to consider the emptiness of legal sovereignty in an interdependent world or the possibilities of regenerating community and democracy through practical development of the formula of subsidiarity. Both Margaret Thatcher and John Major appreciated the vital British *and* European interest in ensuring that pragmatism, not formalism, should become the watchword of a European Union. Sadly, neither proved able to convince the British Conservative Party, let alone Britain's European partners, of the superiority of this position over crudely federalist or nationalist alternatives.

To turn from the particular European dilemma to the more general crisis of the multinational state is to appreciate all the more the imprudence of both these alternatives. For the larger picture suggests that the gap between the extensive units needed for economic and

---

[1] The term 'anti-politics' and the idea of the Cold War as a suspension of politics are derived from the Hungarian writer, George Konrád, *Antipolitics* (London: Quartet, 1984).

military security and the more restricted entities in which personal identity is grounded has widened. Indeed, the change since Carr's day is more radical than this form of words suggests, for the truth is that neither kind of institution can any longer be plausibly defined in territorial or even spatial terms. Nuclear weapons and the potency of terrorist and guerrilla techniques coupled with economic globalisation mean that no territorial state is large enough to offer security through closure. Taken together, the personal politics of gender, sexual orientation, religious faith, and environmentalism, the rarity of contiguous populations with an agreed identity, and the political marginalisation of millions throughout the world by elite technocratic appropriation of formal politics and political institutions mean that personal aspirations cannot be met by any conceivable territorial mosaic, no matter how small the pieces. In Aristotelean terms the situation is no longer amenable, if it ever was, to theoretic reason, but only to practical reason, deliberation, and the exercise of prudence.

To put it another way, the density and complexity of the bureaucratic systems of corporate management, social security, service provision, and military intelligence in which theoretic reason must necessarily hold sway, if water and electricity are to be supplied, planes to reach their destinations, and production to be sustained, is now so complete that the entire structure is at risk – as the experience of the Soviet Union and Yugoslavia has demonstrated – if the fundamental error of the Enlightenment is persisted in. And that error was quite simply the incautious extension of law, rule, bureaucracy, and the whole apparatus by which theoretic reason may be applied to political affairs, to cover issues where contingency, prudence, and discretion – in short pragmatism – were indispensable. In a postmodern age awake to the irrationality of rationality pursued to the limit – whether in the Holocaust's parody of Fordist industrial production or the 'efficient' destruction of Hiroshima and Nagasaki – politics can more clearly be seen to consist less in managing the internal affairs of sovereign and autarkic states and their mutual relations than in using the entire register of forms of governance and pragmatic application of the principle of subsidiarity to reconcile these two forms of rationality.

Carr, following Mannheim, asked the critical question of whose interests were served by any political prescription. The general crisis of the multinational state – in former colonial territories, in the Soviet Union, or, more discreetly, in Britain itself – has drawn attention to the extent to which the project was bound up with the interests of the class of technocrats to which Carr himself belonged: the new Western-educated and *déraciné* urban elites of colonial Africa and Asia, the party cadres of the Communist world, the mass of civil servants and corporate executives who staffed the growing public and private bureaucracies of the United Nations, the European Commission, the major transnational corporations, the world's growing number of great cities, and its swollen national states.

Why should this class – the Lords of the Washington consensus – willingly compromise their current superiority in a bid to avert an uncertain future threat to their preferred manifestations of rationality? Carr's answer might have stressed the enlightened self-interest that leads powers in decline, whether great nineteenth-century employers or leading twentieth-century states, to compromise with rising and revisionist powers.

The current situation is rather different. Whereas the power of the capitalist had a clear material basis and that of the state was rooted in national economy and military force, neither the technocratic class nor the individual citizen has an analogous and specific power-base. Instead Carr's successors in the offices of state and firm depend on the mass of citizens and consumers to legitimate their authority. The best chance is therefore that, having once exhausted strategies of populist mobilisation and neoliberal marginalisation of the world's underclass, they may start to see that they have little option but to embark on a process of emancipation and social inclusion if their own activities are to be legitimated and their security assured in the long run. In many parts of the world it is the negative power of defection and disaffection as much as or more than direct armed challenge to the state that threatens those who rule. The government of Hong Kong by the People's Republic of China may turn out to be a crucial test of whether this search for legitimacy is a sufficient cause of the adoption of pragmatic realism by a powerful and overprincipled bureaucratic state.

As representative of this privileged mandarin class, Carr was at his worst when he abandoned his own prescription of pragmatism in favour of sudden lurches into generalised prophecy and at his best when pointing out the inadvisability of generalisation and the need to deal with cases and situations on their merits. Examples of the former include Carr's conviction that small states were militarily and eco-nomically obsolete and his insistence on a steadily diminishing number of states in Europe and the wider world, falsified in various ways since 1945 by Vietnamese military success, the economic achievements and continued independence of Singapore, or the break-up of Yugoslavia and the Soviet Union. Much more robust, after half a century, are Carr's warnings against binding commitments to future military action, his conviction that the boundary between public and private sectors in Britain 'must be determined by empirical tests, not by the dictates of political prejudice or economic doctrine conceived in other days and in other conditions', and his insistence on the divisibility of world peace, allowing for quite different practical responses to morally comparable situations according to circumstance.[2]

So long as consistency is taken as the measure of fairness, pragmatism and pluralism can easily appear to be the abandonment rather than the application of principle. The first is bound to lead to the seeming inequity of a massive military response to Iraq's 1990 invasion of Kuwait alongside prolonged silence in the face of Indonesian action in East Timor or Turkish occupation of northern Cyprus. Moral pluralism, by which is understood a willingness to recognise and respect the incommensurable difference of other cultures even as one wholeheartedly asserts the claims of one's own, is equally pledged to a contingency and indeterminacy of outcomes which is bound to disturb lovers of consistency. Returning to the passage from Rochester's *Satire* that opens this book, it is enough to conclude that the continuing value of Carr's intervention in international relations lies in its perfect illustration of the conflict between absolute, universalist forms of reason characteristic of the European Enlightenment and a more modest Aristotelean account which places reason on an equal footing with desire. At a moment of supreme national crisis, Carr might easily have adopted Rochester's lines as his motto:

> Thus, whilst against false reasoning I inveigh,
> I own right reason, which I would obey:
> That bounds desires, with a reforming will
> To keep 'em more in vigour, not to kill.

A science of international relations that aspires to anything less is doomed either to scholastic abstraction or to the mundane chronicling of current affairs.

[2] 'State and Industry', *The Times*, 6 December 1941.

Bibliography

Primary

(a) *Public Records Office*
FO371
INF1

(b) *British Library. Add. MSS 55909–55930. Macmillan Archives. Edition Books.*

(c) *News International. Archives of The Times.*

(d) *Royal Institute of International Affairs, Chatham House, 21 St James's Square, London. Records of the Nationalism Working Group.*

(e) *Birmingham University Library. Carr Papers.*

Unpublished theses

Dunne, Timothy. 'International Relations Theory in Britain: The Invention of an International Society Tradition'. University of Oxford, DPhil., 1993.

Press

The Times, 1940–7.

Secondary

Abramsky, C., ed. *Essays in Honour of E. H. Carr*. London: Macmillan, 1974.

Addison, Paul. *The Road to 1945: British Politics and the Second World War.* [London: Cape, 1975] London: Pimlico, 1994.

Axelrod, Robert. *The Evolution of Cooperation.* New York: Basic Books, 1984.

Barraclough, Geoffrey. *An Introduction to Contemporary History.* [London: Watts, 1964] London: Penguin, 1967.

Bayliss, John. 'Britain, the Brussels Pact, and the Continental Commitment', *International Affairs*, 60:4, 1984, pp. 615–29.

Bibliography

The Diplomacy of Pragmatism: Britain and the Formation of NATO, 1942–1949.
Basingstoke: Macmillan, 1993.
Bell, P. M. *John Bull and the Bear: British Public Opinion, Foreign Policy, and the Soviet Union, 1941–1945.* London: Arnold, 1990.
Berki, R. N. *On Political Realism.* London: Dent, 1981.
Bloor, David. *Knowledge and Social Imagery.* London: Routledge & Kegan Paul, 1976.
Booth, Ken. 'Security in Anarchy: Utopian Realism in Theory and Practice', *International Affairs*, 67:3, July 1991, pp. 527–45.
Bosco, Andrea, and Cornelia Navari, eds. *Chatham House and British Foreign Policy, 1919–1945: The Royal Institute of International Affairs During the Inter-War Period.* London: Lothian Foundation, 1994.
Brewin, Christopher. 'Arnold Toynbee and Chatham House'. In Bosco and Navari, *Chatham House and British Foreign Policy*, pp. 137–61.
Buchan, John. *Mr. Standfast.* London: Hodder & Stoughton, 1919.
Bull, Hedley. 'The Theory of International Politics, 1919–1969'. In Porter, *Aberystwyth Papers*, pp. 30–55.
The Anarchical Society: A Study of Order in World Politics. Basingstoke: Macmillan, 1977.
Bullock, Alan. *Ernest Bevin: Foreign Secretary.* Oxford: Oxford University Press, 1985.
Buzan, Barry, Charles Jones, and Richard Little. *The Logic of Anarchy: From Neorealism to Structural Realism.* New York: Columbia University Press, 1993.
Carr, E. H. *Dostoievsky.* Boston: Houghton Mifflin, 1931.
The Romantic Exiles. Boston: Beacon Press, 1933.
Karl Marx: A Study in Fanaticism. London: Dent, 1934.
'Public Opinion as a Safeguard of Peace', *International Affairs*, 15:6, November–December 1936, pp. 846–62.
'The Future of the League – Idealism or Reality?', *Fortnightly*, 140 (new series), July–December 1936, pp. 385–402.
Michael Bakunin. London: Macmillan, 1937.
International Relations since the Peace Treaties. London: Macmillan, 1937.
'Great Britain as a Mediterranean Power'. Cust Foundation Lecture, 1937. University College, Nottingham. Delivered 19 November 1937. Published by the University.
'Europe and the Spanish War', *Fortnightly*, 141 (new series), January–June 1937, pp. 25–34.
'The Twilight of the Comintern', *Fortnightly*, 143 (new series), January–June 1938, pp. 137–47.
Britain: A Study of Foreign Policy from the Versailles Treaty to the Outbreak of War. London: Longman Green, 1939. (Ambassadors at Large: Studies in the Foreign Policies of the Leading Powers, general ed., E. H. Carr.)
The Twenty Years' Crisis, 1919–1939: An Introduction to the Study of International Relations. London: Macmillan, 1939. 2nd edn; London: Macmillan, 1946.

'Honour among Nations', *Fortnightly*, 145 (new series), January–June 1939, pp. 489–500.

The Future of Nations: Independence or Interdependence? London: Kegan Paul, 1941. (The Democratic Order, No. 1.)

Conditions of Peace. London: Macmillan, 1942.

Nationalism and After. London: Macmillan, 1945.

'Democracy in International Affairs'. Cust Foundation Lecture, 1945, University of Nottingham. Delivered 9 November 1945. Published by the University.

The Soviet Impact on the Western World. London: Macmillan, 1946.

German–Soviet Relations Between the Two World Wars, 1919–1939. Baltimore: Johns Hopkins Press, 1951. (The Albert Shaw Lectures on Diplomatic History, 1951.)

The New Society. London: Macmillan, 1951.

What Is History? London: Macmillan, 1962. 2nd edn; London: Penguin, 1987.

'Karl Mannheim'. In E. H. Carr, *From Napoleon to Stalin and Other Essays*, pp. 177–83. Basingstoke: Macmillan, 1980.

Chapman, Stanley. *Merchant Enterprise in Britain from the Industrial Revolution to World War I.* Cambridge: Cambridge University Press, 1992.

Cockett, Richard. *Twilight of Truth: Chamberlain, Appeasement, and the Manipulation of the Press.* London: Weidenfeld & Nicolson, 1989.

Cole, Robert. *Britain and the War of Words in Neutral Europe, 1939–1945: The Art of the Possible.* Basingstoke: Macmillan, 1990.

Colville, John. *The Fringes of Power: 10 Downing Street Diaries, 1939–1955.* New York: W. W. Norton & Co., 1985.

Davies, David. *An International Police Force.* London: Benn, 1932.

Davies, R. W. 'Edward Hallett Carr, 1892–1982'. In *Proceedings of the British Academy, 1983*, vol. LXIX, pp. 472–511. London: Oxford University Press for the British Academy, 1984.

Deudney, Daniel. 'Nuclear Weapons and the Waning of the Real-State', *Daedalus*, 124:2, Spring 1995, pp. 209–31.

Dougherty, James E., and Robert Pfaltzgraff jun. *Contending Theories of International Relations.* 3rd edn; New York: Harper & Row, 1990.

Etherington, Norman. *Theories of Imperialism: War, Conquest, and Capital.* Beckenham: Croom Helm, 1984.

Evans, Graham. 'E. H. Carr and International Relations', *British Journal of International Studies*, 1:2, July 1975, pp. 77–97.

Foster, Alan. 'The Times and Appeasement: The Second Phase'. In Laqueur, *Second World War*, pp. 275–99.

Fox, William T. R. *The Superpowers: The United States, Britain, and the Soviet Union – Their Responsibility for Peace.* New Haven, CT: Yale University Institute of International Studies, 1944.

'E. H. Carr and Political Realism: Vision and Revision', *Review of International Studies*, 11:1, January 1985, pp. 1–16.

Bibliography

Glendinning, Victoria. *Rebecca West: A Life*. London: Weidenfeld & Nicolson, 1987.

Greenwood, Sean. 'Ernest Bevin, France, and "Western Union"': August 1945–February 1946', *European History Quarterly*, 14:3, 1984, pp. 319–38.

'Bevin, the Ruhr, and the Division of Germany: August 1945–December 1946', *Historical Journal*, 29:1, 1986, pp. 203–12.

Hall, James. *Dictionary of Subjects and Symbols in Art*. London: Murray, 1974.

Hallett, John. [E. H. Carr.] 'Nationalism, the World's Bane?', *Fortnightly Review*, 133 (new series), January–June 1933, pp. 694–702.

'The Austrian Background', *Fortnightly Review*, 135 (new series), January–June 1934, pp. 569–76.

Haslam, Jonathan. 'We Need a Faith', *History Today*, 33, August 1983, pp. 36–9.

Headlam-Morley, Sir James. *A Memoir of the Paris Peace Conference, 1919*. Edited by Agnes Headlam-Morley. London: Methuen, 1972.

Herz, J. H. *Political Realism and Political Idealism: A Study in Theories and Realities*. Chicago: University of Chicago Press, 1951.

Hollis, Martin, and Steve Smith. *Explaining and Understanding International Relations*. Oxford: Clarendon Press, 1990.

Holsti, K. J. *The Divided Discipline: Hegemony and Diversity in International Theory*. Boston: Allen & Unwin, 1985.

Howe, Paul. 'The Utopian Realism of E. H. Carr', *Review of International Studies*, 20:3, July 1994, pp. 277–97.

Jenkins, Keith. *Re-thinking History*. London: Routledge, 1991.

On What Is History. London: Routledge, 1995.

John, Ieuan, Moorhead Wright, and John Garnett. 'International Politics at Aberystwyth, 1919–1969'. In Porter, *Aberystwyth Papers*, pp. 86–102.

Jones, Charles. 'E. H. Carr Through Cold War Lenses: Nationalism, Large States, and the Shaping of Opinion'. In Bosco and Navari, *Chatham House and British Foreign Policy*, pp. 163–85.

'E. H. Carr: Ambivalent Realist'. In Francis A. Beer and Robert Hariman, eds., *Post-Realism: The Rhetorical Turn in International Relations*, pp. 95–119. East Lansing: Michigan State University Press, 1996.

'Institutional Forms of British Direct Investment in South America', *Business History*, 39:2, April 1997, pp. 21–41.

'Carr, Mannheim, and a Post-positivist Science of International Relations', *Political Studies*, 45:2, June 1997, pp. 232–46.

Kaiser, David. *Politics and War: European Conflict from Philip II to Hitler*. London: I. B. Tauris, 1990.

Kegley, Charles W., jun. *Controversies in International Relations Theory: Realism and the Neoliberal Challenge*. New York: St Martin's Press, 1995.

Kegley, Charles W., jun., and Eugene Wittkopf. *World Politics: Trend and Transformation*. 4th edn; New York: St Martin's Press, 1993.

Kennan, George F. *Memoirs, 1925–1959*. London: Hutchinson, 1968.

Kennedy, Paul. *The Rise and Fall of the Great Powers: Economic Change and Military Conflict from 1500 to 2000*. New York: Random House, 1988.

Keynes, John Maynard. *The End of Laissez-Faire*. London: Hogarth, 1926.

Knight, Wayne. 'Labourite Britain: America's "Sure Friend"'? The Anglo-Soviet Treaty Issue, 1947', *Diplomatic History*, 7:4, 1983, pp. 267–82.

Konrád, George. *Antipolitics*. London: Quartet, 1984.

Koss, Stephen. *The Rise and Fall of the Political Press in Britain*, vol. II, *The Twentieth Century*. Chapel Hill and London: University of North Carolina Press, 1984.

Kroeber, Karl. 'Frictional Fiction: Walter Scott in the Light of von Clausewitz's *On War*'. In James Pipkin, ed., *English and German Romanticism: Cross-Currents and Controversies*, pp. 251–73. Heidelberg: Carl Winter, 1985.

Labedz, Leopold. 'E. H. Carr: An Historian Overtaken by History', *Survey*, 30:1–2, 1988, pp. 94–111.

Laqueur, Walter, ed. *The Second World War: Essays in Military and Political History*. London: Sage, 1982.

Linklater, Andrew. 'The Transformation of Political Community: E. H. Carr, Critical Theory, and International Relations', *Review of International Studies*, 23:3, July 1997, pp. 321–57. (Eleventh E. H. Carr Memorial Lecture, Aberystwyth, 15 May 1996.)

Little, Richard. 'The Evolution of International Relations as a Social Science'. In R. C. Kent and G. P. Nielsson, eds., *The Study and Teaching of International Relations: A Perspective on Mid-Career Education*, pp. 1–27. London: Pinter, 1980.

Long, David, and Peter Wilson, eds. *Thinkers of the Twenty Years' Crisis: Inter-War Idealism Reassessed*. Oxford: Clarendon, 1995.

McDonald, Iverach. *The History of 'The Times'*, vol. V, *Struggles in War and Peace, 1939–1966*. London: Times Books, 1984.

McKinlay, Robert D., and Richard Little. *Global Problems and World Order*. London: Pinter, 1986.

McLachlan, Donald. *In the Chair: Barrington-Ward of 'The Times', 1927–1948*. London: Weidenfeld & Nicolson, 1971.

McLaine, Ian. *Ministry of Morale: Home Front Morale and the Ministry of Information in World War II*. London: George Allen & Unwin, 1979.

McNeill, William H. *Arnold J. Toynbee: A Life*. New York and Oxford: Oxford University Press, 1989.

Mannheim, Karl. *Ideology and Utopia: An Introduction to the Sociology of Knowledge*. London: Kegan Paul, 1936.

Man and Society in an Age of Reconstruction: Studies in Modern Social Structure. London: Kegan Paul, 1940.

Mansbach, Richard W., and John A. Vasquez. *In Search of Theory: A New Paradigm for Global Politics*. New York: Columbia University Press, 1981.

Mehta, Ved. *Fly and the Fly-Bottle: Encounters with British Intellectuals*. London: Weidenfeld & Nicolson, 1963.

Morgan, Roger. 'E. H. Carr and the Study of International Relations'. In Abramsky, *Essays in Honour of E. H. Carr*, pp. 171–80.

Bibliography

Morgenthau, Hans J. *The Restoration of American Politics*. Chicago: University of Chicago Press, 1962.

Mouffe, Chantal. *The Return of the Political*. London: Verso, 1993.

Nationalism: Its Nature and Consequences. London: Oxford University Press for the Royal Institute of International Affairs, 1939.

Niebuhr, Reinhold. *Moral Man and Immoral Society*. New York: Scribner's, 1932.

Olson, William C. 'The Growth of a Discipline'. In Porter,*Aberystwyth Papers*, pp. 3–29.

O'Neill, Onora. 'The Public Use of Reason', *Political Theory*, 14:4, November 1986, pp. 523–51.

Parmar, Inderjeet. 'Chatham House, the Foreign Policy Process, and the Making of the Anglo-American Alliance'. In Bosco and Navari, *Chatham House and British Foreign Policy, 1919–1945*, pp. 299–318.

Planning for War and Peace: Ten Leading Articles Reprinted from 'The Times'. London: The Times Publishing Co., 1940.

Ponting, Clive. *Churchill*. London: Sinclair-Stevenson, 1994.

Popper, Karl R. *The Open Society and Its Enemies*. London: Routledge & Kegan Paul, 1945.

The Poverty of Historicism. London: Routledge & Kegan Paul, 1957.

Porter, Brian. 'David Davies and the Enforcement of Peace'. In Long and Wilson,*Thinkers of the Twenty Years' Crisis*, pp. 58–78.

Porter, Brian, ed. *The Aberystwyth Papers: International Politics, 1919–1969*. London: Oxford University Press, 1972.

Poznanski, Czeslaw. *The Rights of Nations*. London: Routledge, 1942.

Rogerson, Sidney. *Propaganda in the Next War*. London: Bles, 1938.

Ross, Graham. 'Foreign Office Attitudes to the Soviet Union, 1941–1945'. In Laqueur, *Second World War*, pp. 255–74.

Schmitt, Carl. *Political Romanticism*. Cambridge, MA: MIT Press, 1986.

Scott, Sir Walter. *Old Mortality*. [1816] Edinburgh: Black, 1878.

Smith, Steve. 'Paradigm Dominance in International Relations: The Development of International Relations as a Social Science'. In Hugh C. Dyer and Leon Mangasarian, eds., *The Study of International Relations: The State of the Art*, pp. 3–27. Basingstoke: Macmillan, 1989.

Stebbing, L. Susan. *Ideals and Illusions*. London: C. A. Watts, 1941.

Stone, Norman. 'Grim Eminence', *London Review of Books*, 5:1, 20 January–2 February 1983, pp. 3–8.

Strawson, P. F. 'Freedom and Resentment'. In Strawson, ed., *Studies in the Philosophy of Thought and Action*, pp. 71–96. London: Oxford University Press, 1968.

Stroud, B. 'Wittgenstein and Logical Necessity', *Philosophical Review*, 74, 1965, pp. 504–18.

Taylor, A. J. P. *The Trouble Makers: Dissent over Foreign Policy, 1792–1939*. London: Hamish Hamilton, 1957.

English History, 1914–1945. Oxford: Oxford at the Clarendon Press, 1985.

Thompson, Kenneth W. *Masters of International Thought: Major Twentieth-*

Century Theorists and the World Crisis. Baton Rouge: Louisiana State University Press, 1980.

Morality and Foreign Policy. Baton Rouge and London: Louisiana State University Press, 1980.

Tickner, J. Ann. 'Re-visioning Security'. In Ken Booth and Steve Smith, eds., *International Relations Theory Today,* pp. 175–97. Cambridge: Polity, 1995.

Trevor-Roper, Hugh. 'E. H. Carr's Success Story', *Encounter,* 1962.

Walker, R. B. J. *Inside/Outside: International Relations as Political Theory.* Cambridge: Cambridge University Press, 1993.

Weltman, John J. *World Politics and the Evolution of War.* Baltimore and London: Johns Hopkins University Press, 1995.

Wendt, Alexander. 'Anarchy Is What States Make of It: The Social Construction of Power Politics', *International Organization,* 46:2, Spring 1992, pp. 391–425.

West, Rebecca. *Black Lamb and Grey Falcon: The Record of a Journey Through Yugoslavia in 1937.* 2 vols. London: Macmillan, 1942.

West, W. J. *Truth Betrayed.* London: Duckworth, 1987.

The Truth about Hollis. London: Duckworth, 1989.

What Is Democracy? London: National Peace Council, n.d. [1946].

Wight, Martin. 'Western Values in International Relations'. In Herbert Butterfield and Wight, eds., *Diplomatic Investigations: Essays in the Theory of International Politics,* pp. 89–131. London: George Allen & Unwin, 1966.

Winch, Peter. 'Understanding a Primitive Society', *American Philosophical Quarterly,* 1:4, October 1964, pp. 307–24.

Ethics and Action. London: Routledge & Kegan Paul, 1972.

Wittgenstein, Ludwig. *Remarks on the Foundation of Mathematics.* Oxford: Blackwell, 1956.

Philosophical Investigations. Oxford: Blackwell, 1968.

Index

178

CAMBRIDGE STUDIES IN INTERNATIONAL RELATIONS

Printed in the United States
By Bookmasters